Whiteness and White Privilege i Psychotherapy

This unprecedented, interdisciplinary collection focuses on gender, whiteness, and white privilege, and sheds light on this understudied subject matter in the context of clinical psychology, in both theories and applications.

Psychologists, especially therapists, are often trained to look for issues that are not readily visible, cannot be spoken, and that are commonly taken for granted. Feminist and multi-cultural researchers and practitioners further seek to expose the power structures that benefit them or that unfairly advantage some groups over others. Whiteness has been investigated by sociologists and critical race theorists, but has been largely overlooked by psychologists and psychotherapists, even those who deal with feminist and multi-cultural issues. This volume explores the ways in which gender, whiteness and white privilege intersect in the therapy room, bringing to light that which is often unseen and, thus, unnamed, while examining issues of epistemology, theory, supervision, and practice in feminist therapies.

The various contributions encompass theory, history, empirical research, personal reflections, and practical teaching strategies for the classroom. The authors remind us that whiteness and other forms of privilege are situated among multiple other forces, structures, identities, and experiences, and cannot be examined alone, without context.

This book was originally published as a special issue of *Women & Therapy*.

Andrea L. Dottolo is Assistant Professor of Psychology at Rhode Island College, Providence, RI, USA, and resident scholar at the Women's Studies Research Center at Brandeis University, Waltham, MA, USA. Her research and teaching explores how social identities are constructed and maintained, and the ways in which they are shaped by institutional and political structures.

Ellyn Kaschak is Professor Emerita of Psychology at San Jose State University, CA, USA, Visiting Professor at the United Nations' University for Peace in Costa Rica, and the editor of the journal *Women & Therapy*. She is the author of *Sight Unseen: Gender and Race through Blind Eyes* (2015).

Whiteness and White Privilege in Psychotherapy

Edited by
Andrea L. Dottolo and Ellyn Kaschak

LONDON AND NEW YORK

First published 2016 by Routledge

2 Park Square, Milton Park, Abingdon, Oxfordshire OX14 4RN
711 Third Avenue, New York, NY 10017

Routledge is an imprint of the Taylor & Francis Group, an informa business

First issued in paperback 2018

Introduction, Chapters 1–4, 6–13 © 2016 Taylor & Francis
Chapter 5 © Peggy McIntosh

All rights reserved. No part of this book may be reprinted or reproduced or utilised in any form or by any electronic, mechanical, or other means, now known or hereafter invented, including photocopying and recording, or in any information storage or retrieval system, without permission in writing from the publishers.

Notice:
Product or corporate names may be trademarks or registered trademarks, and are used only for identification and explanation without intent to infringe.

British Library Cataloguing in Publication Data
A catalogue record for this book is available from the British Library

ISBN 13: 978-1-138-64842-5 (hbk)
ISBN 13: 978-1-138-39394-3 (pbk)

Typeset in Adobe Garamond
by RefineCatch Limited, Bungay, Suffolk

Publisher's Note
The publisher accepts responsibility for any inconsistencies that may have arisen during the conversion of this book from journal articles to book chapters, namely the possible inclusion of journal terminology.

Disclaimer
Every effort has been made to contact copyright holders for their permission to reprint material in this book. The publishers would be grateful to hear from any copyright holder who is not here acknowledged and will undertake to rectify any errors or omissions in future editions of this book.

Printed in the United Kingdom
by Henry Ling Limited

Contents

Citation Information — vii
About the Authors — ix

Introduction: Whiteness and White Privilege — 1
Andrea L. Dottolo and Ellyn Kaschak

Part I: Setting the Stage

1. Little White Lies: Racialization and the White/Black Divide — 7
   Ellyn Kaschak

Part II: Cultural Critiques

2. Whiteness in Latina Immigrants: A Venezuelan Perspective — 16
   Elena Padrón

3. The Butterfly Dilemma: Asian Women, Whiteness, and Heterosexual Relationships — 29
   Natalie Porter

4. Whiteness and Disability: Double Marginalization — 42
   Martha E. Banks

Part III: Training

5. Extending the Knapsack: Using the White Privilege Analysis to Examine Conferred Advantage and Disadvantage — 54
   Peggy McIntosh

6. What Do White Counselors and Psychotherapists Need to Know About Race? White Racial Socialization in Counseling and Psychotherapy Training Programs — 68
   Eleonora Bartoli, Keisha L. Bentley-Edwards, Ana María García, Ali Michael, and Audrey Ervin

CONTENTS

7. White Practitioners in Therapeutic Ally-ance: An Intersectional
   Privilege Awareness Training Model   85
   Kim A. Case

8. I Don't See Color, All People Are the Same: Whiteness and Color-
   Blindness as Training and Supervisory Issues   101
   Michi Fu

9. Examining Biases and White Privilege: Classroom Teaching Strategies
   That Promote Cultural Competence   117
   Gina C. Torino

Part IV: Microaggressions and being 'American'

10. Racial Microaggressions, Whiteness, and Feminist Therapy   130
    Silvia L. Mazzula and Kevin L. Nadal

11. The Unbearable Lightness of Being White   149
    Diane M. Adams

12. "American" as a Proxy for "Whiteness": Racial Color-Blindness in
    Everyday Life   163
    Nellie Tran and Susan E. Paterson

13. Slicing White Bre(a)d: Racial Identities, Recipes, and Italian-American
    Women   178
    Andrea L. Dottolo

    Index   199

Citation Information

The chapters in this book were originally published in *Women & Therapy*, volume 38, issues 3–4 (July–December 2015). When citing this material, please use the original page numbering for each article, as follows:

Introduction
Whiteness and White Privilege
Andrea L. Dottolo and Ellyn Kaschak
Women & Therapy, volume 38, issues 3–4 (July–December 2015) pp. 179–184

Chapter 1
Little White Lies: Racialization and the White/Black Divide
Ellyn Kaschak
Women & Therapy, volume 38, issues 3–4 (July–December 2015) pp. 185–193

Chapter 2
Whiteness in Latina Immigrants: A Venezuelan Perspective
Elena Padrón
Women & Therapy, volume 38, issues 3–4 (July–December 2015) pp. 194–206

Chapter 3
The Butterfly Dilemma: Asian Women, Whiteness, and Heterosexual Relationships
Natalie Porter
Women & Therapy, volume 38, issues 3–4 (July–December 2015) pp. 207–219

Chapter 4
Whiteness and Disability: Double Marginalization
Martha E. Banks
Women & Therapy, volume 38, issues 3–4 (July–December 2015) pp. 220–231

Chapter 5
Extending the Knapsack: Using the White Privilege Analysis to Examine Conferred Advantage and Disadvantage
Peggy McIntosh
Women & Therapy, volume 38, issues 3–4 (July–December 2015) pp. 232–245

CITATION INFORMATION

Chapter 6
What Do White Counselors and Psychotherapists Need to Know About Race? White Racial Socialization in Counseling and Psychotherapy Training Programs
Eleonora Bartoli, Keisha L. Bentley-Edwards, Ana María García, Ali Michael, and Audrey Ervin
Women & Therapy, volume 38, issues 3–4 (July–December 2015) pp. 246–262

Chapter 7
White Practitioners in Therapeutic Ally-ance: An Intersectional Privilege Awareness Training Model
Kim A. Case
Women & Therapy, volume 38, issues 3–4 (July–December 2015) pp. 263–278

Chapter 8
I Don't See Color, All People Are the Same: Whiteness and Color-Blindness as Training and Supervisory Issues
Michi Fu
Women & Therapy, volume 38, issues 3–4 (July–December 2015) pp. 279–294

Chapter 9
Examining Biases and White Privilege: Classroom Teaching Strategies That Promote Cultural Competence
Gina C. Torino
Women & Therapy, volume 38, issues 3–4 (July–December 2015) pp. 295–307

Chapter 10
Racial Microaggressions, Whiteness, and Feminist Therapy
Silvia L. Mazzula and Kevin L. Nadal
Women & Therapy, volume 38, issues 3–4 (July–December 2015) pp. 308–326

Chapter 11
The Unbearable Lightness of Being White
Diane M. Adams
Women & Therapy, volume 38, issues 3–4 (July–December 2015) pp. 327–340

Chapter 12
"American" as a Proxy for "Whiteness": Racial Color-Blindness in Everyday Life
Nellie Tran and Susan E. Paterson
Women & Therapy, volume 38, issues 3–4 (July–December 2015) pp. 341–355

Chapter 13
Slicing White Bre(a)d: Racial Identities, Recipes, and Italian-American Women
Andrea L. Dottolo
Women & Therapy, volume 38, issues 3–4 (July–December 2015) pp. 356–376

For any permission-related enquiries please visit:
http://www.tandfonline.com/page/help/permissions

About the Authors

Diane M. Adams is an Associate Professor in the Social Justice Track of the Clinical PsyD Program at the California School of Professional Psychology at Alliant International University in San Francisco and an African American woman. She has a lifelong and professional interest in issues of social justice, oppression, and racism, and in teaching, learning and writing about these issues.

Martha E. Banks is a research neuropsychologist at ABackans DCP, Inc., in Akron, Ohio, and a former professor at The College of Wooster and Kent State University. She is a retired clinical psychologist, whose primary research is on traumatic brain injuries sustained by victims of domestic violence. Dr. Banks was the 2008–2009 President of the Society for the Psychology of Women and is recognized for her professional service, presentations, and publications on women, trauma, and health care.

Eleonora Bartoli, Ph.D. is an Associate Professor and the Director of the graduate program in Counseling at Arcadia University. Her professional and research interests include multicultural counseling competence, White racial socialization, training effectiveness, trauma, and mindfulness. She is currently the Chair of the Masters in Counseling Accreditation Committee (MCAC).

Keisha L. Bentley-Edwards, Ph.D. is an Assistant Professor of Educational Psychology at the University of Texas at Austin. Her work focuses on the racialized experiences of youth and how cultural strengths can be used to support resiliency. She has developed measures of Black racial socialization and racial cohesion, and also studies how White racial socialization can influence interracial dynamics.

Kim A. Case, Ph.D., is Professor of Psychology and Women's Studies and Director of the Psychology Master's program Applied Social Issues sub-plan at the University of Houston-Clear Lake. Her research addresses diversity-course effectiveness, inclusive classroom practices, teaching for social justice, strategies for raising awareness of various forms of privilege, and prejudice confrontation as ally behavior. Her edited book, *"Deconstructing Privilege: Teaching and Learning as Allies in the Classroom,"* (2013) focuses on

ABOUT THE AUTHORS

interdisciplinary strategies for teaching about privilege through an intersectional lens.

Andrea L. Dottolo, Ph.D. is an Assistant Professor of Psychology at Rhode Island College and resident scholar at the Women's Studies Research Center at Brandeis University. Her research and teaching explores how social identities are constructed and maintained and the ways in which they are shaped by institutional and political structures. She was recently the guest editor for a special issue of the *Journal of Lesbian Studies* on white privilege (2014). Her current research with her mother, Carol, focuses on Italian American women, food, and identity.

Audrey Ervin, Ph.D., is an Assistant Professor and the Academic Program Director of the graduate program in Counseling Psychology at Delaware Valley College. Her clinical and research interests focus on multicultural counseling, gender, sexual identity and racial identity. She was the spokesperson for the Association for Women in Psychology.

Michi Fu, Ph.D., is a licensed psychologist specializing in working with culturally diverse clients and communities. She is an Associate Professor at Alliant International University where she teaches courses related to diversity issues. She is also the Statewide Prevention Projects Director of Pacific Clinics, responsible for stigma and discrimination reduction programs and cultural responsive trainings.

Ana María García, Psy.D., is an Associate Professor and the Chair of the Sociology, Anthropology and Criminal Justice Department at Arcadia University. Prior to joining Arcadia she served as Senior Staff Psychologist and Director of Training at the Child Psychiatry Center in Philadelphia, and as Senior Consultant, Project Coordinator, and Director of Client Services for Eclipse Consultant Group, an organization that developed and conducted diversity training in higher education, business, healthcare, and school settings. Dr. García's professional presentations and publications focus on diversity issues, including issues of race, ethnicity, gender and sexual orientation.

Ellyn Kaschak, Ph.D., is a Professor Emerita of Psychology at San José State University, Visiting Professor at the United Nations' University for Peace in Costa Rica and the editor of the journal *Women & Therapy*. She is also the author of 11 edited books, as well as *Engendered Lives: A New Psychology of Women's Experience* and *Sight Unseen: Gender and Race through Blind Eyes*.

Silvia L. Mazzula, Ph.D., is Director of the Latina Researchers Network, an Assistant Professor of Psychology at John Jay College of Criminal Justice,

CUNY, and former President of the Latino Psychological Association of New Jersey. Dr. Mazzula has extensive experience counseling underserved communities. Her research focuses on the intersection of racial cultural psychological processes and mental health, particularly among Latino/a populations.

Peggy McIntosh is Associate Director of the Wellesley Centers for Women at Wellesley College. She is Founder and Senior Associate of the National SEED Project on Inclusive Curriculum (Seeking Educational Equity and Diversity; nationalseedproject.org). Through Jean Baker Miller's Stone Center at Wellesley College she published three papers on "feeling like a fraud" and is working now on the fourth and final one in the series. Much of her work is devoted to systems of privilege and oppression, on which she first published in 1988.

Ali Michael, Ph.D., is the Director of K–12 Consulting and Professional Development at the Center for the Study of Race and Equity in Education at the University of Pennsylvania. She is also the Director and co-founder of the Race Institute for K–12 Educators and the author of *Raising Race Questions: Whiteness and Inquiry in Education*.

Kevin L. Nadal, Ph.D., is the Executive Director of the Center for Lesbian and Gay Studies at the Graduate Center- City University of New York (CUNY), as well as an Associate Professor of Psychology at John Jay College of Criminal Justice- CUNY. He is one of the leading experts on microaggressions, or subtle forms of discrimination towards people of color, women, and lesbian, gay, bisexual, and transgender people. He is the author of several works including "That's So Gay! Microaggressions and the Lesbian, Gay, Bisexual, and Transgender Community" (American Psychological Association, 2013) and "Women and Mental Disorders" (Praeger, 2011).

Elena Padrón, Ph.D., is an Associate Professor at the California School of Professional Psychology of Alliant International University in San Francisco, California. Her research focuses on the developmental psychopathology of attachment, particularly disorganized attachment, and the intergenerational transmission of attachment and trauma. Her clinical expertise is in the area of early childhood mental health and dyadic and family therapy with multicultural populations, especially with Latino families and children exposed to trauma.

Susan E. Paterson received her M.A. in Community Social Psychology from the University of Massachusetts Lowell. She is currently a doctoral student in the Community Well-Being Ph.D. program at the University of Miami.

Natalie Porter has written several papers on the intersections of gender, race, ethnicity, and class from a feminist perspective particularly in the areas of supervision, ethnics, and leadership. As a White woman, she has attempted to write from an antiracist, multicultural perspective as well.

Gina C. Torino, Ph.D., is an Assistant Professor of Human Development and Educational Studies at SUNY Empire State College. Her research interests include the investigation of pedagogical strategies which lead to the development of culturally competent clinicians; processes of White racial identity development, and racial/gender microaggressions.

Nellie Tran is an Assistant Professor at San Diego State University in the Department of Counseling and School Psychology. She is a Community Psychologist interested in the identification and impact of subtle forms of discrimination in varying contexts.

Introduction

Whiteness and White Privilege

ANDREA L. DOTTOLO
Psychology Department, Rhode Island College, Providence, Rhode Island; and Women's Studies Research Center, Brandeis University, Waltham, Massachusetts

ELLYN KASCHAK
Psychology Department, San José State University, San José, California

Psychologists, especially therapists, are often trained to ferret out, search and seize upon that which is not readily visible and cannot be spoken, implicit issues and influences, that are commonly taken for granted. Whether the models invoked are as diverse as those citing unconscious conflicts about love, sex and relationships or the hidden reinforcement of conditioning, psychological epistemologies are interested in making explicit that which is implicit and, in therapeutic approaches, bringing these issues into view. Feminist and multi-cultural researchers and practitioners further seek to expose the power structures that benefit them or that unfairly advantage some groups over others and so have, since their inception, striven to consider such issues as fees and sliding scales, masculinities and normative heterosexuality as unique areas of inquiry. This special issue is dedicated to adding to those issues that of Whiteness and White privilege in the therapy room, bringing to light that which is often unseen and, thus, unnamed.

Whiteness has been investigated by sociologists and critical race theorists, but has been largely overlooked by psychologists and psychotherapists, even those who deal with feminist and multi-cultural issues. The designation "multi-cultural" has, thus far, been reserved for people of color and ethnic groups other than White. Thence comes its otherness, which we aim in this issue to extend to the "non-others." While Whiteness generally carries privilege in European-American contexts, the extent of such privilege depends greatly on principles of intersectionality or mattering. That is, White women and men of different classes, disabilities and sexual orientations are not equally privileged in equivalent circumstances. Additionally, Whiteness is not only about privilege, but includes many other aspects that call out for analysis and investigation. In this volume, we attempt to answer that call.

Psychologists and psychotherapists have investigated racial-ethnic identities in various ways, but most often they use the construct to signify oppressed minorities (Phinney, 1992; Sellers, Smith, Shelton, Rowley & Chavous, 1998). This is not to say that the examination of racial-ethnic identities of marginalized groups in research and practice is not significant or has not advanced the discipline's understanding of race and identity, but instead that racial categories themselves are relational and comparative. An important corresponding component, privileged identities, can easily be overlooked by the well-socialized eye and mind (Kaschak, 2015). Missing a critical interrogation of privileged identities also leads to the failure to confront and claim responsibility for unearned positions in social hierarchies. Morawski (2004) explains:

> Until very recently, race research comprised a psychology of the "other" wherein nonwhite races were the target of investigation. That research presumed, but did not interrogate, a normative psychology of whiteness. Instead, it demonstrated a keen regard for the nature of otherness, all the while largely neglecting the meanings and implications of whiteness. (p. 216)

This "keen regard" also presents itself in the therapeutic context, where clinicians are often taught that race is a characteristic of those who are not White. Traditional psychologies, as well as feminist and multi-cultural approaches, support existing racial arrangements not only by problematizing racial designations other than White and/or directly avoiding the study of privileged identities, but more indirectly and broadly by omitting these characteristics in the study of more general psychological topics, such as human development, personality theory and even neuroscience. Guthrie (1976) famously criticized psychology's racism and inherent biases in favor of Whites in both theory and practice. In an especially powerful collection, Fine, Weis, Pruitt, and Burns (2004) address not only the shortcomings of psychology in understanding Whiteness, but the ways in which the discipline perpetuates inequalities through theory and research findings about topics and clinical tests that seem not to be about race at all. The authors state:

> Psychology, the home of IQ testing, special education, multicultural studies, cross-cultural psychology, intergroup relations, and stereotyping research, has spawned studies of personality, intelligence, motivation, achievement, and other measures of "merit" and competence that have camouflaged the ever-raced biases for ordering the world. ... Whiteness has come to be more than itself, embodying objectivity, normality, truth, knowledge, merit, motivation, achievement, and trustworthiness; it accumulates invisible and unrecognized supports that contribute to the already accumulated and bolstered capital of whiteness. Rarely, however, is it acknowledged that

whiteness demands and constitutes hierarchy, exclusion, and deprivation. The production and maintenance of white privilege is a difficult task. The very academic frameworks and practices of... psychology have worked hard to prop up racial hierarchies, securing the place of select groups within these hierarchies for many years now. A trenchant analysis of the "propping up" function of these fields is long overdue. (p. viii)

By implementing a feminist theoretical framework that highlights whiteness, we hope that this special issue contributes to the dismantling of racial hierarchies, chipping away at some of the props that support them. It is especially important to note that we are not advocating a monolithic whiteness, but emphasize the "mutability and multiplicity of white identities" (Perry, 2002, p. 3). Whiteness, like all other social identities, is shifting, contradictory, and shaped by gender, class, sexuality, age, region and culture (Dottolo & Stewart, 2013; Kaschak, 2010). Authors in this special issue employ scholarship on intersectionality (Collins, 1990; Crenshaw, 1995) and Kaschak's (2011) "mattering map" in order to contextualize and situate whiteness among many other forces and structures of power and privilege.

Kaschak introduces the collection by tracing some of the historical pillars of racism and situating whiteness as a central and primary lens of scholarship and discourse, a way of seeing. Drawing on her own experience, she contextualizes white privilege and queries her own process of learning about whiteness, offering suggestions and strategies for resisting racial binaries in therapy.

The next set of articles presents various cultural critiques of whiteness and white privilege. Padrón examines the construct of Whiteness in Venezuela, a racial framework that differs from the fixed racial categories commonly used in the United States. In Venezuela, where most citizens are of mixed race and where the concept of race is fluid, race and racism take on more complex forms that include dimensions such as social class, eye color, family, education, and even manners. Padrón discusses ways in which culturally defined notions of race can be incorporated into psychotherapy with Latina immigrants to the United States.

Porter explores the racialized messages and representations in the opera *Madame Butterfly,* analyzing how race, gender, and sexuality are configured in heterosexual relationships between White men and Asian women. She discusses how colonial manifestations of whiteness compare with contemporary themes of White privilege and stereotypes, connecting the opera with three recent therapy case studies involving White American husbands and Asian immigrant wives.

Banks interrogates the intersection of race, gender, and disability, demonstrating the cultural and psychological complexities of navigating particular forms of privilege and oppression. For White women, disability impacts on femininity, the part of identity that differentiates them from European American men who hold maximal power and privilege in U.S. culture. Disability represents a health issue, a barrier to social participation, and vulnerability to individual and societal abuse. Banks discusses how the development of a healthy disability identity allows European American women to negotiate being White, women, and disabled.

The next set of articles focuses on teaching and training interventions, offering specific strategies and exercises especially for students and practitioners about Whiteness and White privilege. Peggy McIntosh, often credited with beginning a critical discussion of Whiteness by "unpacking" various forms of white privilege, leads this charge. Her famous essay is included in this special collection, as the exercise she details in her article hinges upon reflections and applications of unearned advantage and dominance in multiple contexts. This practical exercise intends to help clinicians understand how clients' lives are influenced by societal disadvantages and advantages, to encourage a new understanding of self, and to increase empathy towards clients.

Bartoli, Bentley-Edwards, García, Michael, and Ervin purport that multicultural training in academic counseling and psychotherapy programs is often designed to address the needs of minority populations, and it rarely places Whiteness in the spotlight. Using the framework of feminist theory, the authors build on key findings on White racial socialization to outline the skills and awareness needed for White counselors and psychotherapists to promote racial justice in both their individual/counseling and community/advocacy work.

Case introduces a privilege awareness pedagogical model as a framework for White students in clinical training programs learning about White privilege, enhancing multicultural competencies, and developing as effective allies in the therapeutic relationship, or *therapeutic ally-ance*. The model emphasizes intersectionality to address White privilege along with a wide variety of oppressions often neglected in the curriculum, involves personal reflection on biases and assumptions to enhance multicultural competencies, and promotes student learning through social action to dismantle privilege. The pedagogical benefits of the four different activities and assignments are described.

Fu describes several different training methods, using excerpts from previous trainees' correspondences to demonstrate impact and effectiveness of the exercises. She shares her own reflections of the training process and explores how this work shaped her own identity. Recommendations for cultural sensitivity training are also considered. Torino also presents a variety of classroom teaching strategies that have been employed to assist White counseling trainees in developing a non-racist White racial identity and increasing cultural competence. Torino addresses the importance of both cognitive understanding and affective processing of biases and White privilege for White trainees, outlining the efficacy of specific didactic and experiential methods.

The last set of contributions centers on microaggressions and being "American," and the ways in which institutional and social structures benefit whites. Drawing from research and scholarship on feminist therapy and microaggressions, Mazzula and Nadal use a case vignette of a 40-year old African-American woman in treatment for depression with a White female therapist to demonstrate how microaggressions may unwittingly occur in a clinician–client dyad. They underscore the challenges that White therapists may encounter and provide suggestions and recommendations for culturally responsive therapy.

Adams explores the relationship between feelings of superiority, White privilege, White guilt, and a denied White racial identity and how these dynamics are enacted in therapy between White therapist and client in a U.S. context. She discusses the concepts of White privilege, White guilt, color-blind racial ideology, and the invisibility of Whiteness, demonstrating implications for clinical practice and training. Adams situates her experiences as a Black woman in the United States, aptly likening her observations of white privilege to the title of movie/novel, *The Unbearable Lightness of Being*—in this case, of being White.

Tran and Paterson discuss racial color-blindness as a modern strategy used by both Whites and People of Color to mask their discussions of race and privilege. People who endorse racial color-blindness tend to believe that race should not matter and currently does not matter in understanding individuals' lived experiences. Therefore, racially color-blind individuals use strategies to justify their racial privilege and racist beliefs and attitudes. Tran and Paterson explain how one such strategy is to use the term "American" as a proxy for "White" in describing instances of White privilege as norms and to hide discussions of race more generally.

Finally, Dottolo explores how Italian-American women construct, understand, and maintain their ethnic identity in relation to Whiteness and White privilege, especially through food. Using the metaphor of "slicing white *bread*," the "bread" represents white food, a commodity and marker of ethnicity, and also "slicing white *bred*"—how whiteness and being American are linked in important and varied ways. Dottolo argues that food serves as a symbol wherein Italian American women manipulate recipes and use food to navigate and negotiate being both Italian and American, Whiteness, femininity, and social class.

We hope that the contributions in this special issue foster larger conversations about Whiteness and privilege among psychologists- both researchers and practitioners. The articles included here contain theory, history, empirical research, personal reflections, and practical teaching strategies for the classroom. The authors remind us that Whiteness and other forms of privilege are situated among multiple other forces, structures, identities and experiences, and cannot be examined alone, without context. We see this special issue as an attempt to heed a call to action, especially invoked by Fine et al. (2004). We also hope that the issues raised in this collection generate more questions than answers, leading to both more thought and more action.

REFERENCES

Collins, P. H. (1990). *Black feminist thought: Knowledge, consciousness, and the politics of empowerment.* London, United Kingdom: Harper Collins.

Crenshaw, K. W. (1995). Mapping the margins: Intersectionality, identity politics, and violence against women of color. In K. W. Crenshaw, N. Gotanda, G. Peller, & K. Thomas (Eds.), *Critical race theory: The key writings that formed the movement* (pp. 359–383). New York, NY: The New Press.

Dottolo, A. L., & Stewart, A. J. (2013). "I never think about my race": Psychological features of White racial identities. *Qualitative Research in Psychology, 10,* 102–117. doi:10.1080/14780887.2011.586449

Fine, M., Weis, L., Pruitt, L. P., & Burns, A. (2004). Preface. In M. Fine, L. Weis, L. P. Pruitt, & A. Burns (Eds.), *Off white: Readings on power, privilege, and resistance* (pp. vii–x). New York, NY: Routledge.

Guthrie, R. V. (1976). *Even the rat was white: A historical view of psychology.* New York, NY: Harper and Row.

Kaschak, E. (2010) The mattering map: Morphing and multiplicity. In C. Bruns & E. Kaschak (Eds.), *Feminist therapy in the 21st century.* New York, NY: Taylor and Francis.

Kaschak, E. (2011). The mattering map: Multiplicity, metaphor and morphing in contextual theory and practice. *Women & Therapy, 34,* 6–18. doi:10.1080/02703149.2010.532688

Kaschak, E. (2015). *Sight unseen: Gender and race through blind eyes.* New York, NY: Columbia University Press.

Morawski, J. G. (2004). White experimenters, white blood, and other white conditions: Locating the psychologist's race. In M. Fine, L. Weis, L. P. Pruitt, & A. Burns (Eds.), *Off white: Readings on power, privilege, and resistance* (pp. 215–231). New York, NY: Routledge.

Perry, P. (2002). *Shades of white: White kids and racial identities in high school.* Durham, NC: Duke University Press.

Phinney, J. S. (1992). The multigroup ethnic identity measure: A new scale for use with diverse groups. *Journal of Adolescent Research, 7,* 156–172. doi:10.1177/074355489272003

Sellers, R. M., Smith, M. A., Shelton, J. N., Rowley, S. A. J., & Chavous, T. M. (1998). Multidimensional model of racial identity: A reconceptualization of African American racial identity. *Personality and Social Psychology Review, 2*(1), 18–39. doi:10.1207/s15327957pspr0201_2

Little White Lies: Racialization and the White/Black Divide

ELLYN KASCHAK

Psychology Department, San José State University, San José, California

This article emphasizes the importance of considering the history, context and epistemological bases of the use of race and racial categories in North America. Using this contextual grounding, I propose that racial categories are born of racism and not the reverse. I include some salient personal examples of the effects of the construct Whiteness in my own life experience. They are, at the same time, personal, political and cultural. Finally, some suggestions are offered for dealing with the issue of Whiteness, in particular, in feminist therapy, which seeks to uncover power differentials and the personal and political, each embedded in the other.

… *racism is so systematic and white privilege so impossible to escape, that one is, simply, trapped… I have enjoined males of my acquaintance to set themselves against masculinity… Likewise I can set myself against Whiteness.* (Frye, 1983)

INTRODUCTION

Just as there is no femininity without its purported opposite, masculinity, there is no way to approach the topic of Whiteness without including its juxtaposition and opposition to Blackness (and somewhat later to other hues and colors). They are reflections in the same mirror viewed through the eyes of what I have named elsewhere (Kaschak, 1992) the indeterminate cultural observer. This abstract, but real, cultural observer retains and propagates the visually based distortions and demands, to my way of thinking, of the particular culture. It is often difficult for any given individual to resist them, since they are largely unconscious and formed before language could represent them to the conscious mind. They are the very organizing principles of vision. These cultural eyes colonize the eye/brain combination in each of us who can see and, as my recent research (Kaschak, 2015) demonstrates, even those of us who cannot. The indeterminate observer is everywhere and nowhere at once. He is still masculine and will continue to be as long as we live in patriarchal societies. That is, he colonizes the eyes of men and women alike with his masculinist and racist values, including the value of interpersonal and international strategies of violence, war, colonization and corporate dominance. He organizes his vision by visual and physically apparent categories such as gender, race, and sexual orientation. In this article, I will question not only these categories, but the very process involved, focusing on the indeterminate observer in the United States or what is named America in defiance of all the other countries that make up the Americas. The indeterminate observer believes he in nothing more than his own centrality and entitlement.

In recent years, feminist and multi-cultural scholars in the United States have begun to problematize the very idea of Whiteness. In this article, I want to advance that discussion. To begin, I want to use the term racialization, as I also do in my book *Sight Unseen* (Kaschak, 2015), which more accurately describes these visually based cultural constructs. I have come to the conclusion, after much thought and research, that the very system of marking human beings for life as members of a racial category, racialization, is entirely a product of racism and not the reverse. Racism precedes race or racialization. Without it as a foundation, the entire edifice crumbles. What need would there be for the categories of race but to divide and conquer? In the service of those goals, the very concept of race was introduced in American[1] and European societies long ago. It is not enough and not even possible to ferret out the racism apparent or hiding in our racial system. The very idea of categorizing human beings must be rejected as racist and masculinist in its inception and its uses today.

As an ethical imperative, as well as an analysis of power distribution, an invented distinction masked as genetic or biological must be unmasked. Genetically, research has begun to demonstrate that there is simply no such thing as race (Bolnick, 2008; Cavalli-Sforza, Menozzi, & Piazza, 1994; Kaplan, 2011); there is no black and white at all. One has only to use one's eyes to see that this distinction is void. Yet most of us do not see well, as the indeterminate cultural observer colonizes our very eyes, demanding that we do not see what is apparent visually. From where then did this pervasive and damaging idea come?

Various researchers (Roediger, 1991) have noted that the racial designation White arose to describe European explorers, traders and settlers who came into contact with Africans and the indigenous peoples of the Americas. As the New World was developing, West African societies were already practicing slavery and, thus, already had a supply of slaves to trade with Europeans (Roy, 2001).

While both groups were regarded as heathens by "our" Christian forefathers, the colonizers felt that Native Americans did not adapt well to enslavement; in contrast, Africans had already adapted to subjugation by African tribal chiefs. Thus, racial theories were more easily applicable to justify their enslavement (Gossett, 1963).

The first Africans landed in America in 1619. They were not enslaved and operated on a basis of equality with Whites (Bennett, 1988). These Africans in pre-racial America occupied the social status of free persons or indentured servants (Roy, 2001, p. 85). However, facing the birth of a nation and socioeconomic forces, including a worldwide demand for tobacco, cotton and sugar, 17th Century colonial leaders needed a large labor force to meet market demands. Native American populations proved too difficult to submit to enslavement, and "... European Christians were reluctant to enslave other Christians [such as the Irish]" (Roy, 2001).

The colonial leaders decided to " ... base the American economic system on human slavery organized around the distribution of melanin in human skin" (Bennett, 1988). The idea of whiteness was then strengthened by the development of America's free-labor market. White workers demanded they be entitled to a legitimate status of "freeman," a status that combined white supremacy, an exclusively occupational trade and civil rights. To legitimate status differences, laws were enacted that imposed the status of 'slave for life' on enslaved Africans. By virtue of this distinction, White European indentured servants might eventually end their servitude, while Africans could not (Gossett, 1963).

Europeans, prior to the late 1600s, did not use the label, Black, to refer to any "race" of people, Africans included. Only after the racialization of slavery around 1680 did whiteness and blackness come to represent racial categories. "Just before the outbreak of the Civil War, Jefferson Davis told the United States Senate 'One of the reconciling features of the existence [of Negro slavery] is the fact that it raises every white man to the same general level, that it dignifies and exalts every white man by the presence of a lower race." (Banton, 1966)

Just as masculinity and femininity, male and female are not equivalent and symmetrical categories, neither are Black and White, even allowing for the more contemporary Brown. Although dichotomous, they do not provide equal access to power and other resources. According to Kincheloe (1999), " ... a pedagogy of whiteness reveals such power-related processes to whites and non-whites alike, exposing how members of both groups are stripped of self-knowledge" (p. 163). No one would dispute the fact that Whiteness still carries the embedded meanings of superiority and the other categories of "lesser than" as they darken in color. Other groups include, in contemporary American parlance, those generally and arbitrarily considered Brown, including Latinos, Asians (previously yellow) and Native Americans (previously red). The color wheel itself has revolved in the eyes of the indeterminate observer. I will not pursue the implications of these supposed racial distinctions in this article, as I believe that the most important aspect of Whiteness is its early and continued distinction from Blackness.

To expose this false perspective even further, there has been, since colonial times, a triple conflation of White, European, and Christian that implies moral and cultural superiority first codified within the language of race in 15th century Spain and adopted into the colonial discourse of white superiority and non-white inferiority in the New World (Bennett, 1998).

THE POLITICAL IS PERSONAL

As a child, I was not a White person, but matured into one rapidly at about the age of ten in an invented American version of racial puberty. As part of the G.I. Bill put in effect after World War II, the American government adjusted their very definition of Whiteness to include Hebrews, as we were named in the official records of the time. They were offering mortgages to returning GIs to enable them to live in the newly built suburbs of Long Island. This was an early program in Affirmative Action for Jewish men only. My father qualified for this program and was able to secure a $10,000 mortgage that bought him a small tract house in Valley Stream, the very first town over the city line, as was said colloquially. By government fiat, we were permitted to live in these communities and thereafter were White people, joining the Irish and the Italians before us (Brodkin, 1998). No one spoke of it and I only learned as an adult that, during my childhood, I was not White. No wonder I feel queasy about the distinction.

As I approached this form of racial adolescence, instead of my body developing curves and secondary sex characteristics of the other officially recognized puberty, it began to turn white. I know this sounds physically impossible and that is precisely because it is. This does not disturb the indeterminate observer, who vision overrides physical reality. I still retain contingent white skin privilege in the United States. It is not impervious to dissolution. There is a simple question that causes it to dissolve. It lasts until the question can be posed, "What kind of name is that (often code for "Are you a Jew?")." Full membership in the Whiteness club still demands Christianity, as it did from the start.

Although I am in a body that American eyes see as White, there is actually nothing white about it. In fact, the color of my skin falls somewhere on the visual spectrum between pink and yellow. To place this color combination within a bodily context, my body is also recognizable as female and now as old. All this is the minimum amount of information immediately available to anyone who reads the American visual code. Judging visually is unconscious and, as research demonstrates, takes only a few seconds (Kaschak, 2015). It is not possible for our human brains to defer or refuse these split second decisions.

Which combinations of seen attributes are salient at a given moment depends on context. It is the multiplicity of characteristics in context to which our human eyes/minds attribute meaning. I am a particular kind of White person, as judged from the outside. There are those whose skin color is lighter than mine and are not members of the White group, including many Latin Americans whom I know. There are Europeans who are darker than many of these Latins, but are still considered White. Color itself cannot explain these distinctions, so what can? How is our very vision and perception so carefully colonized that we cannot see what is in front of our own eyes?

The human perceptual system is designed to organize visual images into patterns and then to relegate as much as possible to the unconscious mind. The most ordinary task would be impossible without this organizing system. These patterns are organized by issues of meaning or mattering. In this way, the consciousness-lowering that we call socialization creates these meanings and, like a cultural magician, makes them disappear from view. Of course, like magic, this is only an optical illusion. The racism or sexism is still alive and well, but hidden from sight.

In Costa Rica, where I live now, skin color is not a particularly salient concern. There I am a Gringa or, more politely, an ex-pat. I have lived there at least part time since my early twenties, but I will always and forever be a foreigner. I am not at all thought of as White. The Costa Ricans have their categories, but race is not as high on the list as is nationality, which is inherited throughout the generations. If your ancestors were from Italy and you have an Italian surname, you will forever after be referred to as Italian. Or Polish. Or Jewish. There are many other systems on the planet that serve to reduce people to categories, focusing instead on ethnic groups, tribes or clans, but a review of them is beyond the scope of this article. Suffice it to say, racialization is a culturally meaningful concept; it matters to North Americans.

Multi-cultural psychology is unique to the U.S. It is as Western as the dominant culture itself and takes for granted Western values and categories for sorting human beings. Thus, it is in extreme danger of mirroring the categories of American racism unquestioningly. From a larger global perspective, things are not so black and white, nor are people. As another example, although I am bi-lingual and bi-cultural, it is in the wrong direction for North American multi-cultural perspectives to see those categories. They do not exist, and where does that leave me and others in my position? Partially invisible.

Looking in the cultural mirror from another angle, Costa Ricans who come to the United States are known as Latinos or Hispanics and automatically all considered Brown or People of Color, although they fit awkwardly into all three American racial designations. Most are considered to be White in Costa Rica, but a brief plane trip can change all that. However, Latino is not a race and is not even a nationality, but many nationalities. Spaniards, ancestors of the majority of Costa Ricans, are generally considered to be White. Here we expose an additional hidden geographical meaning of Whiteness. To be precise, Europeans are White; Latinos are not.

A friend of mine who is a member of the racialized group African-American had an illuminating experience one day in a café in Paris. She was, of course, getting their famously atrocious service. She reflexively attributed it to racialization, as she had learned through many hard lessons in the American South of her childhood. On further investigation, she discovered that she was indeed being treated badly, but it was because she was an American. She had never thought of herself as an American, but always as a particular kind of American, an African-American. The Parisian waiters did not perceive that distinction.

Whiteness then is not so much a personal quality as it is a reflection of power embedded in the very structure and functioning of American culture. One of the functions of the indeterminate observer is to metabolize the outlandish into the ordinary, taken-for-granted. In that process, the seen becomes unseen, the visible becomes invisible, and the racism and sexism taken for granted and named ordinary life.

THERAPEUTIC INTERSECTIONS

The way that feminists and psychotherapists know to combat this unconscious colonization of the eyes and mind begins with the indelicate art of consciousness-raising or "Seeing with beginner's eyes." This process of "bringing into awareness" is part and parcel of every effective therapeutic approach, although in itself does not necessarily bring about change (Kaschak, 1992). Within the paradigm of feminist therapy, consciousness-raising serves to permit the individual to discern that what seems an individual problem instead involves membership in a culturally meaningful group. That is, the problem belongs to all racialized and genderized people, although differently depending on other aspects of their experience and identity. The correct level of analysis can lead to a more effective solution.

Thus, feminist therapy supports the development as a practice and an art of the ability to notice and to question cultural realities. Feminist and culturally sensitive therapy is one context in which this process can occur or, at least, begin. Buddhist practice and group analysis, as used to occur in consciousness-raising groups, are others.

Whiteness has to be made visible long before it can be made irrelevant. The first step is to defy the pressures of color-blindness and begin to name the obvious. The first step in the process of consciousness-raising is noticing and involves de-familiarizing (Friedman, 2011; 2012) the quotidian. Such a first step is fraught with danger, as it involves naming each White person as such, undermining the system by invoking it. This must occur carefully and not mirror in any way White racism, but must instead occur as a call to consciousness. Only then can these distortions be resisted. As a start, in any circumstance in which the speaker would identify someone as Black or Brown, they might begin the practice of identifying the White persons as well. It would sound something like the following: "I passed a White man on the street today, who was hassling another White man. I was afraid that a fight would break out and crossed the street."

Consciousness-raising and power analysis, two irreducible aspects of feminist psychotherapy, along with gender analysis, shed light on what easily can become unconscious and taken-for-granted. The feminist call to consciousness of the yet unnamed category of gender ushered in an intellectual and cultural revolution that cannot be undone. These very same steps can be applied to the cultural racialization. Careful attention facilitates the process of naming into visibility that which has been relegated to the invisible. Conscious-raising allows what has been made invisible through the learning process of consciousness-lowering that each culture designs for each individual to become visible. Whiteness is one of the most important aspects of this socialization process, becoming the invisible, default position for racialization. That is, it becomes the race that is not one, especially among Whites in the Western nations.

Feminist therapy analyzes personal and structural power. Feminist therapists, but especially those designated as White, must deal with the deleterious consequences and effects of Whiteness, while, at the same time, rejecting its very existence. Much as many feminist men have opposed masculinity, so must we all resist being seen as White, Black or Brown, being sorted and compartmentalized by the amount of melanin in the skin, being reduced to a visual category. Whiteness is not an identity, but an historical category that damages all who come into contact with it.

Resistance occurs on two levels. First, as I have indicated here, the very sorting principle must be rejected. Secondly, the power differential, as manifested in the sense of entitlement also associated with masculinity (Kaschak, 1992) must be refused over and over. In no way does such resistance rectify historical and material inequities and their accompanying human damage, but it can contribute to its future reduction.

Feminist therapy was originally opposed to the idea of individual, confidential, separated therapy, except in temporary and urgent circumstances (Kaschak, 1976). This crucial aspect of intervention has been entirely lost as feminist therapy has become a profession instead of a revolution, a way of earning a living instead of resisting racism and misogyny. By participating in professionalized feminist therapy, women and men are separated from each other and from the very process of group consciousness that lies at the root of feminist therapy. In this way, they are also separated from the collective action necessary for social change. I lament this loss that consolidates power and awareness in the relationship with the therapist. I think it is a mistake of huge proportions for feminists. Racism, like misogyny, classism, etc. cannot be opposed individually, for they are not at all individual issues or characteristics.

While Whiteness acquires meaning only in context, Whiteness is also the invisible context for meaning-making, that is, for what matters. From it flow the categories and meanings that come to matter in everyday life. It becomes the norm, the default position that need not even be named to exist and to provide definition.

In the four decades since I began teaching and training therapists, I have had the opportunity to discuss these issues with many generations of students. The semester invariably begins, all these years later, with several students protesting that the subject matter is not about them and that a course in Gender and Ethnicity should be an elective for women and ethnic minorities. White students consistently begin by saying that they have no ethnicity and are just regular or "White bread" Americans. The course, I hope, changes their minds. And isn't that just what education is about, changing minds?

Just as the official romantic narrative of the media remains predominantly heterosexual and in other agents of the indeterminate observer's influence, so is the history of racism described in the language of "progress" rather than of domination and hallucination. The choice of language deceives us. There is no progress involved in dismantling a system that never should have been put in place.

I believe that feminists, multi-culturalists and all people need to stop legitimizing the Black/White/Brown categories and stop using White as the invisible or default position. Racialization is a hallucination that must be cured and such "cures" are the purview of psychotherapy. Americans are hypnotized by the indeterminate cultural observer into seeing black and white where there is an infinite spectrum of browns, pinks, yellows, etc. and no black or white at all. In recent years, we have even invented the color brown where yellow and red were once used.

I prefer to consider gender, race, class and sexual orientation as multiplicities rather than intersections, as they combine and recombine in unique and complex ways and do not simply overlap. These are not just intersections, attributions that are simply additive or even subtractive; they are multipliers and, paradoxically, as they multiply, they divide.

I reject the categories. Why do we still see through their eyes? For it to be effective, training in racial socialization must move beyond an awareness of privilege and biases to an understanding of racial hierarchies, one's place in them, as well as one's role in preserving (or questioning) the status quo. Multi-cultural concepts should not just reflect these categories, but should seek to destroy them, to define the discourse.

NOTE

1. To avoid linguistic awkwardness, I will refer to the United States as American and its residents as Americans in various places. The reader should be aware that this reference is a product and preference of the American indeterminate observer and is being used in order not to introduce confusion into the narrative. Note that all of Latin America, as well as Canada, are also American. In most of Latin America, we are known as North America and are considered imperious when naming ourselves Americans.

REFERENCES

Banton, M. (1966). Race as a Social Category. Race VIII:1.

Bolnick, D. A. (2008). Individual ancestry inference and the reification of race as a biological phenomenon. In B. A. Koenig, S. S. Richardson, & S.-J. Lee (Eds.), *Revisiting race in a genomic age* (pp. 70–88). New Brunswick, NJ: Rutgers University Press.

Bennett, A. (1998). Who was White? The disappearance of Non-European White identities and the formation of European racial Whiteness. *Ethnic and Racial Studies, 21*(6), 1029–1055. doi:10.1080/01419879808565651

Brodkin, K. (1999). *How Jews became White folks and what that says about race in America.* New Brunswick, NJ: Rutgers University Press.

Cavalli-Sforza, L. L., Menozzi, P., & Piazza, A. (1994). *The history and geography of human genes.* Princeton, NJ: Princeton University Press.

Friedman, A. (2011). Toward a sociology of perception: Sight, sex and gender. *Cultural Sociology, 5*(2), 187–206. doi:10.1177/1749975511400696

Friedman, A. M. (2012). Believing not seeing: A blind phenomenology of sexed bodies. *Symbolic Interaction, 35*(3), 284–300. doi:10.1002/symb.25

Frye, M. (1983). *On being white, the politics of reality: Essays in feminist theory.* Freedom, CA: The Crossing Press, pp. 12.

Gossett, T. F. (1963). *Race: The history of an idea.* Dallas, TX: Southern University Press.

Kaplan, J. M. (2011). "Race": What biology can tell us about a social construct. *Encyclopedia of Life Sciences (ELS).* Chichester, UK: John Wiley & Sons, Ltd.

Kaschak, E. (1976). Sociotherapy. An ecological model for psychotherapy with women. *Psychotherapy: Theory, Research and Practice, 13,* 61–63. doi:10.1037/h0086487

Kaschak, E. (1992). *Engendered lives: A new psychology of women's experience.* New York, NY: Basic Books.

Kaschak, E. (2015). *Sight unseen: Gender and race through blind eyes.* New York, NY: Columbia University Press.

Kincheloe. J. L. (1999). The struggle to define and reinvent Whiteness: A pedagogical analysis. *College Literature, 26*(3), 162–194.

Roediger, D. R. (1991). *The wages of Whiteness: Race and the making of the American working class.* New York, NY: Verso.

Roy, W. G. (2001). *Making societies: The historical construction of our world.* Thousand Oaks, CA: Pine Forge Press.

Whiteness in Latina Immigrants: A Venezuelan Perspective

ELENA PADRÓN

California School of Professional Psychology, Alliant International University, San Francisco, California

This article examines the construct of Whiteness in Venezuela, which requires a framework that differs from the fixed racial categories commonly used in the United States. In Venezuela, where most citizens are of mixed race and where the concept of race is fluid, race and racism take on more complex forms that include dimensions such as social class, eye color, family, education, and even manners. This means that Whiteness and privilege do not always go hand in hand. I discuss ways in which this culturally defined notion of race can be incorporated into psychotherapy with Latina immigrants to the United States.

De la Cadena (2001) described how in many Latin American countries, visitors may observe a "relative ease with which pervasive and very visible discriminatory practices coexist with the denial of racism" (p. 16). Some might claim that the process of *mestizaje*, or widespread racial mixing, that took place in Venezuela, and which resulted in a great majority of its current population being of "mixed race," implies that there is no significant racism in that country. I start from the principle of critical race theory, which states that racism is ubiquitous in American society (Delgado & Stefancic, 2013), and argue that this applies to Venezuelan society as well.

However, in order to truly understand how race and racism affect clients from Latin American countries, therapists in the United States must guard from a natural tendency to simply apply the American understanding of race to those clients, as if it were universal. If we do not take into account historical, socio-political, and cultural views of race across different countries, we might find ourselves attempting to "educate" clients who emigrated from foreign countries about what their understanding of race "should" be. In such cases, we would run the risk that American cultural biases could distort our understanding of immigrant clients. This is similar to a process Carter (1998) has termed cultural encapsulation, which he has described as having the potential to interfere with the effectiveness of psychotherapy when the cultural values of therapist and client differ.

There was an interesting discussion about race that took place in the comment section of the *American Psychologist*, which illustrates the perils of cross-national assumptions about race. Sue, Capodilupo, Nadal, and Torino (2008) replied to a comment made by Harris (2008), who had questioned their labeling of an incident personally experienced by Sue as a micro-aggression. Sue et al. (2008) described Harris and other commenters as "well-intentioned Whites" (p. 277), who tended to deny the reality of people of color (POC) in order to impose their own reality. In other words, Sue and his colleagues attributed Harris's disagreements with their own views to his "White" privilege. Interestingly, Harris (2008) then responded by claiming that a micro-aggression had been committed against himself:

> I must admit to some anger and even more disbelief at a significant error. I am a native of La República Bolivariana de Venezuela and as such identify as a LatinoAmericano. While I personally dislike the term POC, the fact remains that per Sue et al.'s use of the definition, I fit into that categorical nomenclature. (p. 22)

In the same volume, Sue (2009) apologized to Harris for his error regarding Harris's identity. When referring to micro-aggressions against POCs in the United States, Sue and colleagues (2008) stated that "it seems truly arrogant for any White person to define and impose their racial reality on marginalized groups." I wholeheartedly agree with this sentiment, and would like to take it even further, to the *cross-national* level. The application of American assumptions of race onto an individual from Venezuela could be seen as a form of oppression via national privilege.

The United States of America often calls itself merely "America." In fact, there is no alternative to the term "American" to refer to cultural products, practices, or individuals from this country. It could be said that this implicitly denies the existence of other countries in the American continent, most of which are Latin American countries. The effect is akin to, for example, the United Kingdom calling itself "Europe." In many ways, the United States holds power over other countries, dominating the world stage and playing an important role in the socio-political history of many Latino countries. Besides its economic and military power, the culture of the United States has been exported across the world, and its ample resources have allowed academicians and advocates of equality, access to excellent educational opportunities and to the means to communicate their perspectives to the world. The American rhetoric about race is highly developed, owing in part to its First World status.

If race is indeed a cultural invention (Smedley & Smedley, 2011), then therapists must understand the societies from which immigrant clients came, in order to fully integrate considerations of race into the therapeutic relationship. In this paper, I will attempt to provide such an understanding, specifically for therapists working with women who emmigrated from Venezuela. Díaz-Lázaro, Verdinelli, and Cohen (2012) state that, within the context of Empowerment Feminist Therapy with Latina immigrants, the socio-political histories of their home countries must be given careful consideration in therapy, owing to the important role they may play in the clients' presentations. I have chosen the example of Venezuela, partly because I am a Venezuelan woman who immigrated to the United States, and partly because I want to underscore that Latin America is not homogenous with regard to race and racism, and that therefore each country deserves its own consideration.

BRIEF HISTORICAL CONTEXT OF VENEZUELA

There are differences between the Spanish colonization of Latin America and the English colonization of North America, which are important to take into account when interpreting the discrepant ways in which the construct of race is conceived in these regions. In the mid-16th century the Spanish settled in Venezuela. As a result, many indigenous communities were decimated, while only a minority—mainly those located in remote rural areas—were able to retain their independent culture (Nichols, 2013). Pollock (1986) explains that, while the English settled in relatively small and specific regions, the Spanish conquered a much larger area, quickly spreading across Latin America, massacring large portions of the millions of Indigenous people, and raping and mixing with Indigenous women to produce mixed-race children; in contrast, North America remained mostly White and unmixed.

In Latin America, the majority of these indigenous communities were incorporated, together with Africans, by the Spanish in the *encomienda* system, in which both groups worked for European-born, or their *criollo* descendants, who were landowners appointed by the Spanish crown (Keen & Haynes, 2003; Montañez, Sánchez, & Salinas, 2003; Nichols, 2013). In Venezuela, particular forms of racial mixing took place:

> In the cities, slaves, European-descended immigrants, and free people of colour lived side by side in rigidly regulated social position. (….) In the rural and coastal areas, however, less-wealthy white overseers, African slaves, free people of colour, and indigenous people all interacted and intermarried regularly with limited white contact.

> While a few examples of remote tribes or isolated coastal cities represented small spaces wherein African and indigenous cultural heritage persisted in colonial Venezuela, economics and geography created a more general mixing of the population. (Nichols, 2013, p. 173)

By the 19th century, despite the racial mixing and the fact that different racial groups lived side by side in some areas of Venezuela, there were nevertheless marked differences in what each of these groups represented and in the power they held. Most Indigenous people were of mixed race, became known as *pardos* or *mestizos*, and held economically disadvantaged positions in the social hierarchy (Nichols, 2013; Pollock, 1986). Even at a greater disadvantage, were the non-mixed Indigenous or Black people, and *mulatos* (Pollock, 1986), who were seen at the time as barbaric, and judged to be lacking in decency and morality (Cunill Grau, 1987; Nichols, 2013; Nichols & Morse, 2010).

After the end of the colonial period, there was a project to produce "coffee with milk" citizens, the result of racist social and immigration policies as well as belief systems, which favored the whitening of the Venezuelan population as a way to cleanse the effect of non-white racial traits (Nichols, 2013). Immigration policies gave preference to those from Europe, while creating obstacles for non-Whites (Wright, 1988). Nichols (2013) aptly claims that in the history of Venezuela it has always been "understood that more milk is better than more coffee" (p. 173).

Even given this history of exclusion and discrimination, Hooker (2005) warns against the interpretation that current discrimination of Black and Indigenous people in Latin America is merely the result of historic practices; she underscores that socioeconomic disparities are also partly due to ongoing racial discrimination practices—which persist even after controlling for education—such as income inequality and restricted power to participate in politics and legislation. This author also explains that, while Indigenous people in Latin America have been able to claim some social and legal rights, Blacks are at a relative disadvantage, despite being a larger minority.

THE RACIAL CONTINUUM IN VENEZUELA

Estimates from the mid-twentieth century place the "mixed race" portion at approximately 70% of the total population of Venezuela (Library of Congress, Federal Research Division, 1993; Wright, 1993). Nevertheless, one should be aware that the literal translation of a word from one language to the other does not necessarily also carry with it an equivalent meaning. A qualitative study by Gulbas (2013) found that, when forced to choose among only three specific racial categories, Venezuelan women predominantly chose "Black"; this was followed by "*morena*" (i.e., brown), with "White" as the least endorsed category. It is important to note that this pattern was present across all social classes. This indicates an important difference between Venezuelan society and the pattern in the United States, where the White phenotype predominates in upper and middle classes, while POCs are statistically more likely to be in the lower socioeconomic classes. Therefore, when placed within the social context, being of "mixed race" in Venezuela does not necessarily have the same meaning it does in the United States.

Carter (1998) argues that, despite the fact that in the United States they tend to be grouped under one category, "Hispanics cut across all racial lines" (p. 43). England (2010) refers to the systems used in some Latin American countries as a "racial continuum," which she contrasts with the "racial binary of the 'North'" (p. 195). Venezuelans do not tend to divide themselves into discrete categorical racial groups in the same way individuals tend to do in the United States. In fact, the Venezuelan census has not collected race information since 1854 (Nichols, 2013). Wright (1993) reports that the Venezuelan government argued that this omission was purposely committed so as not to arise painful memories of slavery; I regard this claim will strike the reader, as it does me, as an attempt to disguise racism.

The fact is that, for women in modern Venezuela, the checkbox question of race—though not racism itself—is particularly foreign. This may also apply to other Latina immigrants to the United States. A recent study of women, comparing open-ended answers against the federally defined racial and ethnic categories, found that, while immigrants responded to checkbox questions of ethnicity, they tended to leave blank the box for race (Eisenhower, Suyemoto, Lucchese, & Canenguez, 2013). Interestingly, the authors compared open-ended questions with the checkbox approach, and found that most of the women who left unchecked the question of race, responded to the open-ended question of race by self-identifying as Latinas. Immigrants in general had the lowest rates of agreement between open-ended and checkbox questions. Eisenhower et al. (2013) concluded that the checkbox approach to race is especially ill-suited for Latinas and immigrant women in the United States, adding that "the lived experiences of many immigrants may not be captured by the NIH measure" (p. 4).

THE "CULTURALIST" NOTION OF RACE IN VENEZUELA

Carter (1998) has argued that "race organizes culture in the United States" (p. 44). While in North America race has greater ties to phenotype, in Latin America race is defined more complexly and is very closely related to culture (De la Cadena, 2001; Pitt-Rivers 1973). In fact, De la Cadena (2001) has argued that in Latin America, culture organizes and subordinates phenotypic markers of race. In Venezuela specifically, race (i.e., the socially constructed framework on the basis of which individuals are grouped and treated in society) is defined based on dimensions of ethnic origin, social class, social setting, skin color, facial features, hair type, eye color, clothing style, behavior, education level and career, the location of an individual's home, and even morality and decency (Gulbas, 2013; Nichols, 2013; Wright, 1988).

This multivariate construction of race implies that a singular focus on skin color in order to determine an individual's standing in Venezuelan society would likely lead to erroneous conclusions. Nichols (2013) argues that "in Venezuela, skin colour alone is a problematic marker of status and family position" (p. 175). For example, De la Cadena (2001) explains that individuals who would be considered White in the United States might not be considered White in certain Latin American countries, and that "brown skinned individuals can be white" in Latin America (p.16). This last statement puts in evidence that a Venezuelan woman who may be perceived as "brown-skinned" by American standards, may in fact self-identify as White, and is likely to enjoy some privileges associated with Whiteness, while in Venezuela. These privileges would presumably disappear upon immigration to the United States.

There are important implications of this culturalist notion of race. A certain level of understanding of the cultural context, of the behaviors and practices that are considered desirable, and of nuanced markers of social class, are required in order to better understand the experiences of oppression and privilege of Venezuelans. There is a saying in the Spanish language that, while it was not intended to apply to racism, captures the essence of this point quite well: "*Como te ven te tratan, si te ven mal te maltratan,*" which can be translated as: "However they perceive you is how they will treat you; if they perceive you badly, they will mistreat you." It is important to consider that this "perception" is not merely based on skin color, and it is certainly not restricted to the phenotypic aspects of race. This means that race is defined *through* culture in Latin America (De la Cadena, 2001).

The multicultural mental health literature in the United States has often used the terms culture and race interchangeably (Carter, 1998). However, this lack of differentiation is especially problematic when attempting to reconcile the notion of race in Latin America with that of the United States. The racial worldview tends to dominate in the United States, which means that sociocultural factors are subordinated to what are thought to be biological markers of race (Carter, 1998; Smedley & Smedley, 2011). Carter (1998) states that "in its original use, race referred to a biological taxonomy that was applied to humans and represented the assumption that a group's shared genetic heritage was evident from physical characteristics (Guthrie, 1976; Johnson, 1990)" (p. 13). This author argues that in the United States race is defined through phenotype, or physical characteristics, and particularly through skin color; as such, it has been used to rank and classify individuals into social strata. However, several authors have contended that this notion of skin color as a marker of race, and this understanding of race as reflecting an inherent, innate, and unchangeable quality of an individual, are misguided (Carter, 1998; Smedley & Smedley, 2011; Pinderhughes, 1989).

When race is defined mostly through physical characteristics, which are perceived to be biologically fixed, this carries with it the consequence that racial identity, as well as its corresponding social status, are also fixed. This notion of race is especially at odds with the more fluid conception reflected in the culturalist definition of race used in countries like Venezuela. Specifically, due to the inclusion of dimensions unrelated to factors that in popular culture are thought to be hereditary markers of race (e.g., skin color), the culturalist notion of race allows for the possibility that an individual's race can in fact change within their lifetime, and that an individual's race can differ from that of her ancestors—who may nevertheless have a similar phenotype. Consider, for instance, aspects such as education, income, style of dress, and behavior, which are also given weight when attributing social status and racial identity in Venezuela. Unlike skin color, these additional aspects can in fact be subject to transformation across an individual's lifetime; they can be affected by opportunity, resources, oppression, social influence, and even choice.

Indeed, "culturalist definitions of race, which endowed education with almost eugenic might, were central to the invention and legislation of Latin American nations" (De la Cadena, 2001, p. 17). Nichols (2013) explains that in Venezuela, by the end of the nineteenth century, there existed:

> (...) The possibility of racial whitening through the acquisition of funds, status or land. From this phenomenon comes the widely repeated saying 'money whitens'. All cafe´ con leche citizens could use wealth and power to bolster their claim to a position of 'decency' (p. 173).

This constitutes a very significant departure from the apparently innate and immutable understanding of race in the United States.

HIDDEN RACISM IN VENEZUELA

Racial mixing and racial democracy were historically seen as defining characteristics of Latin American countries and as sources of pride, in response to European views that Latin Americans were inferior (Golash-Boza & Bonilla-Silva, 2013). But, defining race through culture can also lead to a corresponding form of "culturalist racism." Hoetnik (1967) argued that, even the more fluid boundaries of the continuum approach to race, have the undercurrent of European racism and slavery. Quintero (2012) has called this apparent racial democracy in Venezuela a myth that attempts to negate the historic hierarchical differences between groups.

One of the implications of this history is that in Venezuelan society there might be hidden racist attitudes, covered by a denial of racism. In an attempt to uncover racist attitudes regarding Afro-Venezuelans, Montañez and colleagues (2003) designed an instrument composed of both close-ended and open-ended questions, and piloted it with 60 Venezuelans, asking them to provide their opinion of the instrument. The authors expressed being quite surprised by the intense emotional reactions that the instrument brought about. Some of these reactions included rejection of the questions and labeling of the questions themselves as discriminatory. This was probably due to the reticence of Venezuelans to openly speak about racism when presented with the issue very directly. Participants also criticized the model itself, reporting that the instrument was based on Black-and-White thinking, as opposed to a continuum.

Given their understanding that racial prejudice in Venezuela tends to be rather ambivalent and intermittent, as opposed to overt, Montañez and colleagues (2003) proceeded to revise the instrument in order to make it more culturally appropriate and evoke less defensiveness. One of the major aspects of the revision was that they moved away from the model of Black and White relations, and instead framed the questions from a perspective of *mestizaje*. For instance, self-identification of race was introduced by the statement that the mixed race population of Venezuela consisted mainly of three components: White, Indigenous, and Black. Respondents were then permitted to identify to how many of these component groups they were biologically related (thereby allowing individuals to endorse more than one category). Subsequently, participants were asked to express, in their own words, how they self-identified within the *mestizo* population of Venezuela. The detailed results of the study are beyond the scope of this paper. Suffice it to say that the revised version of the measure was believed by the authors to be a more accurate reflection of latent racist attitudes in Venezuela. This fascinating study can offer therapists a useful model for how to approach discussions of race with Latina immigrants.

CONCLUSIONS AND CLINICAL IMPLICATIONS

In this article, I have argued that psychotherapists in the United States are at risk of allowing nationalism and power-over to erode the therapeutic relationship if they insist on solely applying an American definition of race when working with Latina immigrants. To attempt to label the particular form of race which exists in Venezuela as "better" or "worse" than that which exists in the United States is misguided. Just like the myth of racial democracy has had the negative implication of making it very difficult to address the problem directly, it has also minimized overt racial conflict. The lack of overt racial conflict in turn has complex implications. For instance, it may be interpreted as the silencing of the voices of the oppressed; and, it is also important to note that racially motivated crime and White supremacist organizations are nearly unheard of in Venezuela.

I believe mental health providers will be best poised to serve immigrant Venezuelans if they understand the history and reality of race in their clients' country of origin, rather than merely attempting to impose the lessons learned by individuals from the United States throughout *their* own history. With regard to the provision of psychotherapy in the United States, Carter (1998) argues that "racial boundaries limit mental health professionals' capacity to help visible racial/ethnic group members (i.e., Black, Asian, Hispanic, and Indian Americans), and some White individuals, on their terms and from their perspectives" (p. 11). This sentiment could be extended and underscored in the case of immigrants.

The issues discussed in this paper have implications for psychotherapy with immigrant Latinas in the United States, and especially Venezuelans. The question of race is usually brought up even before the initial meeting with the therapist; it tends to be included as a checkbox in paperwork that clients must complete during the screening or intake process. Ruiz (2012) states that:

> An RCT [Relational Cultural Theory] framework that includes an assessment of sociopolitical and cultural factors can help clinicians understand which of these factors may be contributing to her experience of disconnections. In addition, relating to less acculturated Latina immigrants in a manner consistent with their cultural values can be helpful in establishing mutually empathic connections. (p. 77)

Therapists treating Latina immigrants might be well advised to revise their paperwork to allow for open-ended answers. This would prevent a microaggression from occurring even before the therapeutic relationship begins. Another option would be to allow clients to check the box as "immigrant", note the country they immigrated from, and then have more open-ended and extensive face-to-face discussions in session with the therapist. Of course, the discussions about race should not be limited to the first session, and should rather be ongoing. This is especially true for clients from countries like Venezuela, for whom multiple dimensions must be analyzed and discussed in order to truly understand their race-related experiences and identities.

I hope that by now the reader understands that one must not assume that phenotype reflects self-identified race. Recently, a trainee who was consulting with me regarding a case, described her adolescent client, who was an immigrant Latino, by stating "he says he's White, but he's *not* White"; she reached this conclusion based largely on her client's skin color. While this could in fact be a case of internalized racism on the part of the young client, it is also important that psychotherapists in this country understand that they do not hold the ultimate truth with regard to an individual's race, especially when one considers that race is a socially defined construct and that immigrants, by definition, come from societies that differ from those within the United States. Other assumptions that should not be made by the therapist during these discussions include that phenotypic Whiteness and privilege go together, or its counterpart, that phenotypic non-Whiteness and lack of privilege go together.

As a light-skinned, green-eyed, daughter of immigrants from the Canary Islands, who was born and raised in Venezuela, I identify as Venezuelan and Latina. Interestingly, this is similar to the way Harris (2008) and the immigrant women in the NIH study self-identified in the open-ended format (Eisenhower et al., 2013). However, when invited to a meeting for "faculty of color" at my university, I sought consultation with a senior, female, African-American faculty member whom I highly respect. I shared with her my uncertainty about whether I belonged in that meeting. On the one hand, I identified as Latina, but on the other hand my phenotype and my upper-middle-class upbringing in Venezuela had offered me privileges that I should not deny. It was my responsibility to remember and maintain these privileges in consciousness, in order to actively work against potential implicit discriminatory attitudes in myself and in my work. I expressed to her that I felt quite guilty about being invited. However, since I left Venezuela, one of my most important career goals has been to serve the impoverished and immigrant Latino community in the United States, especially women and young children. Because of this common goal, and due to my identification and alignment with the Latino community in the United States, I wanted to attend that meeting. My African-American colleague and mentor warmly told me not to worry, and that I was in fact a "POC."

Some time later, during a different exchange with a small group of faculty, a White colleague mentioned their concern that our program "did not have any Latino faculty members." Having worked alongside this colleague for several years, I felt attacked by this comment; it affected me physically, emotionally, and mentally for several days, and even weeks. My colleague was kind enough to have an honest and respectful conversation with me after this incident. Nevertheless, I confess that I have never quite recovered from it. I think that this sentiment did not just reflect this particular colleague's view, but it also likely represented the, perhaps unconscious, views of other colleagues. Further, this comment gave voice to an experience I had been repeatedly having for years, but that had never been so directly spoken. Unfortunately, this was not the only incident of this kind. The message was strong and clear: as a price for immigrating, and owing to my phenotype, my identity had been invalidated; I was not a "real Latina."

Somewhat unknowingly, I internalized this message. I told myself that it was more important to honor and understand the experiences of Latinos in the United States who did carry within them the weight of oppression as POCs, and that my own relatively privileged experience should not be brought into the dialogue. I saw this silence as a way of taking responsibility for my privilege. I consciously decided to compartmentalize my Venezuelan side at work, in order to keep it away from the public sphere. Ruiz (2012) described a similar process within the context of Relational Cultural Therapy with Latina immigrants: following repeated experiences of disconnection, "in their yearning to connect with others, individuals learn to keep valuable aspects of their experience out of their relationships to maintain or 'stay in relationship'" (p. 69).

In my case, this strategy was challenged when I was invited to contribute to this special issue. At first I felt like an impostor, as someone who was not qualified for this task of providing a Latina perspective. I then realized that writing this article would also be an opportunity to expose others to a different understanding of race regarding Venezuelan clients, which could potentially benefit those clients. I also understood that I was paying the price of inauthenticity by keeping quiet and that, especially owing to my privileged education and current status as a faculty member, I had a responsibility to at least attempt to contribute to the ongoing dialogue.

Most importantly, I realized that it was healthier to self-identify than to wait for others to define me in order to avoid conflict and discomfort. I believe that my approval for permanent residency in the interim also provided me some courage. Having been officially labeled as more than a "guest worker," I now find myself more comfortable owning who I am and less afraid of speaking up, contributing more during meetings and being more willing to (respectfully) disagree with my colleagues—in general, not just regarding race. My hope is that I have provided some useful insights to allow for open-ended discussions of race and privilege in clinical work with immigrant Latinas, and especially Venezuelans, in a way that will in turn facilitate validation of *their* unique, multidimensional, identities.

REFERENCES

Carter, R. T. (1998). *The influence of race and racial identity in psychotherapy: Toward a racially inclusive model.* New York, NY: Wiley.

Cunill Grau, P. (1987). *Geografía del poblamiento venezolano en el siglo XIX.* Caracas, Venezuela: Ediciones de la Presidencia de la República.

De la Cadena, M. (2001). Reconstructing race: Racism, culture and mestizaje in Latin America. *NACLA Report on the Americas, 34*(6), 16.

Delgado, R., & Stefancic, J. (Eds.). (2013). *Critical race theory: The cutting edge* (3rd. ed.). Philadelphia, PA: Temple University Press.

Díaz-Lázaro, C. M., Verdinelli, S., & Cohen, B. B. (2012). Empowerment feminist therapy with latina immigrants: Honoring the complexity and socio-cultural contexts of clients' lives. *Women & Therapy, 35*(1–2), 80–92. doi:10.1080/02703149.2012.634730

Eisenhower, A., Suyemoto, K., Lucchese, F., & Canenguez, K. (2013). Which box should I check?: Examining standard check box approaches to measuring race and ethnicity. *Health Services Research*, *49*, 1034–1055. doi:10.1111/1475-6773.12132

England, S. (2010). Mixed and multiracial in Trinidad and Honduras: Rethinking mixed-race identities in Latin America and the Caribbean. *Ethnic and Racial Studies*, *33*(2), 195–213. doi:10.1080/01419870903040169

Golash-Boza, T., & Bonilla-Silva, E. (2013). Rethinking race, racism, identity and ideology in Latin America. *Ethnic and Racial Studies*, *36*(10), 1485–1489. doi:10.1080/01419870.2013.808357

Gulbas, L. E. (2013). Embodying racism: Race, rhinoplasty, and self-esteem in Venezuela. *Qualitative Health Research*, *23*(3), 326–335. doi:10.1177/1049732312468335

Guthrie, R. (1976). *Even the rat was white: A historical view of psychology*. New York, NY: Harper & Row.

Harris, R. S., Jr. (2008). Racial microaggression? How do you know? *American Psychologist*, *63*(4), 275–276. doi:10.1037/0003-066x.63.4.275

Hoetnik, H. (1967). *The two variants in Caribbean race relations: A contribution to the sociology of segmented societies*. London, UK: Oxford University Press.

Hooker, J. (2005). Indigenous inclusion/black exclusion: Race, ethnicity and multicultural citizenship in Latin America. *Journal of Latin American Studies*, *37*(2), 285–310. doi:10.1017/s0022216x05009016

Johnson, S. D. (1990). Toward clarifying culture, race, and ethnicity in the context of multicultural counseling. *Journal of Multicultural Counseling and Development*, *18*(1), 41–50. doi:10.1002/j.2161-1912.1990.tb00435.x

Keen, B., & Haynes, K. (2003). *A history of Latin America*. (7th ed.). Boston, MA: Wadsworth Publishing.

Library of Congress, Federal Research Division. (1993). Venezuela: A country study. Retrieved from http://lcweb2.loc.gov/frd/cs/vetoc.html

Montañez, L., Sánchez, L. M., & Salinas, J. F. (2003). Proyecto "Imagen del Negro en la Venezuela de Hoy": Una Reflexión Metodológica. *Revista Interamericana de Psicología*, *37*(1), 31–49.

Nichols, E. G. (2013). "Decent girls with good hair": Beauty, morality and race in Venezuela. *Feminist Theory*, *14*(2), 171–185. doi:10.1177/1464700113483243

Nichols, E. G., & Morse, K. J. (2010). *Venezuela*. Santa Barbara, CA: ABC-Clio.

Pinderhughes, E. (1989). *Understanding race, ethnicity and power: The key to efficacy on clinical practice* (1st ed.). New York, NY: Free Press.

Pitt-Rivers, J. (1973). Race in Latin America: The concept of "raza". *European Journal of Sociology*, *14*(1), 3–31. doi:10.1017/s0003975600002630

Pollock, G. H. (1986). Simon Bolivar: Revolutionary, liberator, and idealist. *The Annual of Psychoanalysis*, *14*, 59–76.

Quintero, P. (2012). La invención de la democracia racial en Venezuela. *Tabula Rasa*, *16*, 161–185.

Ruiz, E. (2012). Understanding Latina immigrants using relational cultural theory. *Women & Therapy*, *35*(1–2), 68–79. doi:10.1080/02703149.2012.634727

Smedley, A., & Smedley, B. D. (2011). *Race in North America: Origin and evolution of a worldview* (4th ed.). Boulder, CO: Westview Press.

Sue, D. W. (2009). Racial microaggressions and worldviews. *American Psychologist*, *64*(3), 220–221. doi:10.1037/a0015310

Sue, D. W., Capodilupo, C. M., Nadal, K. L., & Torino, G. C. (2008, June 5). Racial microaggressions and the power to define reality. *American Psychologist, 63,* 277–279. doi:10.1037/0003-066x.63.4.277

Wright, W. R. (1988). The Todd Duncan affair: Acción Democrática and the myth of racial democracy in Venezuela. *The Americas, 44,* 441–459. doi:10.2307/1006969

Wright, W. R. (1993). *Café con leche: Race, class, and national image in Venezuela.* Austin, TX: University of Texas Press.

The Butterfly Dilemma: Asian Women, Whiteness, and Heterosexual Relationships

NATALIE PORTER

California School of Professional Psychology, Alliant International University, San Francisco, California

Critical Whiteness theory explores Whiteness as a form of power and privilege that originated in Western countries and has been dispersed globally. Its form is particular to location and its interaction with race, ethnicity, nationality, class, and gender. Two ways it has operated historically is through making the norms of Whiteness universal and the marker of reason and rationality. This article examines Whiteness through two lenses, the colonial-era opera, Madame Butterfly, *and three recent therapy case studies involving White American husbands and Asian immigrant wives. Although the women in these therapy cases have emigrated from different Asian countries and cultures, the treatment toward them suggests that colonial-era images and stereotypes of Asian women still resonate in contemporary White American culture and are impervious to national or cultural boundaries. A comparison of the opera's themes with those of the therapy cases suggest how historical and social constructions of Whiteness continue to promote inequality in heterosexual relationships comprised of White American males and Asian females. Feminist, multicultural analyses of the therapy cases are provided to highlight more egalitarian treatment of the women in therapy, in their families, and in the broader society. The intersectionality of gender with ethnicity and culture is discussed for these Asian women who experience the homogenization of their identities in spite of having immigrated to the U.S. from distinct cultures.*

In the opening act of *Madame Butterfly*, Benjamin Franklin Pinkerton, a lieutenant on a U.S. Navy warship, has arrived at his new house in Nagasaki, Japan to marry his new bride, 15 year old Cio-cio san, or "Butterfly" (Ilica & Giacosa, 1906). Laughing, Pinkerton informs the American consul, Sharpless, who is there for the wedding, that he has purchased the house for 999 years, but the contract can be cancelled each month. He adds that he intends to apply the marriage contract in the same way, "... I'm marrying in Japanese fashion, tied up for nine hundred and ninety-nine years, free, though, to annul the marriage monthly" (Ilica & Giacosa, 1906, p. 10). The young bride arrives with friends and family for the marriage ceremony, ecstatic at the prospect of true love and leaving her life of poverty behind. In her quest to please her husband and become "American," she has renounced Buddhism to adopt Christianity. Her family disowns her; she views the loss of her family as a necessary sacrifice for her new life.

In 2 months, the Navy frigate and Pinkerton have sailed back to the U.S., where Pinkerton plans to find a "real American bride" (Ilica & Giacosa, 1906, p. 12). Butterfly, almost penniless, continues to scan the horizon daily in search of his returning ship. Her confidence in his return "when the red-breasted robins are busy nesting" (Ilica & Giacosa, 1906, p. 39) is unwavering in spite of the three seasons of robins' nesting that have passed. Pinkerton does return and hearing that Butterfly has borne his son sends his new American wife to collect him. Butterfly, believing that he will be better off in America, turns him over before killing herself with a ceremonial knife used by her father for the same purpose (Ilica & Giacosa, 1906).

Madame Butterfly provides a vantage point for understanding the construction of Whiteness, as well as its role of power and domination in a global context. The opera remains the most popular in the U.S. (Metropolitan Opera, 2014) suggesting that the colonial-era stereotypes and images of Asian women still resonate in White American culture. Three therapy case studies involving contemporary relationships beween White American husbands and their Asian, immigrant wives of various nationalities will be compared to the opera's themes to explore how these historical social constructions of Whiteness continue to influence power and inequality in heterosexual relationships.

Kincheloe (1999) describes two ways in which Whiteness operates. The first is "the white privilege of universalizing its characteristics as the 'proper ways to be'" (p. 162). The second is the equation of reason and rationality with Whiteness:

> ... Whiteness would be framed in rationalistic terms–Whiteness representing orderliness, rationality, and self-control and non-Whiteness as chaos, irrationality, violence, and the breakdown of self-regulation. Rationality emerged as the conceptual base around which civilization and savagery could be delineated (Alcoff, 1995; Giroux, 1992; Keating, 1995). (pp. 163–164)

"Whiteness is 'knowing' that you are born to rule" (Hewitt, 2005).

The power of Whiteness is the power to make White patriarchal norms the universal signifier even as they apply to other racial/ethnic groups, such as non-White women like Butterfly. These universal norms propagate the dominance of maleness and heterosexuality, as well as of white supremacy. (Risman, 2004). From this standpoint, *Madame Butterfly* is not, as it is typically described, merely about star-crossed lovers (Blue, 2014), the exoticism of the Orient (McKenzie, 2004; Said, 1978), or Cio-cio san's undying love for Pinkerton (Ilica & Giacosa, 1906), but a tale romanticizing power and the "right" to possess and colonize women and countries. It provides a window for identifying a Western construction of Whiteness and gender within a "foreign" culture at the turn of the 19th century, including the the invisibility of Whiteness, hidden under its surrogates of civility, propriety, and universal standards (Kincheloe, 1999). This window provides a point of comparison to examine how Whiteness is manifested in heterosexual relationships in the U.S. between White men and Asian women more than 100 years later and how its interactions with gender, ethnicity, and class have persisted or evolved. We can learn a great deal from studying Whiteness in non-White geographies, as in the case of the opera. Studying the juxtaposition of women who have immigrated to the U.S. and coupled with White U.S. American men will shed light on how power and inequality are manifested today for women in an immigrant context. This article primarily addresses how these Asian women are stereotypically *perceived* in their relationships with White men, the adaptations they must make, and how many of their individual or cultural characteristics are made invisible.

The relationship between Pinkerton and Butterfly exemplifies power differentials in a context where the protagonist is perfectly at ease with the "rightness" of this arrangement. For Pinkerton, Butterfly is a prize in his colonial, global quest for adventure and pleasure. Butterfly is there for the taking, and he has the right to consume her, to break her wings (Ilica & Giacosa, 1906). His callousness toward his young bride mirrors his contempt toward Japanese culture and cultural values different than his own. His actions, his attitudes, his position in Japan all speak to Whiteness as constructed at the turn of the 19th century in relation to the East—militaristic, imperialistic, and arrogant. Pinkerton shows his condescension for the names, customs, the etiquette, and the nuances of the Japanese. He self-confidently personifies Whiteness as the standard bearer of norms, the frame through which all should be measured or judged (Hewitt, 2005) without the self-awareness that his judgments reflect only one worldview rather than "truth". He is unaware that he does not "see" Japanese culture except through the lens of his own experience (Kincheloe, 1999). Cio-cio san represents his right to conquer, ". . . though in the quest her frail wings should be broken" (Ilica & Giacosa, 1906, p. 11). When Cio-cio san asks Pinkerton whether it is true that the men where he comes from catch and pin the wings of butterflies. Pinkerton explains that it is done so they cannot escape- "I have caught you" (Ilica & Giacosa, 1906, p. 34).

Butterfly has become emblematic of the stereotype of Asian exoticism and the idealized image of a beautiful and innocent, submissive and fragile, yet seductive and sexual woman who falls hopelessly in love with a westerner and will sacrifice all for this love (Fukui, 2013; Kim, 2010; Kondo, 1990; Lu, 1997; Woan, 2008). Said (1978) underscored the relationship between Orientalism and Sexism depicted through media such as *Madame Butterfly*, "[Orientalism] view[s] itself and its subject matter with sexist blinders.... [The local] women are usually the creatures of a male power-fantasy. They express unlimited sensuality, they are more or less stupid, and above all they are willing... (p. 188). Kwan (1998) adds that the "Oriental Woman is a fictive creation, an invention of the western imagination deployed to justify sexual exploitation, dominance and not infrequently, violence to Asian women" (p. 100).

The relationship between Butterfly and Pinkerton is still described today in most opera guides and by many critics as an "ethnic misconception" (Plumley, 2014, p. 39) or "misguided love" (Jenkins, 2014). This analysis neglects to understand Butterfly in the context of her circumstances, her need for survival in a harsh world where she is poor and dependent on the financial support of her patrons. Her plight springs from more than unrequited love. Cio-cio san's story is closer to that of a mail-order bride, the poor immigrant woman who is trading what she has to offer, her youth, beauty, and servitude for the rewards of survival. By marrying Pinkerton and renouncing her religion, her family, and her cultural traditions in Nagasaki, she has symbolically emigrated from Japan. She lives alone on the hill with her maid as isolated as if she had crossed the ocean. She desires to assimilate as quickly and completely as possible. Her goal, signaled by her insistence on being referred to as Mrs. Pinkerton, is to leave her poverty behind by gaining access to the White world. Cio-cio san unquestioningly seems to believe that this American life will be better. She derides her maid for praying to the Japanese God, because, "Lazy and idle are the gods of Japan. The God my husband prays to will give an answer far more quickly to those who bow before him." (Ilica & Giacosa, 1906, p. 36). Contrary to opera reviews where she is considered childish, foolish, and mad (Blue, 2014), Butterfly has actually demonstrated that she is brave enough to risk all for the chance of a new life. She has witnessed the prosperity of her husband and his people; she too has bought into the notion that this prosperity equates with cultural and morale superiority. What she learns as time goes on is that as a woman of color, a foreigner, it is not intended for her to share in this prosperity.

The women in the three following therapy cases are immigrant women from three distinct Asian countries: India, Thailand, and the Filipino Republic. The cases illustrate themes related to the understanding of Whiteness and intersectionality (Crenshaw, 1995), particularly the interaction of gender, social class, culture, and immigration in heterosexual relationships. My focus is primarily on the commonalities of how they are perceived in the U.S. in the context of white privilege and the adaptations they make as socially marginalized, immigrant women. In spite of their national and cultural differences from each other, these women are frequently lumped together in the U.S. as "Asian." They all made great sacrifices to move to the United States. They left families, countries, and cultures to embark on new lives. Two of the women came to work and met their husbands in the United States. One woman, a professional in her own country, came for "love," at the cost of her profession. They all had children in the United States, with child-rearing departing substantially from what they expected or would have experienced in their home countries. For the most part, these differences brought them to therapy; two came for family therapy and one for individual. In the first case I served as a consultant to the therapist in a graduate therapy seminar; in the other two cases I served as the clinical supervisor to the therapists. In order to maintain confidentiality, I have disguised the clients' identities.

In the three cases presented, the hegemony of White culture and patriarchy are apparent. The women are relegated to invisible and subservient roles in spite of their substantial strengths. From a White woman's perspective, their adaptations may also seem confounding in that they appear to accept and even promote the roles projected onto them. This aspect of intersectionality is important in understanding how the experiences and perspectives of immigrant women may vary greatly from that of women from the dominant culture. Mahalingam, Balan, and Haritatos (2008) propose that identity development for immigrant women is a fluid and dynamic process, where identities are shaped by the social, cultural, and historical forces of their home country in relation to their migration experiences and circumstances and perspectives on the new, host culture. These processes frequently emphasize the differences between immigrants and the host culture, and one adaptation is for immigrants to construct their own idealized identities in contrast to how they are viewed in the dominant culture (Espiritu, 2001; Mahalingam et al., 2008; Mahalingam & Leu, 2005; Ong, 1999).

Asian women who have immigrated to the United States from many distinct and complex cultures frequently experience the homogenization of their identities as Asian-American women. Their response may be to essentialize gender and idealize patriarchy as represented in their home countries (Mahalingam & Leu, 2005). They do so to set themselves apart from White women and from the dominant culture's version of who they are. One way in which Asian immigrant women essentialize themselves is as possessing superior family values, as being more chaste, virtuous, and family-oriented than U.S. White women (Espiritu, 2001; Mahalingam et al., 2008; Mahalingam & Leu, 2005). The historical context represented by the Butterfly stereotype connects to their idealization of chasteness because of the sexual exploitation they experienced in their home countries at the hands of White, American military men stationed throughout Asia (Mahalingam & Leu, 2005). In each of the three therapy cases, the Butterfly myth can be seen as a basis for how these women are perceived and the identities they have constructed in opposition to that myth. These idealized beliefs about gender serve to increase their psychological well-being as first generation immigrants (Mahalingam et al., 2008), but it also perpetuates their subservient, invisible roles (Pessar, 1999).

In the first example, a pre-adolescent boy, James, was referred to therapy for learning and social difficulties in school. He attends a competitive private school with an immersion program in an Asian culture different from his own. His father, Ned, is White, originally from the U.S. Midwest, and the mother, Teresa, is Asian, from a rural agricultural area of the Filipino Republic. The parents met several years after the mother had immigrated, and she has had a successful career as a surgical nurse for 15 years. The father is working from home as a computer consultant after losing his job 2 years ago. The father accompanied James to therapy ostensibly because of the flexibility in his schedule. When the therapist encouraged the mother's participation, the father stated that she probably did not have much to offer given her language skills and lack of understanding of American culture. When the mother did attend, she remained silent, deferring to the father even when questions were directly posed to her. Although she was the primary breadwinner for the family and performed most of the household chores, the therapist noticed that she was marginalized in the home; her contributions were viewed as either inconsequential or negative. Themes of James' therapy portrayed his mother as eating disgusting, "smelly" food and Filipino society as old, lawless, and dangerous and U.S. society as modern, orderly and safe, with tasty food. His father was drawn as the breadwinner with his mother hidden in the kitchen. Both parents desperately wanted their son to fit in to U.S. culture, and the mother did not share much of her language or culture, although she had brought her family to visit her country once.

However, James' temperament and physical appearance favored his mother. He was shy and did not like to participate in roughhouse play or group competitive sports, activities prized by his father. The therapist observed that the boy had negatively internalized the discrepancy between who he appeared to be (Filipino) and what he valued (American). The therapist understood that an essential goal of the therapy would need to be to elevate the family's respect for the mother and her culture:

> ...[James] dismisses his mother despite their shared attributes and appearance. Over-identification with his father has manifested in an internalized racism that emerges both through condescension to his mother as a second class un-assimilated citizen (despite her role as primary wage earner, highly respected career in the medical field and dual degrees) and in reference to bicultural students as "others" and "Asian-looking." Acculturative dissonance at home and in school are added layers within two contexts that are incongruent with [James's] developing cultural identity. (Katz, 2014, p. 12)

The mother, Teresa, was not as open to the goal of connecting James back to her culture as the therapist had hoped. Initially it was easy to blame her continued deference on the father's control. Over time, as the father became less sure of his own convictions, Teresa's active role in maintaining the patriarchal values became more apparent.

Kincheloe (1999) points out the self-loathing that can be inherent when equating White society with universal norms of appropriateness. The family identified their concerns in a personal and individual context and in essentialist terms: the father saw himself as "right" because he understood the dominant culture and was male, and the mother assented because she could not possibly possess his cultural fluency, although she in fact was more successful in this culture on many levels. She provided economic stability to her family in spite of her immigrant "shortcomings." However her strengths seemed invisible to her husband, who could only envision his son's worth as derived from an "All-American template." Like Butterfly, Teresa believes that American culture was better. She has "rejected" hers to raise James as American as possible. Similar to other Filipina women, she has constructed her identity so that her family values including subservience to her husband take precedence (Mahalingam & Leu, 2005) in spite of what she has to offer to her son. Like Butterfly, she felt compelled to relinquish her son to her husband.

This second example provides a contrasting story. Unlike the first, where Teresa came to the United States for economic gain and status relative to women in her home country, the woman in this case, Daya, lost both status and the fruits of being economically well off. She came to therapy ostensibly for becoming unable to meet her family responsibilities, for example, not having dinner ready on time or "forgetting" to do laundry. She had met a White American professional living in India and subsequently moved to the U.S. to marry him (Porter, 2014). Her family objected to Daya marrying outside of their cultural and caste traditions, although they were less opposed to her moving to the United States Daya had worked as a dentist in India, but was unable to get licensed in the U.S. without repeating most of her education. Her husband has dissuaded her from doing so because of the expense and time away from the family. Daya agreed that her goals were not attainable, but she become increasingly depressed. Her husband spent long hours working away from home; Daya was left with attending to the house and family and did not feel that she had the time to pursue friends or other interests. She had grown progressively isolated. Daya's husband balked at socializing in the Indian community, where he said he felt like an outsider, but did not recognize how Daya may feel the same way at his work and family events.

Daya's plight highlights the dilemma of constructing an essentialized identity that prevented her from advocating more for her own interests. In Mahalingam and Leu's (2005) research on professional Indian woman working in the United States, the women contrasted themselves with American woman on the dimensions of being more committed to their marriages and families. In Daya's case, this commitment to family is manifested through her surrendering her work and personal goals because they are costly and time consuming. At this juncture, her well-being is compromised by her acquiescence. One course of the therapy was to reduce Daya's isolation by encouraging her to become connected to social and support groups of Indian woman. As she did so, she was able to assert herself more in the relationship while continuing to feel true to her cultural values.

In India, Daya's identity included her professional, economic, and social statuses. Her professional career was enabled by greater support for domestic duties. Taking care of the house and children were tasks for which she would have been aided by her extended family and household servants. In the United States, she perceived her social status to have been diminished by both her lack of household support and her lack of participation in the workforce (Mahalingam & Leu, 2005). Because her husband equated high quality of life solely with living in the United States, he did not consider that Daya might think hers was better in India, surrounded by family, social and household support, and a meaningful profession. Childcare concerns were found to be prevalent among professional Indian women in the United States. in Mahalingam and Leu's (2005) study. The women of their study were in the United States on work visas in the computer industry. They found that given the lack of household support, many women sent their children back to India to be raised when family members were not available to stay and assist them in the United States. It is ironic that for many Indian women, the Butterfly dilemma of giving their children a better life may require them to return them to their former "foreign" home. For the most part the Indian women in Mahalingam and Leu (2005)'s study had maintained their resilience and well-being by maintaining strong ties with and a sense of superiority about their home cultures.

The third case pertains to the reactions of the therapists toward a couple that included a White, U.S. male (Dave), and an Asian, Thai woman (Rose). She had separated from her husband and was seeking therapy 6 months later, because the adolescent son was refusing to spend time with her. Rose had originally emigrated from northern Thailand and had put herself through community college while working. She had married Dave, a salesman who was away on business much of the time, and was raising two children. She had returned to school to become a pharmacist, a path supported by her husband, who saw it as an investment in the economic future of the family. Rose was going to school as well as handling all household chores and childcare. After 14 years of marriage and a year of pharmacy school, Rose asked for a separation. She moved into a small apartment so that Dave and the children could keep the house. She returned to the house to take care of the children almost weekly while Dave was traveling. When he was not away, the arrangement was for the children, a son and a daughter, to visit her at her apartment. Rose still participated in all family holidays at the home to ensure that the children were disrupted as little as possible. At the last family holiday dinner, Dave and Rose had begun to argue over their separation; Dave hit Rose and threatened her with a knife. She left the home before the dinner was on the table. After this incident, her son had refused to visit her anymore and would not speak to her when she stayed at the family home.

During the history-gathering it came out that Dave had been physically violent at other times during their marriage, as well as being controlling of Rose's schedule and activities. She had no relatives in the United States and between working and household duties had had little time to develop relationships with other Thai people. She had assimilated as fully as possible in dress, food, and customs to please her husband, and she had shared little of her former life or her heritage with her children.

Rose's own sense of colonization had emerged when she returned to university. As she encountered other immigrants and people of color who were interested in her cultural heritage, she began to resent how much she had endeavored to assimilate and forego her identity. She realized that she was invisible to her children in many ways. When she attempted to present a more bicultural picture of herself, her family was puzzled, amused, and annoyed. Her husband saw her as regressing to an earlier, unsophisticated version of herself.

The son blamed his mother for abandoning the family in spite of the prior domestic violence. The children expressed their confusion and pain about their mother's role in their lives in that she was continuously "in" and "out;" just as they felt they were a family again, she would return to her own place. One of the goals of the therapy needed to be to clarify the boundaries between Dave and Rose and the children. Their plan to maintain so much of their former life was painful for all. The therapists interpreted Rose's behavior as selfish ambivalence. I saw it as paralyzing guilt. Rose had constructed her identity similar to many of the women in Mahalingam and Leu (2005)'s study as more moral, less individualistic, less likely to divorce, and more family and child oriented. Rose had broken all of her own rules.

The therapists were quite angry and impatient with Rose's inability to set firmer boundaries. The therapy issues are not unusual in divorce cases, so the intensity of their reactions were of interest to me. As time when on, I interpreted the supervisees' impatience as somehow related to her status as a woman of color and an immigrant. The White supervisees seemed to be able to identify more with the husband, and like the husband, they felt that Rose should be more grateful for the opportunities she had been "given." However, similar to the other two examples, Rose had done quite well on her own prior to meeting Dave; she had emigrated from a rural area on the other side of the world on her own, perfected her English, held a job, cared for a family, and pursued an education.

The therapists in this case had to explore their own preconceptions about her background, and the normalcy they attributed to her mandate to fit in here and be grateful—to be the good model Asian woman. She had willingly vacated her home for the sake of her children and husband, but initially in the therapists' eyes she had not gone far enough. She should have stayed married. In working with this client, the White therapists had to explore how they also saw her assimilated self as more "normal" and her desire to explore her more authentic, Thai self as "selfish."

These three therapy cases share several commonalities. The three women were educated and successful, yet seen by their spouses and themselves as dependent and not particularly competent. In the case of their husbands, perhaps this portrayal was more in the eye of the beholder. In a study of men who select mail order brides, they often saw themselves as more conservative and traditional and seeking spouses who were not pushy American women (Scholes, 1997). For the women, they too had seemed to internalize the qualities they considered essential differences from White women in the United States In addition, the women lacked family and other social supports in the United States so they were more reliant on their spouses. In this climate of seeing them as dependent, their social acumen and their significant accomplishments were minimized.

The three women had assimilated in most ways to U.S. culture, leaving their own cultural rituals and values behind. Each of the women presented manifested the interactions among race, ethnicity, nationality, gender, class, and immigration in different ways that depended on home and host country contexts. For the most part, they all seemed to have adopted the belief that the "proper" standards were those encountered in the United States. American life was the "regular" life, at least for their husbands and children to whom they took a back seat. However, at the same time, they rejected aspects of American life for themselves, particularly the values they perceived as belong to White American women, whom they considered less family-oriented or self-sacrificing. Like Cio-cio san, they had dedicated themselves to pleasing their husbands by fitting in. In two of the examples, their children knew little of their heritage and saw themselves as White. The mothers were shadowy figures not fully fleshed out, which rendered them somewhat invisible to the children. The children then fully identified with White culture, and had been deprived of participating in a rich, mixed heritage.

These themes of therapy are not uncommon ones for White women in couples or family therapy. Women in the United States who adhere to traditional gender roles may also essentialize themselves as family oriented first and foremost and minimize their own needs relative to those of their family. Their needs may also be invisible to the family, their actions unappreciated. These differences may be ones of degree. However, these women lacked the family and social supports that their White, American counterparts would possess. They were also considered by their partners to be unable to negotiate the culture, understand its values or rear their children steeped in the "American way." Their cultures for the most part remained hidden from their children. Their spouses did not seem to question the normality of their assimilation rather than creating bicultural families. In some ways Teresa, Daya, and Rose, like Butterfly, had given up their children to White America.

Although most contemporary American critics or opera-goers are aware of and even offended by the racist undercurrents of *Madame Butterfly* (Parker, 2007; Plumley, 2014), the opera plays on and remains hugely popular. We allow ourselves to believe that we love the love story but hate the racism, justifying its imperialistic message as from a different era. The three therapy cases presented suggest that the themes of the opera resonate today through the expectation of subordination of Asian women in relationships with Western men, albeit in forms more nuanced and underground. In "Butterfly's Revenge" Fukui (2013) suggests that it is White men who are the prisoners of their own exotic desires, allowing Asian women to take advantage of these fantasies. However, social and sexual inequalities between White men and Asian women are perpetuated even when individual Asian women construct their roles as instrumental rather than as victims.

The exoticization of the Asian woman has permitted her sexual and social exploitation in ways that would be unacceptable if committed upon White women (Kwan, 1998). Simultaneously the myth implies that White women are aggressive and undesirable, further dividing White and Asian women (Kwan, 1998) and essentializing their identities (Mahalingam & Leu, 2005). The story of Butterfly in its many versions is fundamental to this present day exploitation, for as Woan (2008) has proposed, Western imperialism is the root cause of this inequality. The retelling of these Butterfly myths with all of its imperialistic undertones perpetuates our White privilege as well as gender privilege in spite of our protests to the contrary.

REFERENCES

Alcoff, L. (2000). Mestizo identity. In R. Bernasconi & T. Lott (Eds.), *The idea of race*. (pp. 139–160). Indianapolis, IN: Hackett Publishing Company.

Blue, R. W. (2014). *San Francisco Opera director Nicola Luisotte on Madame Butterfly. San Francisco Opera Program 2013–2014* (p. 43). Seattle, WA: Encore Arts Programs.

Crenshaw, K. (1995). *The intersection of race and gender: Critical race theory: The key writings that formed the movement*. New York, NY: New Press.

Espiritu, Y. L. (2001). We don't sleep around like White girls do: Family, culture and gender in Filipina American lives. *Signs: Journal of Women in Culture and Society, 26*, 415–440. doi:10.1086/495599

Fukui, M. (2013). Madame Butterfly's revenge. *Griffith Review Edition 40: Women & Power*. Retrieved from https://griffithreview.com/articles/madame-butterflys-revenge/.

Giroux, H. (1992). *Border crossings: Cultural workers and the politics of education.* New York, NY: Routledge.

Hewitt, R. (2005). *White backlash and the politics of multiculturalism.* Cambridge, UK: Cambridge University Press.

Ilica, I., & Giacosa, C. [Elkin, R. H., English Version]. (1906). *Libretto: Madame Butterfly: A Japanese tragedy.* New York, NY: G. Ricordi & Company. Retrieved from https://archive.org/stream/madambutterflyja00pucc#page/n1/mode/2up.

Jenkins, C. (2014). *New York City Opera Project: Madame Butterfly.* Retrieved from //www.columbia.edu/itc/music/NYCO/butterfly/luther.html

Katz, M. (2014). James: A clinical case presentation. Unpublished paper. Advanced Clinical Seminar, California School of Professional Psychology, San Francisco, CA.

Keating, A. 1995. Interrogating "whiteness," (de) constructing "race". *College English, 57,* 901–918. Retrieved from //0-search.proquest.com.library.alliant.edu/docview/236933459?accountid=25255.

Kim, H. (2010). The Madame Butterfly controversy: Cio-Cio San's gender, racial, and cultural construction in Orientalist metaphysics. *PEAR (Yonsei Journal of International Studies), 2,* 121–129. Retrieved from http://yonseijournal.files.wordpress.com/2012/08/butterfly.pdf

Kincheloe, J. L. (1999). The struggle to define and reinvent whiteness: A pedagogical analysis. *College Literature, 26,* 162. Retrieved from //www.virginia.edu/woodson/courses/aas102%20(spring%2001)/articles/kincheloe.html.

Kondo, D. K. (1990). M. Butterfly: Orientalism, gender and a critique of essentialist identity. *Cultural Critique, Fall, 16,* 5–29. Retrieved from //www.jstor.org/discover/10.2307/1354343?uid=2&uid=4&sid=21103981039231

Kwan, P. (1998). Invention, inversion and intervention: The Oriental woman in the world of Suzie Wong, M. Butterfly, and the adventures of Priscilla, queen of the desert. *Asian American Law Journal, 99,* 100–137. Retrieved from //scholarship.law.berkeley.edu/aalj/vol5/iss1/5.

Lu, L. (1997). Critical visions: The representation and resistance of Asian women. In S. Shah (Ed.), *Dragon ladies: Asian American feminists breathe fire* (pp. 17–28). Boston, MA: South End Press.

Mahalingam, R., Balan, S., & Haritatos, J. (2008). Engendering immigrant psychology: An intersectionality perspective. *Sex Roles, 59,* 326–336. doi:10.1007/s11199-008-9495-2

Mahalingam, R., & Leu, J. (2005). Culture, essentialism, immigration and representations of gender. *Theory & Psychology, 15,* 839–860. doi:10.1177/0959354305059335

McKenzie, L. (2004). *Madame Chrysantheme as an item of nineteenth-century French Japonaiserie* (Doctoral Dissertation). Christchurch, New Zealand: University of Canterbury. Retrieved from //ir.canterbury.ac.nz/handle/10092/4687

Metropolitan Opera. (2014). *Madame Butterfly educator guide.* Retrieved from //www.metopera.org/metopera/about/education/educatorguides/content.aspx?customid=5414

Ong, A. (1999). *Flexible citizenship: The cultural logics of transnationality.* Durham, NC: Duke University Press.

Parker, R. (2007). One fine obscenity. *The Guardian.* Retrieved from //www.theguardian.com/music/2007/feb/13/classicalmusicandopera.reviews

Pessar, P. R. (1999). Engendering migration studies: The case of new immigrants in the United States. *American Behavioral Scientist, 42*, 577–600. doi:10.1177/ 00027649921954372

Plumley, G. (2014). *Culture clash: Puccini's Madame Butterfly. San Francisco Opera Program 2013–2014* (pp. 39–43). Seattle, WA: Encore Arts Programs.

Porter, N. (2014). Women, culture, and social justice: Supervision across the intersections. In C. A. Falender, E. P. Shafranske, & C. J. Falicov (Eds.), *Multiculturalism and diversity in clinical supervision: A competency-based approach* (pp. 59–82). Washington, DC: American Psychological Association.

Risman, B. J. (2004). Gender as a social structure: Theory wrestling with activism. *Gender & Society, 18*, 429–450. doi:10.1177/0891243204265349

Said, E. (1978). *Orientalism*. London, UK: Routledge & Kegan Paul.

Scholes, R. J. (1997). How many mail-order brides? *Immigration Review, 28*, 7–10. Retrieved from //cis.org/MailOrderBrides.

Woan, S. (2008). White sexual imperialism: A theory of Asian feminist jurisprudence. *Washington & Lee Journal of Civil Rights & Social Justice, 14*, 275. Retrieved from //scholarlycommons.law.wlu.edu/crsj/vol14/iss2/5.

Whiteness and Disability: Double Marginalization

MARTHA E. BANKS

Research & Development Division, ABackans DCP, Inc., Akron, Ohio

Whiteness involves a set of privileges that are lost or removed when a person becomes, or is perceived to be, disabled. For European American women, disability impacts femininity, the part of identity that differentiates them from European American men who hold maximal power and privilege in U.S. society. Disability represents a health issue, a barrier to social participation, and vulnerability to individual and societal abuse. Development of a healthy disability identity allows European American women to negotiate the multicultural situation of being White, women, and disabled.

If you are going to write about Women with Disabilities, remember to write about the White women first. Any others can come later.[1]

U.S. society, similar to other nations with a history of colonization by Europeans, in the guise of a meritocracy, is actually a hierarchy with social status determined by gender, ability, status, age, sexual orientation and identity, geography, immigration status, religion, ethnicity, and socioeconomic status. The greatest privilege has been accorded by able-bodied, middle-age, heterosexual, suburban, U.S.-born, Protestant, European American men of high socioeconomic status to themselves, including the privilege to define "acceptable" traits of those different from them (Banks, 2012). Their status, and that of European-American women, accords them "Whiteness," a level of humanity (Robinson, 2012) and ethnic invisibility (Sue, 2004) not accorded to other people. Historically, in the United States, Whiteness was equated with freedom, with Black people being considered as property and then as members of a species to be held separate from White people (Brown, 2014). Although Whiteness has generally been considered along ethnic lines and ascribed to European Americans, it is critical to recognize that Whiteness involves skin color with both interethnic and intraethnic implications in media portrayal, education, employment, incarceration, and health care (Banks, 2014; Brown, 2014; Norwood & Foreman, 2014). This article/chapter focuses on how Whiteness impacts the specific challenges of health, femininity, social status and barriers to social participation, and abuse experienced by women with disabilities. Having a disability places a person in a marginalized group with a history of oppression. Attention is also given to the role of disability identity as a personal resource.

HEALTH AND DISABILITY

Disability is generally recognized as a health condition. The Americans with Disabilities Act (1994) defines disability as:

1. [Having] a physical or mental impairment that substantially limits one or more major life activities of such individual;
2. [Having] a record of such an impairment; or
3. Being regarded as having such an impairment.

Approximately 20.5% of European-American women and girls are identified as having disabilities. Although this is the same *overall* percentage as African-American women and girls, it is important to note that European American women are less likely to have disabilities at each age group, reflecting an ethnic health disparity (Table 1; Steinmetz, 2006). The overall percentage masks the fact that African-American women with disabilities (WWD) die significantly younger than European American WWD. *Life itself is the result, in part, of privilege.* To ignore that fact or to hide the disparities at different ages is to engage in the privileged practice of "racial color-blindness": denial, distortion, and minimization of race and racism in the United States (Todd,

TABLE 1 Rates of disability by ethnicity

Age	Female, White*, Not Hispanic	Female, Black*
All Ages	20.5%	20.5%
Less than 15 years	6.3%	8.3%
15 to 24 years	9.7%	11.1%
25 to 64 years	17.4%	21.5%
65 years and older	54.9%	64.9%

Table adapted from Steinmetz (2006).
*The terms "White, Not Hispanic" and "Black" are used by the author.

Spanierman, & Aber, 2010). "Whiteness and its invisibility serve as a default standard that makes it difficult to see how it may unfairly intrude into the lives of racial/ethnic minority groups" (Sue, 2004, p. 762). By keeping Whiteness invisible and omitting discourse about privilege, systems of oppression and resulting social hierarchies are maintained (Rossatto, 2011). Silence about women's Whiteness impedes discussion of the impact of disability on perceptions of the femininity and womanhood of WWD.

FEMININITY, WOMANHOOD, AND DISABILITY

In the United States, the ideal physical model of women, with emphasis on feminine attractiveness, is based on European women's bodies, albeit in distortion of shape and color (Murnen, 2011; Norwood & Foreman, 2014). Images of beauty, romance, and reproductive rights are components of femininity, the most visible manifestation of which is body image, the perception by self and others of bodily form (Bagley, Character, & Shelton, 2003). For European American women, bodily form contributes to their own and others' perceptions of conformity to externally defined femininity (Cole & Zucker, 2007; Halim et al., 2013) with an emphasis on attractiveness in the context of romance.

Visible disability appears to be noticed more quickly than other personal characteristics (Rohmer & Louvet, 2009). There are few media images of romantic relationships that include WWD (Ostrove & Coffman, 2012), although, as noted by Crawford and Ostrove (2003), there are images of men with disabilities (MWD) as heroes or superheroes; that makes those men desirable as heterosexual intimate partners. In general, U.S. society is lacking in images of WWD in lesbian, bisexual, or other sexual minority relationships. For WWD, there can be a struggle between the desire for love and conflict with fetishists who seek them due to the presence of specific disabilities, such as amputations (Solvang, 2007).

Romantic love is generally considered to lead to formalized or informal family relationships, including parenting. In the absence of disability, one privilege of Whiteness for women is presumed competence to make decisions about one's body with respect to sexual activity, pregnancy, and childbirth. For WWD, there are barriers to their reproductive rights that temporarily abled European American women do not experience. West (2006) described the ways in which U.S. society celebrates European-American women's beauty, attractiveness, sexual activity, pregnancy, childbirth, and motherhood, while simultaneously denigrating or disparaging the very same attributes and activities of African-American women. European American WWD find themselves thrust into negative categories similar to those of African-American women (with and without disabilities). Stereotypes of WWD, particularly conflation of disability with intellectual limitation, interfere with their reproductive rights. Mukherjee, Reis, and Heller (2003) described a woman with an acquired disability who struggled with the decision to have a child, due to societal discouragement. European American WWD have a seldom-discussed history that includes eugenics (Rembis, 2009) or sterilization (Tilley, Walmsley, Earle, & Atkinson, 2012), similar to that experienced by African-American women (Welch, 2002). Femininity and reproductive issues represent one facet of the social status of WWD. In order to understand some of the other issues, it is important to consider the mindsets that contribute to stereotypes about PWD and the barriers that prevent their full participation in society.

SOCIAL STATUS AND BARRIERS TO SOCIAL PARTICIPATION

The portrayal of social status has taken place for centuries through the arts and religion (Robinson, 2012). Social stratification has been enforced through repetition of stereotypes and abusive punishment or threats of such abuse of those who are not at the top of the social hierarchy (Burrell, 2010). For European American WWD, there has been an evolution of the ways in which disability is perceived (Banks, 2010, 2013; Pledger, 2003; Seelman, 2004a, 2004b, 2004c). Originally, the medical or epidemiological model focused on individual weakness or inadequacy, blaming the "guilt" of WWD or their ancestors for physical and mental disabling conditions. The social model recognized social barriers that interfered with function; a well-known example would be stairs that prevent entry into buildings for people using wheelchairs. Under the social model, socioeconomic effects of disability are experienced when people are disabled by a lack of resources to meet their needs. The potential of people to contribute and add economic value to society is often underestimated in PWD unless they are given equal rights and equally suitable facilities and opportunities as others. The relative model considered ability in context, focusing on the specific situations in which PWD experienced limitations. A cultural minority model acknowledged oppression by the maintenance of known barriers and the low priority placed on barrier removal and support for health care and personal assistance for PWD. The integrative model pays attention to multiple roles and varying levels of agency, recognizing that PWD need access to appropriate health care, accommodation in education and employment, and rights involved in full social participation. Mona et al. (2005) observed that physical and social environments are seldom designed to meet the needs and capacities of WWD, so that they experience a disproportionate stress burden that could be eased or relieved by supports for self-determined life activities, relevant personal assistance, and removal of physical access barriers.

The barriers identified in the social and integrative models can involve mindsets that support their creation and maintenance. Campbell (2009) indicated that messages about disability are pervasive and that "disability may be tolerated but in the final instance, is inherently negative. We are all, regardless of our status, shaped and formed by the politics of ableism" (p. 20).

Campbell defined ableism as "attitudes and barriers contributing to the subordination of people with disabilities in liberal society" (p. 21); the manifestation/implementation of ableist attitudes is disableism: "a set of assumptions and practices promoting the differential or unequal treatment of people because of actual or presumed disabilities" (p. 21). She added: "[A]bleism can be associated with the production of ableness, the perfect body and, by default, the implication that disability is the loss of ableness" (p. 21). In contrast, "Disableism relates to the production of disability and fits well into a socially constructed understanding of disability" (p. 21).

Thus, ableism is, like institutionalized racism and sexism, a system by which mainstream society devalues PWD, while privileging people without disabilities; disableism involves the actual discrimination. Human worth and intelligence are equated with being able-bodied and able-minded, while disability is conflated with stupidity and worthlessness; this is parallel to the privileging of Whiteness over "Color" and maleness over femaleness. For European Americans, disability diminishes their Whiteness similar to the way that hypodescent defines the ethnicity of people by the lowest social status of their ancestors. For European-American women, disability increases their social distance from European-American men and, thus, decreases their privilege.

The social and integrative models of disability, in contrast to ableism, are based on a distinction between the terms "impairment" and "disability." Impairment refers to the actual attributes (or loss of attributes) of a person, whether in terms of limbs, organs, or psychological function, while the term disability is used to refer to restrictions caused by society when it does not give equivalent accommodation to the needs of individuals with impairments. Thus, attempts to change PWD, often derived from a medical model, can be both prejudiced (ableist) and discriminatory (disableist) (Pledger, 2003).

Therapists need to be mindful of Campbell's warning that "The pathologization of disability has meant that therapy predominantly concentrates on normalization and is not necessarily directed to attending to the harms of ableism ([that is] living with prejudice)" (Campbell, 2009, pp. 23–24). Campbell (2009) described internalized ableism, which leads PWD to as strive for "a state of near-ablebodiedness, or at the very least to effect a state of passing" (p. 27). For internalized ableism to occur there needs to be an existing presumption of compulsory ableness (Campbell, 2009). Internalized disableism, on the other hand, involves acceptance of disabled status as unchangeable fate, sometimes accompanied by blaming of one's self for having a disability. European American WWD are at risk for internalized disableism, particularly when they are struggling to adjust to acquired disability with concomitant loss of privilege.

The worst manifestation of disableism is abuse. The problems of abuse experienced by WWD have been silenced in the same ways as Whiteness.

ABUSE

"[O]ur cultural obsession with bodily perfection as the expected norm can result in tacit acceptance of the mistreatment of disabled women" (Mona, Cameron, & Crawford, 2005, p. 239). Mona and colleagues (2005) observed "Cultural notions of women with disabilities are predicated on images of helplessness, vulnerability, asexuality, and perpetual childlike innocence... The perception that women with disabilities are sexless beings further solidifies our cultural denial regarding the prevalence of sexual assault in this population" (p. 238–239).

Discrimination and harassment, as well as intimate partner violence can lead to physical and mental illness for women (Paludi, Wilmot, & Speach, 2010). That illness can become disabling, interfering with ability to participate in paid employment. The result is poverty and financial dependence; in 2012, 15.2% of WWD lived in poverty as compared to 11.8% of MWD (Nazarov & Lee, 2012).

There are several types of abuse experienced by WWD (Banks, 2010). Disability-related emotional abuse includes neglect and threats of or actual abandonment. Withholding of assistive devices or not allowing personal assistance are forms of disability-related physical abuse. WWD are vulnerable to disability-related sexual abuse, such as inappropriate sexual touching during assistance. For women who need assistance for sexual activity, there might be confusion between helping and actual participation. In institutional settings for PWD, WWD are at risk for sexual abuse by staff under the guise of provision of healthcare. They often lack protection from male patients in inpatient settings; those men are seldom held accountable for the abuse. Helping professionals also abuse WWD, as exemplified by personal assistants' rough handling or therapists' misattribution of psychological presenting complaints to physical disability. WWD are at risk for financial abuse when family members or other people purchase personal items with the care recipient's money, and when personal assistants work short hours but receive full pay. Disability-related abuse was reported almost exclusively by European American women (McFarlane et al., 2001). Robinson-Whelen et al. (2010) identified several societal circumstances, such as lack of resources and therapist misattribution of psychological symptoms to "expected" reactions to physical disability, which might account for this ethnic difference in reporting abuse, but they omitted an analysis of ethnic privilege.

Mona and colleagues (2005) described issues for PWD, using a social/minority model of disability, including "restricted access to economic and cultural institutions," and "repeated experience of stigma and discrimination." They noted "Many people with disabilities consider themselves to be bicultural, in that they must become experts at successfully navigating between disabled and nondisabled worlds" (Mona et al., 2005, p. 232). For European American women, the sense of being "bicultural" appears to involve only two cultures: "disabled" and "nondisabled." As WWD, European American women retain some White privilege. That differentiates them from women of color with disabilities whose survival involves a multicultural perspective, understanding their culture(s) of color, European American culture, *and* the disabled and nondisabled worlds. European American WWD, who are elderly, members of sexual minority groups, living in rural areas, immigrants, members of nonmainstream religions, and/or poor, also deal with multiculturalism as a survival strategy, but they do so with overwhelming, but seldom acknowledged, White privilege. The White or European-American part of their identity remains invisible.

One area in which Whiteness might be a barrier rather than a privilege is psychotherapy. In a parallel to the silence around Whiteness, ableism has led to overlooking the stress experienced by "successful" disabled people as reflected in suicide rates, substance abuse, and depression (Campbell, 2009). Campbell (2009) noted "One might be led to believe that the pathologization of the disability 'problem' has, in contrast to matters of race, meant an acceptance and awareness of internalized ableism (pp. 23–24). The consideration of "success" generally presumes Whiteness. Racial stereotypes of members of marginalized populations include substance abuse, but such problems are incompatible with images of Whiteness, particularly for European American women. As a result, European American WWD might not be assessed or referred for needed substance abuse treatment. Gibson (2009) recognized that countertransference of temporarily abled therapists working with clients with disabilities includes a sense of vulnerability, and in some cases, outright fear (Altschuler & Katz, 2010; Levitas & Hurley, 2007; Watermeyer, 2012). For European American therapists, societal racism serves as a protection from that sense of vulnerability due to distancing from clients of color with disabilities, but the countertransference is more problematic with European American clients with disabilities. Under that circumstance, Whiteness is a liability for WWD rather than a privilege. Therapists are aware of the loss of privilege that is a reality for PWD, especially under circumstances in which therapists are called upon to provide support for disability compensation (Mischoulon, 2002).

In order to survive and thrive in a society tainted with ableism, WWD need to develop healthy identities that undergird the resilience needed to cope under the societal oppression.

DISABILITY IDENTITY

White WWD experience being simultaneously oppressors and oppressed, and therefore, can be expected to experience high levels of psychological stress (American Psychological Association, 2007). Such stress is considerably reduced for all PWD who develop disability identities. Gibson (2009) described the process of building a disability identity as parallel to development of ethnic identity (Helms, 2007). The process, which is not linear, includes struggle between unhealthy acceptance of stereotypes and healthy acceptance of self and others as individuals. Enns (2010) described the purpose of identity development as movement from unquestioned internalized oppression or privilege to flexibility and positive attitudes toward and about groups with which a person identifies and some people perceive as different. Ultimately, development of a disability identity allows PWD to advocate for themselves and others. Williams exemplified the maturity of a healthy disability identity as she described how her disability is a significant part of her self-identity "and if I took that away I would lose a major part of who I am as a person" (Williams & Upadhyay, 2003, p. 151).

People in racial/ethnic minority groups usually develop in an environment that includes other people who face similar discrimination. There are obvious role models who demonstrate coping strategies and varying levels of pride in the racial/ethnic identity. "The experience for People with Disabilities is different in that many who have early onset disabilities are unlikely to grow up with other people with similar disabilities, and those with late onset disabilities are very unlikely to have role models with whom they identify" (Banks & Ackerman, 2006, p. 58).

One of the advantages of White privilege with respect to disability was described by Devlieger and Albrecht (2000) as "The visible disability Community—disability advocates and scholars—in the United States is largely White, adult, educated, middle class, and empowered" (p. 51). As a result, the disability research is primarily focused on European American, adult, educated, middle class, and empowered People with Disabilities (PWD), with the goal of empowering similar people. Banks (2010) noted that members of that population "have the facility to find each other and work together" (p. 221). In so doing, they have been able to take advantage of their White privilege to participate in defining disability.

SUMMARY

This article/chapter has provided a brief consideration of health, femininity, social status, abuse, and identity as they impact the lives of European American WWD. It is difficult to address the interaction of those concerns with social status and, specifically, privilege, without open discussion of Whiteness (Sue, 2004; Yeung, Spanierman, & Landrum-Brown, 2013). With increased emphasis on empirically supported treatment and attempts to decrease health disparities, attention to cultural issues would be incomplete without the intersection of Whiteness, gender, and disability (Chin, Yee, & Banks, 2014).

NOTE

1. Unsolicited advice as the author embarked on the editorship of her first book.

REFERENCES

Altschuler, J., & Katz, A. D. (2010). Keeping your eye on the process: Body image, older women, and countertransference. *Journal of Gerontological Social Work*, *53*(3), 200–214. doi:10.1080/01634370903507589

American Psychological Association. (2007). Guidelines for psychological practice with girls and women. *American Psychologist*, *62*, 949–979. doi:10.1037/0003-066X.62.9.949

Bagley, C., Character, C. A., & Shelton, L. (2003). Eating disorders among urban and rural African American and European American women. In M. E. Banks & E. Kaschak (Eds.), *Women with visible and invisible disabilities: Multiple intersections, multiple issues, multiple therapies* (pp. 57–79). New York, NY: Haworth Press.

Banks, M. E. (2010). 2009 Division 35 presidential address: Feminist psychology and women with Disabilities: An emerging alliance. *Psychology of Women Quarterly*, *34*, 431–442. doi:10.1111/j.1471-6402.2010.01593.x

Banks, M. E. (2012). Multiple minority identities and mental health: Social and research implications of diversity within and between groups. In R. Nettles & R. Balter (Eds.), *Multiple minority identities: Applications for practice, research, and training* (pp. 35–58). New York, NY: Springer.

Banks, M. E. (2013). Women of Color with Disabilities. In L. Comas-Díaz & B. Greene (Eds.), *Psychological health of women of color: Intersections, challenges, and opportunities* (pp. 219–231). Westport, CT: Praeger.

Banks, M. E., & Ackerman, R. J. (2006). Health disparities: Focus on disability. In K. J. Hagglund & A. W. Heinemann (Eds.), *Handbook of applied disability and rehabilitation research* (pp. 45–70). New York, NY: Springer.

Banks, T. L. (2014). A darker shade of pale revisited: disaggregated Blackness and colorism in the, "post-racial" Obama era. In K. J. Norwood (Ed.), *Color matters: Skin tone and the myth of a post-racial America* (pp. 95–117). New York, NY: Routledge.

Brown, K. D. (2014). The rise and fall of the one-drop rule: How the importance of color came to eclipse race. In K. J. Norwood (Ed.), *Color matters: Skin tone and the myth of a post-racial America* (pp. 44–94). New York, NY: Routledge.

Burrell, T. (2010). *Brainwashed: Challenging the myth of Black inferiority*. New York: SmileyBooks.

Campbell, F. K. (2009). Disability harms: Exploring internalized ableism. In C. A. Marshall, E. Kendall, M. E. Banks, & R. M. S. Gover (Eds.), *Disabilities: Insights from across fields and around the world. Volume 1: The experience: Definitions, causes, and consequences* (pp. 19–33). Westport, CT: Praeger.

Chin, J. L., Yee, B. W. K., & Banks, M. E. (2014). Women health and behavior health issues in health care reform. *Journal of Social Work in Disability and Rehabilitation*, *13*, 122–138. doi:10.1080/1536710X.2013.870509

Cole, E. R., & Zucker, A. N. (2007). Black and white women's perspectives on femininity. *Cultural Diversity and Ethnic Minority Psychology*, *13*(1), 1–9. doi:10.1037/1099-9809.13.1.1

Crawford, D., & Ostrove, J. M. (2003). Representations of disability and the interpersonal relationships of women with disabilities. In M. E. Banks & E. Kaschak

(Eds.), *Women with visible and invisible disabilities: Multiple intersections, multiple issues, multiple therapies* (pp. 179–194). New York, NY: Haworth Press.

Devlieger, P. J., & Albrecht, G. L. (2000). Your experience is not my experience: The concept and experience of disability on Chicago's Near West Side. *Journal of Disability Policy Studies, 11*, 51–60. doi:10.1177/104420730001100115

Enns, C. Z. (2010). Locational feminisms and feminist social identity analysis. *Professional Psychology: Research and Practice, 41*(4), 333–339. doi:10.1037/a0020260

Gibson, J. (2009). Navigating societal norms: The psychological implications of living in the United States with a disability. In C. A. Marshall, E. Kendall, M. E. Banks, & R. M. S. Gover (Eds.), *Disabilities: Insights from across fields and around the world. Volume 2: The context: Environmental, social, and cultural considerations* (pp. 139–150). Westport, CT: Praeger.

Halim, M. L., Ruble, D. N., Tamis-LeMonda, C. S., Zosuls, K. M., Lurye, L. E., & Greulich, F. K. (2013). Pink frilly dresses and the avoidance of all things "girly": Children's appearance rigidity and cognitive theories of gender development. *Developmental Psychology, 50*(4), 1091–1101. doi:10.1037/a0034906

Helms, J. E. (2007). Some better practices for measuring racial and ethnic identity constructs. *Journal of Counseling Psychology, 54*(3), 235–246. doi:10.1037/0022-0167.54.3.235

Levitas, A. S., & Hurley, A. D. (2007). Overmedication as a manifestation of countertransference. *Mental Health Aspects of Developmental Disabilities, 10*(2), 68–72.

McFarlane, J., Hughes, R. B., Nosek, M. A., Groff, J. Y., Swedlend, N., & Mullen, P. D. (2001). Abuse Assessment Screen-Disability (AAS-D): Measuring frequency, type, and perpetrator of abuse toward women with physical disabilities. *Journal of Women's Health & Gender-Based Medicine, 10*, 861–866. doi:10.1089/152460901753285750

Mischoulon, D. (2002). Potential pitfalls to the therapeutic relationship arising from disability claims. *Psychiatric Annals, 32*(5), 299–302. doi:10.3928/0048-5713-20020501-07

Mona, L. R., Cameron, R. P., & Crawford, D. (2005). Stress and trauma in the lives of women with disabilities. In K. A. Kendall-Tackett (Ed.), *Handbook of women, stress, and trauma* (pp. 229–244). New York, NY: Brunner-Routledge.

Mukherjee, D., Reis, J. P., & Heller, W. (2003). Women living with traumatic brain injury: Social isolation, emotional functioning and implications for psychotherapy. In M. E. Banks & E. Kaschak (Eds.), *Women with visible and invisible disabilities: Multiple intersections, multiple issues, multiple therapies* (pp. 1–26). New York, NY: Haworth Press.

Murnen, S. K. (2011). Gender and body images. In T. F. Cash & L. Smolak (Eds.), *Body image: A handbook of science, practice, and prevention* (2nd ed., pp. 173–179). New York, NY: Guilford Press.

Nazarov, Z, & Lee, C. G. (2012). *Disability Statistics from the Current Population Survey (CPS)*. Ithaca, NY: Cornell University Rehabilitation Research and Training Center on Disability Demographics and Statistics (StatsRRTC). Retrieved from www.disabilitystatistics.org

Norwood, K. J., & Foreman, V. S. (2014). The ubiquitousness of colorism: Then and now. In K. J. Norwood (Ed.), *Color matters: Skin tone and the myth of a post-racial America* (pp. 9–28). New York, NY: Routledge.

Ostrove, J. M., & Coffman, S. L. (2012). The psychology of love in the context of physical disability: Reframing culture, exposing oppression, narrating resistance. In M. A. Paludi (Ed.), *The psychology of love* (Vols. 1–4, pp. 95–110). Santa Barbara, CA: Praeger/ABC-CLIO.

Paludi, M. A., Wilmot, J., & Speach, L. (2010). Intimate partner violence as a workplace concern: Impact on women's emotional and physical well-being and careers. In M. A. Paludi (Ed.), *Feminism and women's rights worldwide. Vol. 2. Mental and physical health* (pp. 103–137). Santa Barbara, CA: Praeger.

Pledger, C. (2003). Discourse on disability and rehabilitation issues: Opportunities for psychology. *American Psychologist, 58*(4), 279–284. doi:10.1037/0003-066X.58.4.279

Rembis, M. A. (2009). (Re)defining disability in the 'genetic age': Behavioral genetics, 'new' eugenics and the future of impairment. *Disability & Society, 24*(5), 585–597. doi:10.1080/09687590903010941

Robinson, E. A. (2012). *Race and theology*. Nashville, TN: Abington.

Robinson-Whelen, S., Hughes, R. B., Powers, L. E., Oschwald, M., Renker, P., Swank, P. R., & Curry, M. A. (2010). Efficacy of a computerized abuse and safety assessment intervention for Women with disabilities: A randomized controlled trial. *Rehabilitation Psychology, 55*, 97–107. doi:10.1037/a0019422

Rohmer, O., & Louvet, E. (2009). Describing persons with disability: Salience of disability, gender, and ethnicity. *Rehabilitation Psychology, 54*(1), 76–82. doi:10.1037/a0014445

Rossatto, C. A. (2011). Schooling future oppressors: Teaching global communities about White privilege. In C. A. Rossatto (Ed.), *Teaching for global community: Overcoming the divide and conquer strategies of the oppressor* (pp. 105–124). Charlotte, NC: Information Age Publishing.

Seelman, K. (2004a). Trends in rehabilitation and disability: Transition from a medical model to an integrative model (part 1). *Disability World, 22*, January–March. Retrieved from http://www.disabilityworld.org/01-03_04/access/rehabtrends1.shtml

Seelman, K. (2004b). Trends in rehabilitation and disability: Transition from a medical model to an integrative model (part 2). *Disability World, 22*, January–March. Retrieved from http://www.disabilityworld.org/01-03_04/access/rehabtrends1.shtml

Seelman, K. (2004c). Trends in rehabilitation and disability: Transition from a medical model to an integrative model (part 3). *Disability World, 22*, January–March. Retrieved from http://www.disabilityworld.org/01-03_04/access/rehabtrends1.shtml

Solvang, P. (2007). The amputee body desired: Beauty destabilized? Disability re-valued? *Sexuality and Disability, 25*(2), 51–64. doi:10.1007/s11195-007-9036-x

Steinmetz, E. (2006, May). *Americans with disabilities: 2002, Current Population Reports, 70–107*. Washington, DC: U.S. Census Bureau.

Sue, D. W. (2004). Whiteness and ethnocentric monoculturalism: Making the "invisible" visible. *American Psychologist, 59*(8), 761–769. doi:10.1037/0003-066X.59.8.761

Tilley, E., Walmsley, J., Earle, S., & Atkinson, D. (2012). 'The silence is roaring': Sterilization, reproductive rights and women with intellectual disabilities. *Disability & Society, 27*(3), 413–426. doi:10.1080/09687599.2012.654991

Todd, N. R., Spanierman, L. B., & Aber, M. S. (2010). White students reflecting on whiteness: Understanding emotional responses. *Journal of Diversity in Higher Education, 3*(2), 97–110. doi:10.1037/a0019299

Watermeyer, B. (2012). Disability and countertransference in group psychotherapy: Connecting social oppression with the clinical frame. *International Journal of Group Psychotherapy, 62*(3), 392–417. doi:10.1521/ijgp.2012.62.3.392

Welch, K. C. (2002). The Bell Curve and the politics of negrophobia. In J. M. Fish (Ed.), *Race and intelligence: Separating science from myth* (pp. 177–198). Mahwah, NJ: Lawrence Erlbaum Associates.

West, T. C. (2006). *Disruptive Christian ethics: When racism and women's lives matter*. Louisville, KY: Westminster John Knox Press.

Williams, M., & Upadhyay, W. S. (2003). To be or not be disabled. In M. E. Banks & E. Kaschak (Eds.), *Women with visible and invisible disabilities: Multiple intersections, multiple issues, multiple therapies* (pp. 145–154). New York, NY: Haworth.

Yeung, J. G., Spanierman, L. B., & Landrum-Brown, J. (2013). "Being White in a multicultural society": Critical whiteness pedagogy in a dialogue course. *Journal of Diversity in Higher Education, 6*(1), 17–32. doi:10.1037/a0031632

Extending the Knapsack: Using the White Privilege Analysis to Examine Conferred Advantage and Disadvantage

PEGGY MCINTOSH
Wellesley Centers for Women, Wellesley College, Wellesley, Massachusetts

This article describes a self-awareness activity that utilizes a directed reading on privilege and a small-group discussion format to examine unearned disadvantage and unearned advantage in one's life. This exercise can help clinicians to better understand systemic and individual sources of power and privilege in society. Beginning with my previous work on white privilege, students can extend this analysis to other domains of privilege, including, for example, gender, class, sexuality, age, nationality, and physical ability, to name a few. The primary goals of this reflective exercise are to help clinicians understand how clients' lives are influenced by societal disadvantages and advantages, to encourage a new understanding of oneself, and to increase empathy towards clients.

INTRODUCTION

This activity was designed to help participants recognize their own privileges and disadvantages—an important element of self-awareness. This activity and its accompanying directed reading have been used by over 40,000 individuals from various disciplines and professions. It has been found to be especially useful in raising awareness and encouraging self-reflection in

© Peggy McIntosh

those practitioners working in clinical professions. In most professional, human-service training programs, practitioners are encouraged to acquire specific knowledge and understanding about the groups that they serve clinically. Unfortunately, many clinical programs do not help practitioners examine their own locations in social structures or systems and the associated privileges and disadvantages afforded to them by their respective social locations.

The exercise described in this chapter provides a systemic and an individual framework for better understanding of privilege and power in society and the role that they play in each clinician's life. The exercise also encourages an examination of the link between the inner and outer operations of power. The primary aim of this exercise is to help clinicians become more aware of how power has worked in their own lives and to increase their ability to imagine how social forces may have affected others. It draws attention to one's experiences of both privilege and oppression, and posits that we all experience both in our lives.

For some participants, this exercise may be a very early experience (perhaps the first occasion) of becoming aware of unearned advantages and disadvantages. As such, this may be a participant's first experience in seeing that their life (with all its associated successes and failures) is significantly related to arbitrary membership in groups whose status has been favored or disfavored within societal hierarchies (e.g., gender-based or race-based hierarchies). Engagement in this activity allows participants to consider that their own arbitrarily assigned social locations (as a function of gender, race, social class, ability level, and so forth) have as much to do (or more to do) with their accomplishments and struggles as do their individual efforts. It has been my experience that participants often go through a period of self-reflection following this activity and develop a clearer understanding of how their ascribed societal status (as a function of group memberships) has affected and shaped their life experiences.

This exercise, although intensely personal and "political," was constructed to avoid eliciting any feelings of blame, shame and guilt. It was designed to reduce the fear of talking about how power relations affect one's daily experience, and to increase the clinician's ability to talk about privilege and oppression. It is believed that through participation in this exercise and focused supervision, clinicians will gain new insights and empowerment.

RATIONALE

At this time, most people in the United States (U.S.) are unaware of how societal power (and its associated privileges) strongly influences life outcomes. The U.S. educational system generally rests on the myth of meritocracy—that people get what they individually want, work for, earn, and deserve. Therefore, those in positions of power (including many clinicians) tend to think of themselves as truly superior rather than as having been favored by hierarchical social systems that empower people differentially. Individuals who are in the helping professions may unintentionally be condescending toward clients or colleagues who have less access to financial resources, education, security, confidence, and well-being. For example, Caucasian practitioners may be quite unaware of the dominance of the white majority culture in shaping their paradigms, workplaces, and their sense of themselves. This brief exercise serves many as an introduction to seeing societal forces that they have been taught not to notice.

ACTIVITY INSTRUCTIONS

The facilitator should prepare for the group activity by reading my previous publications on the topic (i.e., *White Privilege and Male Privilege: A Personal Account of Coming to See Correspondences Through work in Women's Studies* (McIntosh, 1988) and *White Privilege: Unpacking the Invisible Knapsack* (McIntosh, 1989)). Additional resources for the facilitator and for participants can be found at The National SEED Project on Inclusive Curriculum (Seeking Educational Equity and Diversity, http://www.nationalseedproject.org). It is especially important that the facilitator be thoughtful and open, because this groundbreaking work in race relations requires honesty and candor. In addition, it is important to remember that the facilitator is not an expert but is a co-learner and participant.

This self-awareness exercise usually takes about an hour to complete and is best done in a group setting (with any number of members from two to fifty). The facilitator distributes "White Privilege: Unpacking the Invisible Knapsack" (1989) so that every participant has a copy (see Appendix A). Facilitators should be mindful of varying reading levels and speeds when assigning this reading, but in most cases, a 15-minute time period will suffice.

The directions given here are for groups of two. After all participants have had a chance to read the paper, participants should divide into dyads. This self-awareness exercise does not work with three people in a group, as three group members will not all be able to speak within the tightly allotted time, which is usually one minute each. If the group is larger, the facilitator is encouraged to ask anyone who does not have a partner to stand and find another person who is not yet matched. The facilitator should volunteer to be the partner of anyone who is still unpaired.

The facilitator should announce, "Don't begin to discuss this topic yet. First you need to find out which of you is speaker #1." The facilitator waits until the room or auditorium is quiet and then asks, "In your pair, which of you has the earliest birthday in the year?" The first speaker can then be designated by whichever of the dyad's members has the *latest* birthday in the year. After everyone has quieted down again, the facilitator gives the instructions to the first speaker, (see below) before starting to the exercise.

The facilitator's instructions to the first speaker should go as follows:

> Speaker #1, please tell your talking partner for one minute, uninterrupted, about one or more ways in which you have had unearned disadvantage in your life. You did not ask for it. It was circumstantial. But in some ways it has made your life harder. It is not a matter for blame, shame and guilt. You didn't invent the systems you were born into. You did not invent your disadvantages. They are not your fault but in some ways they have given you difficulty. Your disadvantage may have to do with your place in the birth order in your family, or whether you were the sex of child your parents wanted. Your disadvantage may come from your parents' relation to money or to education; what language you spoke at home; your neighborhood; Your gender, ethnicity, race, religion, sexual orientation, physical appearance, stereotypes about your family; your physical coordination; your handedness—were you left handed? What else is there that gave you some unearned disadvantage? Please tell your partner about one or more of these things that have arbitrarily set you back and made your life harder, through no fault of your own. Whatever you say is for your partner alone, not to be repeated to anyone else.

Although this is a lengthy introduction for the first speaker in this exercise, it has the advantage of giving both partners some time to think through what they might want to say. Additionally, some participants need a little more time to consider all the factors that can be discussed in relation to privilege because the article can make some worry that the *only* topic that they will be asked to talk about is race. Realizing that privilege comes in a variety of forms can come as a relief to some, especially those who have strong reactions to the topics of race and gender.

At the end of the minute, the facilitator should firmly and quickly cut the speaker off as the minute ends, and then give the instructions for the second speaker to begin. The facilitator must not be informal even if the group is only one pair. The method is very intentionally structured and is not effective for awareness-raising when it is not firmly followed. The purpose of the strict structure is to not unwittingly afford one participant more advantage or disadvantage than another in terms of time spent talking.

Now comes the time for the second speaker. Instructions for the second speaker include:

> Speaker #2, your role is extremely weird. Normally if you had listened to someone telling for a full minute about things that have made their life difficult, you would show that you have been listening. But do not do that. This is not a social event. Start fresh. Pretend you are the first speaker and that nothing has been said. Do not empathize, echo, piggyback, or show that you have heard anything that the first person has said. This is your minute. Please tell your talking partner about one or more of

> your experiences of having unearned disadvantage in the world. You did not ask for it and it is not your fault. It is not a matter for blame, shame or guilt, but it has made life harder for you in some ways. It could include many things that I have already mentioned, or others like hair, or body type, or being short or tall or having a certain kind of voice, or your gender, race, ethnicity, religion, sexual orientation, class, your parents' reputation, your neighbors, your siblings and relatives, and so on.

The facilitator once again monitors the "talk time" for the speaker and cuts off the speaker at 1 minute. Next, the facilitator shares the following instructions and provides examples of unearned advantages if necessary:

> Now we go to the second part of this exercise. As you may have guessed, this second part is an opportunity to share some of your experiences of unearned advantage. Unearned advantage is privilege that was given to you arbitrarily. It is not a matter of blame, shame, or guilt, but it has helped you out and made life easier for you in some ways. It can have to do with any of the factors that created disadvantages to some people, but in this case you were on the lucky side. You are talking about circumstances that helped you. Speaker #1, please tell your talking partner about one or more ways that you have had unearned advantage in your life as a function of your race, class, gender or anything else that has helped you through no virtue of your own.

Speaker #1 is given 1 minute to talk on this subject and then speaker #2 is given the following instructions:

> "Even if you were about to say what you partner has said, start fresh and speak from your own experience. Please tell your partner about your unearned advantage." To highlight the subtlety and the complexity of privilege, here I usually give several new and different examples of unearned advantage related to living in the United States. These include coming to expect hot and cold running water, which is not available to most people on the face of the earth; having a currency that buys a lot of goods from other places in the world; or having your nation's language spoken in virtually all airports in the world.

After these exchanges, it is advisable for the facilitator to communicate the following, "I know it can feel brutal to be cut off after 60 seconds, especially when you are talking about difficult things, but the author of this activity (Peggy McIntosh) refers to this aspect of the exercise as 'the Autocratic Administration of Time in the Service of Democratic Distribution of Time.' Abrupt though it may feel, the reality is that time *is not* democratically distributed in our personal lives or professional locations." The facilitator should explain that with this method, "Talkers must talk less and listen more. People who usually do not talk get to talk, if they like. And since each person is speaking about their own experience, they cannot be questioned. This is their experience and something on which they are the sole authority." Furthermore, the topic being presented is one's own experience of what I call the *politics of unearned circumstance*, and it is something that no other person can question or second-guess. What each person has experienced is what that person has experienced.

This process of taking turns speaking about one's own experience and listening to another person's experience is something that I have named Serial Testimony. In brief, it is a mode of timed discourse that requires participants to take turns speaking about personal *experience* as opposed to opinions, in a setting where they are not cross-examined, questioned, agreed or disagreed with. I have found it to be more useful than traditional forms of professional discourse, instruction, and counseling, many of which reflect hierarchies of power and privilege. I attribute part of the success of the National SEED Project on Inclusive Curriculum, now in its 27th year, to this kind of lateral pedagogy. This kind of speaking and listening process respects the experience of all participants. Serial Testimony allows people to make sense of their own experience while hearing about others' lives. It allows for what I call "deeply personal group work."

If a person wishes not to talk about their unearned privilege and disadvantage, they should let their partner know before the exercise begins. Infrequently, individuals decline to participate in the activity and leave the room before it begins. An effective facilitator, when orienting the group to the activity, should inform them that they will have an opportunity to talk about some of their experiences of disadvantage and privilege—which can make them feel vulnerable and challenged, but probably also rewarded. This type of statement allows participants the chance to decide whether they want to participate fully in the activity or not.

As additional guidance to the facilitator, debriefing after this exercise is not recommended since debriefing can be seen as a filtering mechanism that leaves out some of what has been said and tends to overgeneralize. Debriefing can also turn into a popularity contest, wherein some people's comments are spotlighted, while others are ignored. In my experience, a debrief can destroy (in just a few seconds) the rare and precious honesty of testimony produced in the whole group when each person knows they may speak for one minute and no one will interrupt, question, or even mention what they have said. I feel that the tendency to debrief is an enculturated and mostly unconscious reflex on the part of a facilitator or teacher to regain control, to be in charge, to indicate to people what they should have heard, or what was most significant.

However, shared conversation following the exercise can be beneficial. Victor Lee Lewis sometimes asks participants whether they have any "new learnings" from this exercise. He requests that that those who choose to participate at this stage only speak to what they have learned from doing the exercise, avoiding what their partner said. The testimony should emphasize the "new learning" acquired and not knowledge or insight that they had when they walked into the room. Listeners often find that other people's comments illuminate or resonate with their own experience of doing the exercise. The "new learnings" comments should follow the Serial Testimony format and remarks should be short and to the point (no more than 30 seconds in duration). This helps prevent participants from trying to outdo each other in their observations and allows the facilitator to remain as a participant rather than being re-installed as the authority or authorizer.

EXAMPLES

The Invisible Knapsack paper and the exercise described here have had a powerful effect on both people of color and white people. It has helped many people of color feel relief after years of experiencing subtle (and not so subtle) resistance by white people to their pursuit of self-respect, advancement and well-being. This resistance sometimes takes the form of direct interference from white individuals but, at other times, it appears more indirect in nature such as the white assumptions underlying organizations run by the white majority. The resistance and lack of support felt by people of color today may not include outright racist incidents; most often the resistance comes from a pervasive and intractable lack of trust by white society regarding the worth, abilities and deservedness of people who are not white. I feel that all disadvantaged people suffer under privilege systems that advance those around them while neglecting them, but most have not been able to name what they are suffering from. After all, in the United States, societal and educational structures have not taught them to see or name systems of privilege, for such teaching would blow away the myth of meritocracy – that everyone gets what they deserve.

Despite the incredible variety of settings, professional grouping, and diverse circumstances of my presentations, when I have talked about how I came to see I have white skin privilege, there has been a very singular response from participants. In fact, regardless of whether they are people of color, poor people, gay and lesbian people, biracial people, and/or immigrants, participants often thank me profusely. They report that they now feel validated, and feel "less crazy." I have given them some names for the power dynamics they have experienced at the hands of more privileged people or institutions. Furthermore, the "Knapsack" reading on privilege followed by the exercise helps many white people realize they have been born into a favored and dominant group in the United States, whose social and financial power benefitted them without their having earned all of their prominence. Most whites report they did not know they had racial experiences and often thought of themselves as "just normal," while "others" had race. Most white readers can relate to the examples I gave regarding my own unearned freedom of choice and comparative ease of mind and action, within societal frameworks and institutions that support "me and my kind." Participants in this exercise are also helped to see and testify to the phenomena of systemic privilege and disadvantage in their own lives, seeing more clearly how they are embedded in cultural frameworks such as language, manners, assumptions, education, medicine, and law enforcement. Many find this hour-long exercise to be transformative and I have heard again and again, from people in all stations of life, "Your work changed my life."

MEASURING PROGRESS

I believe that working in helping professions tends to encourage one to feel superior, on a vertical axis, to those being helped. The exercise on privilege and disadvantage encourages thoughtful people to think twice about whether they have really earned their positions or how circumstances of birth may have propelled them upward or downward arbitrarily. They may develop more empathy for others after they have realized how much their placement in social structures worked for or against them without their knowing it. Helpers may realize that they have developed traits of arrogance or feelings of virtue because they have benefited from a society that favors their groups. They may come to question whether the strengths that their social groups reward are in fact broadly useful to humans' well-being.

CONCLUSION

As I see it, there is a hypothetical line of social justice running parallel to the ground. Below it people or groups are pushed down in a variety of ways. Above it, people and groups are pushed upward in a variety of ways. I believe that all of us have a combination of experiences that place us both above and below the hypothetical line of social justice. An hour spent doing this exercise can be fascinating, shocking, chastening, illuminating, disconcerting, or enlightening. Those who refer to this paper and activity as "transformative" have sometimes said that they feel they have been relocated and reoriented in the world, or even the universe. This is a testament to the power of seeing systemically rather than only in terms of individuals, and to the power of understanding that there is an unjust "upside" in addition to the unjust "downside" in circumstances to which we were born.

ACKNOWLEDGMENTS

This article includes an authorized excerpt of McIntosh's original white privilege article, "White Privilege and Male Privilege: A Personal Account of Coming to See Correspondences through Work in Women's Studies,"

Working Paper 189 (1988), Wellesley Centers for Women, Wellesley College, MA, 02481. © Peggy McIntosh 1988.

ADDITIONAL RESOURCES

Butler, S., (Producer)., & Butler, S. (Director). (2006). *Mirrors of privilege: Making whiteness visible.* Oakland, CA: World Trust Educational Services, Inc.

Case, K. (2013). *Deconstructing privilege: Teaching and learning as allies in the classroom.* New York, NY: Routledge.

Dill, B. T., & Zambrana, R. E. (Eds.). (2009). *Emerging intersections: Race, class and gender in theory, policy and practice.* New Brunswick, NJ: Rutgers University Press.

Ferber, A. L. (1998). *White man falling: Race, gender, and white supremacy.* Lanham, MD: Roman and Littlefield.

Ferber, A. L., & Kimmel, M. S. (Eds.), (2010). *Privilege: A reader* (2nd ed.). Boulder, CO: Westview Press.

Kendall, F. E. (2006). *Understanding white privilege: Creating pathways to authentic relationships across race.* New York, NY: Routledge.

McIntosh, P. (2012). Reflections and future directions for privilege studies. *Journal of Social Issues, 68*(1), 194–206. doi:10.1111/j.1540-4560.2011.01744.x

McIntosh, P. (2013). Teaching about privilege: Transforming learned ignorance into usable knowledge. Foreword to Case, Kim. (2013). *Deconstructing privilege: Teaching and learning as allies in the classroom.* New York, NY: Routledge.

Rich, A. (1984). *Notes toward a politics of location, in Blood, Bread, and Poetry: Selected Prose 1979–1985.* New York, NY: W.W. Norton.

Wildman, S. M., Armstrong, M. J., Davis, A. D., & Grillo, T. (1996). *Privilege revealed: How invisible preference undermines America.* New York, NY: New York University Press.

REFERENCES

McIntosh, P. (1988). White privilege and male privilege: A personal account of coming to see correspondences through work in women's studies (Working paper no. 189). Wellesley, MA: Wellesley Centers for Women.

McIntosh, P. (1989). White privilege: Unpacking the invisible knapsack. *Peace and Freedom, July/August,* 10–12. Philadelphia, PA: Women's International League for Peace and Freedom.

APPENDIX A

White Privilege: Unpacking the Invisible Knapsack

© McIntosh, P. (1989). *Peace and Freedom Magazine, July/August,* 10–12. Philadelphia, PA: Women's International League for Peace and Freedom.

Through work to bring materials from Women's Studies into the rest of the curriculum, I have often noticed men's unwillingness to grant that they are over-privileged, even though they may grant that women are disadvantaged. They may say they will work to improve women's status, in the society, the university, or the curriculum, but they can't or won't support the idea of lessening men's. Denials which amount to taboos surround the subject of advantages which men gain from women's disadvantages. These denials protect male privilege from being fully acknowledged, lessened or ended.

Thinking through unacknowledged male privilege as a phenomenon, I realized that, since hierarchies in our society are interlocking, there was most likely a phenomenon of white privilege that was similarly denied and protected. As a white person, I realized I had been taught about racism as something that puts others at a disadvantage, but had been taught not to see one of its corollary aspects, white privilege, which puts me at an advantage.

I think whites are carefully taught not to recognize white privilege, as males are taught not to recognize male privilege. So I have begun in an untutored way to ask what it is like to have white privilege. I have come to see white privilege as an invisible package of unearned assets that I can count on cashing in each day, but about which I was "meant" to remain oblivious. White privilege is like an invisible weightless knapsack of special provisions, maps, passports, codebooks, visas, clothes, tools and blank checks.

Describing white privilege makes one newly accountable. As we in Women's Studies work to reveal male privilege and ask men to give up some of their power, so one who writes about white privilege must ask, "Having described it, what will I do to lessen or end it?"

After I realized the extent to which men work from a base of unacknowledged privilege, I understood that much of their oppressiveness was unconscious. Then I remembered the frequent charges from women of color that white women whom they encounter are oppressive.

I began to understand why we are justly seen as oppressive, even when we don't see ourselves that way. I began to count the ways in which I enjoy unearned skin privilege and have been conditioned into oblivion about its existence.

My schooling gave me no training in seeing myself as an oppressor, as an unfairly advantaged person, or as a participant in a damaged culture. I was taught to see myself as an individual whose moral state depended on her individual moral will. My schooling followed the pattern my colleague Elizabeth Minnich has pointed out: whites are taught to think of their lives as morally neutral, normative, and average, and also ideal, so that when we work to benefit others, this is seen as work which will allow "them" to be more like "us."

I decided to try to work on myself at least by identifying some of the daily effects of white privilege in my life. I have chosen those conditions which

I think in my case *attach somewhat more to skin-color privilege* than to class, religion, ethnic status, or geographic location, though of course all these other factors are intricately intertwined. As far as I can see, my African American co-workers, friends, and acquaintances with whom I come into daily or frequent contact in this particular time, place and line of work cannot count on most of these conditions:

1. I can if I wish arrange to be in the company of people of my race most of the time.
2. If I should need to move, I can be pretty sure of renting or purchasing housing in an area which I can afford and in which I would want to live.
3. I can be pretty sure that my neighbors in such a location will be neutral or pleasant to me.
4. I can go shopping alone most of the time, pretty well assured that I will not be followed or harassed.
5. I can turn on the television or open to the front page of the paper and see people of my race widely represented.
6. When I am told about our national heritage or about "civilization," I am shown that people of my color made it what it is.
7. I can be sure that my children will be given curricular materials that testify to the existence of their race.
8. If want to, I can be pretty sure of finding a publisher for this piece on white privilege.
9. I can go into a music shop and count on finding the music of my race represented, into a supermarket and find the staple foods that fit with my cultural traditions, into a hairdresser's shop and find someone who can cut my hair.
10. Whether I use checks, credit cards or cash, I can count on my skin color not to work against the appearance of financial reliability.
11. I can arrange to protect my children most of the time from people who might not like them.
12. I can swear, or dress in second-hand clothes, or not answer letters, without having people attribute these choices to the bad morals, the poverty, or the illiteracy of my race.
13. I can speak in public to a powerful male group without putting my race on trial.
14. I can do well in a challenging situation without being called a credit to my race.
15. I am never asked to speak for all the people of my racial group.
16. I can remain oblivious of the language and customs of persons of color who constitute the world's majority without feeling in my culture any penalty for such oblivion.
17. I can criticize our government and talk about how much I fear its policies and behavior without being seen as a cultural outsider.

18. I can be pretty sure that if I ask to talk to "the person in charge," I will be facing a person of my race.
19. If a traffic cop pulls me over or if the IRS audits my tax return, I can be sure I haven't been singled out because of my race.
20. I can easily buy posters, postcards, picture books, greeting cards, dolls, toys, and children's magazines featuring people of my race.
21. I can go home from most meetings of organizations I belong to feeling somewhat tied in, rather than isolated, out-of-place, outnumbered, unheard, held at a distance, or feared.
22. I can take a job with an affirmative action employer without having co-workers on the job suspect that I got it because of my race.
23. I can choose public accommodations without fearing that people of my race cannot get in or will be mistreated in the places I have chosen.
24. I can be sure that if I need legal or medical help, my race will not work against me.
25. If my day, week, or year is going badly, I need not ask of each negative episode or situation whether it has racial overtones.
26. I can choose blemish cover or bandages in "flesh" color and have them more less match my skin.

I repeatedly forgot each of the realizations on this list until I wrote it down. For me, white privilege has turned out to be an elusive and fugitive subject. The pressure to avoid it is great, for in facing it I must give up the myth of meritocracy. If these things are true, this is not such a free country; one's life is not what one makes it; many doors open for certain people through no virtues of their own.

In unpacking this invisible knapsack of white privilege, I have listed conditions of daily experience that I once took for granted. Nor did I think of any of these prerequisites as bad for the holder. I now think that we need a more finely differentiated taxonomy of privilege, for some of these varieties are only what one would want for everyone in a just society, and others give license to be ignorant, oblivious, arrogant and destructive.

I see a pattern running through the matrix of white privilege, a pattern of assumptions that were passed on to me as a white person. There was one main piece of cultural turf; it was my own turf, and I was among those who could control the turf. *My skin color was an asset for any move I was educated to want to make.* I could think of myself as belonging in major ways and of making social systems work for me. I could freely disparage, fear, neglect, or be oblivious to anything outside of the dominant cultural forms. Being of the main culture, I could also criticize it fairly freely.

In proportion as my racial group was being made confident, comfortable, and oblivious, other groups were likely being made inconfident, uncomfortable, and alienated. Whiteness protected me from many kinds of hostility, distress and violence which I was being subtly trained to visit, in turn, upon people of color.

For this reason, the word "privilege" now seems to me misleading. We usually think of privilege as being a favored state, whether earned or conferred by birth or luck. Yet some of the conditions I have described here work systematically to overempower certain groups. Such privilege simply *confers dominance* because of one's race or sex.

I want, then, to distinguish between earned strength and unearned power conferred systemically. Power from unearned privilege can look like strength when it is in fact permission to escape or to dominate. But not all of the privileges on my list are inevitably damaging. Some, like the expectation that neighbors will be decent to you, or that your race will not count against you in court, should be the norm in a just society. Others, like the privilege to ignore less powerful people, distort the humanity of the holders as well as the ignored groups.

We might at least start by distinguishing between positive advantages, which we can work to spread, and negative types of advantage, which unless rejected will always reinforce our present hierarchies. For example, the feeling that one belongs within the human circle, as Native Americans say, should not be seen as privilege for a few. Ideally it is an *unearned entitlement*. At present, since only a few have it, it is an *unearned advantage* for them. This paper results from a process of coming to see that some of the power that I originally saw as attendant on being a human being in the United States consisted in unearned advantage and conferred dominance.

I have met very few men who are truly distressed about systemic, unearned male advantage and conferred dominance. And so one question for me and others like me is whether we will be like them, or whether we will get truly distressed, even outraged, about unearned race advantage and conferred dominance, and, if so, what will we do to lessen them. In any case, we need to do more work in identifying how they actually affect our daily lives. Many, perhaps most, of our white students in the U.S. think that racism doesn't affect them because they are not people of color; they do not see "whiteness" as a racial identity. In addition, since race and sex are not the only advantaging systems at work, we need similarly to examine the daily experience of having age advantage, or ethnic advantage, or physical ability, or advantage related to nationality, religion, or sexual orientation.

Difficulties and dangers surrounding the task of finding parallels are many. Since racism, sexism, and heterosexism are not the same, the advantages associated with them should not be seen as the same. In addition, it is hard to disentangle aspects of unearned advantage which rest more on social class, economic class, race, religion, sex, and ethnic identity than on other factors. Still, all of the oppressions are interlocking, as the Combahee River Collective Statement of 1977 continues to remind us eloquently.

One factor seems clear about all of the interlocking oppressions. They take both active forms, which we can see, and embedded forms, which as a member of the dominant group one is taught not to see. In my class and place, I did not see myself as a racist because I was taught to recognize racism only in individual acts of meanness by members of my group, never in invisible systems conferring unsought racial dominance on my group from birth.

Disapproving of the systems won't be enough to change them. I was taught to think that racism could end if white individuals changed their attitudes. But a "white" skin in the United States opens many doors for whites whether or not we approve of the way dominance has been conferred on us. Individual acts can palliate, but cannot end, these problems.

To redesign social systems, we need first to acknowledge their colossal unseen dimensions. The silences and denials surrounding privilege are the key political tool here. They keep the thinking about equality or equity incomplete, protecting unearned advantage and conferred dominance by making these taboo subjects. Most talk by whites about equal opportunity seems to me now to be about equal opportunity to try to get into a position of dominance while denying that *systems* of dominance exist.

It seems to me that obliviousness about white advantage, like obliviousness about male advantage, is kept strongly inculturated in the United States so as to maintain the myth of meritocracy, the myth that democratic choice is equally available to all. Keeping most people unaware that freedom of confident action is there for just a small number of people props up those in power and serves to keep power in the hands of the same groups that have most of it already.

Although systemic change takes many decades, there are pressing questions for me and I imagine for some others like me if we raise our daily consciousness on the perquisites of being light-skinned. What will we do with such knowledge? As we know from watching men, it is an open question whether we will choose to use unearned advantage to weaken hidden systems of advantage, and whether we will use any of our arbitrarily awarded power to try to reconstruct power systems on a broader base.

What Do White Counselors and Psychotherapists Need to Know About Race? White Racial Socialization in Counseling and Psychotherapy Training Programs

ELEONORA BARTOLI
Department of Psychology, Arcadia University, Glenside, Pennsylvania

KEISHA L. BENTLEY-EDWARDS
Department of Educational Psychology, University of Texas at Austin, Austin, Texas

ANA MARÍA GARCÍA
Department of Sociology, Anthropology, and Criminal Justice, Arcadia University, Glenside, Pennsylvania

ALI MICHAEL
Center for the Study of Race and Equity in Education, University of Pennsylvania, Philadelphia, Pennsylvania

AUDREY ERVIN
Department of Counseling Psychology, Delaware Valley University, Doylestown, Pennsylvania

Multicultural training in academic counseling and psychotherapy programs is often designed to address the needs of minority populations, and it rarely places Whiteness in the spotlight. Its structure, in fact, risks mirroring the very dynamics embedded in White privilege. Using the framework of feminist theory, we build on key findings on White racial socialization—which has a profound impact on the quality of communication and interaction within and across racial groups—to outline the skills and awareness needed for White counselors and psychotherapists to promote racial justice in both their individual/counseling and community/advocacy work.

FROM MULTICULTURALISM TO SOCIAL JUSTICE

The centrality of the therapeutic relationship is one of several forces that have propelled counseling and psychology training programs to adopt a multicultural lens, as there are few contexts where that quality of communication and interaction matters more than in the relationship between counselor and client (whether the client is an individual or a community). There has been marked progress over the past thirty years in coverage of knowledge and awareness around diversity in counseling and psychotherapy training programs (Arredondo, Tovar-Blank, & Parham, 2008; D'Andrea & Heckman, 2008; Sue, Arredondo, & McDavis, 1992), as well as in the integration of guidelines for competent multicultural practice into the professional standards of counseling organizations, accrediting bodies, and licensing boards (American Counseling Association, 2005; American Psychological Association, 2010; Fawcett & Evans, 2013). Facilitating multicultural competence has become central to ethical clinical and counseling training, with its responsibility resting on training programs and clinical supervisors (Inman & DeBoer Kreider, 2013; Sue & Sue, 2012).

That said, multicultural training in counseling and psychotherapy training programs have focused primarily on the impact of particular identities, especially racial identity, on the therapeutic relationship and process (Helms, 1993; Pinderhughes, 1989; Ponterotto, Gretchen, Utsey, Rieger, & Austin, 2002; Wei, Chao, Tsai, & Botello-Zamarron, 2012). By focusing on the race of the client and the counselor, the field for the most part has studied how "minorities" experience the world, how mental health or illness are shaped by such experiences (e.g., racism), or how racial differences impact the power dynamic within the therapeutic relationship. While such an approach does begin to acknowledge the privilege of Whiteness, it does not problematize the very method of inquiry that places Whiteness as the standard referent from which viewpoint we study those who are "other" or "different."

Further, while the multicultural movement has provided a foundation for dialogue as well as a heightened appreciation for multiple perspectives, when matters of race come up in the therapeutic relationships (or the classroom, or faculty meeting), it is not uncommon for resistance and defensiveness to arise. The discomfort emerges from being challenged in one's view of oneself or one's experience of the world and it gets in the way of authentic and intentional dialogue—where race can remain central, and genuine transformation can occur. Partly because of this discomfort (which also preserves the normativity of Whiteness), counseling and psychotherapy training programs have relied on an additive model of race and gender. This model ultimately frames all women (whether clients or psychotherapists) as essentially the same, with individual race variances (e.g., we are women who happen to be Black or White, or my client is just like me except she is Latina). This additive model encourages a "victim competition" (i.e., who experiences the most oppression, given one's multiple minority identity statuses) that is counterproductive and distracting in one's attempt to fully hear, acknowledge, appreciate, and validate another's experience/reality (the latter being the only way of developing safe and authentic relationships). By isolating identities, we are both minimizing and making one-dimensional a complex social life, and continuing to identify the location of "the problem" in "the other."

Multicultural training has also focused primarily on developing students' self-awareness. In this context, we would argue that it is insufficient to understand one's own racial identity or work on internalized stereotypes and misconceptions of self and others, as injustice and oppression are not simply individual problems and cannot be resolved only with individual solutions. We argue that self-awareness needs to be promoted in tandem with the examination of our particular social locations and statuses, scripts and roles. Fully understanding oneself and one's impact on others demands that we look at our position in the social landscape, at how it is managed in comparison to another social group, and at our relationship to dominant cultural power and social order. While self-awareness has its value, it doesn't make us immune to the forces that shape our lives, whether we approve of them or not.

Feminists of Color have written extensively about moving from an additive model of race to one of intersectionality (Collins, 1990; Crenshaw, 1993), which "emphasizes the interlocking effects of race, class, gender, and sexuality, highlighting the ways in which categories of identity and structures of inequality are mutually constituted and defy separation into discrete categories of analysis" (Thornton Dill & Kohlman, 2012, p.154). For instance, women experience oppression and constraint (a) as an individual in their own personal biography, (b) as a member of a social group with particular social status, and (c) as a participant in, and producer of, social institutions (Collins, 1990). In other words, personal identity and attitudes are grafted onto existing social and cultural processes; these structures then often produce outcomes that are worse for women of Color or poor White women. Therefore, fully understanding oneself and one's impact on others must include not simply self-reflection, but an understanding of the social scripts and structures that frame the very conversation and enable the existing power structure.

This shift from an individual to a structural perspective moves the conversation from one of multiculturalism to one of social justice. Once we view the individual within a social network of relationships and structures, we can begin to detangle power and personality. This perspective was summarized long ago by the feminist principle "the personal is political," indicating that one's private and public selves are interrelated and interdependent. For example, rape and violence, once conceptualized as personal and private, are now viewed as a social problems linked to heteronormative practices and gender norms. In psychotherapy or teaching, we are confronted by power differentials between "expert" and "novice," or by notions of sickness and health. In each, we reflect our own racial social status, with its privileges or burdens.

We see evidence of this in individual White feminists who might struggle with how to be both a member of a privileged group by race or heterosexual marriage, and a member of a disenfranchised group by gender. The discomfort generated by this dissonance forces some White feminists to maintain a coherent narrative of oppression based on gender by denying the racial scripts of privilege (Gillman, 2007). From this space, roles are enacted and reinforced that allow White feminists to render invisible and inconsequential their statuses of power and privilege. As helpers, teachers, and activists we have many well-rehearsed roles and scripts that rid us of racist responsibility (e.g., I teach a multicultural course), provide us with an alibi for why we are post-racist (Gillman, 2007), and defines us as "the good one"—somehow supposedly impermeable to the social structure in which we are embedded.

If we want to truly move from an additive multicultural model to a social justice model, we need to interrogate not only our personal life experiences, but the ways that we serve the larger social system. We must move psychotherapists and faculty to see social action and social change as inextricably tied to the healing and restorative process. It is from this perspective that we offer an analysis of the importance of racial socialization of White students in counseling and psychotherapy training programs, and propose guidelines for the inclusion of social justice principles both in the structure of counseling and psychology programs and the curriculum delivered to students.

RACIAL SOCIALIZATION

Definition of Racial Socialization

Racial socialization is the way individuals learn about, interpret, and interact with members of their own and other racial/ethnic groups (Bentley, Adams, & Stevenson, 2009). Using both explicit and implicit messages, informants such as parent, teachers, and psychotherapists communicate to youth their perceptions of racial hierarchies, how to manage racial conflict, and norms for interacting with people based on their racial/ethnic background. Although coping with racial strife typically involves members of different racial groups, providing the skills for navigating racial tension has primarily rested on the shoulders of ethnic minorities. These expectations have resulted in racial socialization literature focusing almost exclusively on racial ethnic minorities, largely neglecting such processes within White families. Although a critical analysis of White racial socialization (WRS) is crucial to understanding intergroup dynamics, it is largely missing within the field of Whiteness studies (Fine, 2004; Helms, 1993; Rowe, Bennett, & Atkinson, 1994).

Racial socialization of Whites must account for their unique position within North American culture and the specific ways in which Whites understand race. It is important to recognize that the aims of WRS are unique and diametrically opposed to the goals of People of Color (POC). For example, the overarching goals of Black racial socialization are to promote safety, positive self-regard, and adaptability to different contexts (Bentley et al., 2009). The primary focus of WRS is to ease racial tension while also promoting positive self-regard. For Whites this means denying vs. acknowledging race, and avoiding vs. seeking multicultural relationships and contexts – where the opposite is true for the racial socialization of youth of Color (Bartoli et al., 2014). Thus, the multiculturalism messages in WRS may capriciously promote cultural diversity while demanding an adherence to White spaces and cultural norms. Further, while racial socialization of youth of Color is often explicit and strategic (e.g., parents of Color telling their sons to be particularly non-threatening to the police), WRS tends to occur via implicit and theoretical means grounded in censorship and what "not to do" (e.g., White parents telling their children not to say anything that makes others think they might be racist).

Prior research by Bartoli et al. (2014) has identified broad constructs salient to WRS, such as aversion for being perceived as racist, denial of the significance of race, promotion of racial hierarchies, and idealization of colorblindness. These constructs have implications for the specific racial stress, appraisal, and coping strategies utilized by White psychotherapists and their clients in same race interactions as well as multicultural contexts. Colorblindness, however ineffective in practice, is a common strategy conveyed in WRS (Bartoli et al., 2014; Pahlke, Bigler, & Suizzo, 2012); it is fostered by the intent to erase racial bias and promote interracial relationships, while in fact it promotes existing racial inequalities and segregation. This means that the goal of much of current forms of WRS (i.e., to erase racial tension) is in direct contrast to its outcomes (increased racial conflict and opportunities for biased behavior).

The Unique Need for Racial Socialization in Counseling and Psychotherapy Training Programs

As mentioned above, multicultural competence in psychotherapists is typically based on an additive model, most often delivered with a White counselor and an ethnic minority client in mind (Gushue, Constantine, & Sciarra, 2008). Multicultural competencies are usually not appraised or deemed significant when White psychotherapists are treating members of their own race. Where it has long been acknowledged that it is imperative for psychotherapists to provide gender socialization (Hare-Mustin, 1978; Kryzanowski & Stewin, 1985) to improve interpersonal dynamics and self-perceptions, imparting racial socialization in the therapeutic setting has not been given equal attention – even though similar challenges in social development may need to be addressed (from parents seeking advice on how to promote the social development of their children, to adult clients' anxiety around social interactions). In fact, psychotherapists are in a unique position to aid in the racial socialization processes of their clients (Brown, Blackmon,

Schumacher, & Urbanski, 2013; McCreary, Cunningham, Ingram, & Fife, 2006) to improve social functioning.

For it to be effective, training in racial socialization must move beyond an awareness of privilege and biases to an understanding of racial hierarchies, one's place in them, as well as one's role in preserving (or questioning) the status quo. Racial socialization would provide psychotherapists with the tools to appraise a client's interpersonal difficulties based on race as a barrier to healthy relationships at work, school, or community. Further, when psychotherapists are cognizant of the enduring nature of challenges to racial justice, they will be better able to engender improved coping in their ethnic minority clients, rather than discounting racial conflict as purely situational or as a matter of personal responsibility. Thus, multicultural competence training should be grounded in viewing all clients as racial beings impacted by racial hierarchies, with varying levels of racial identity development. Racial socialization must also avoid attempts to isolate identities when convenient (or rather inconvenient), as this is in direct opposition to the realities created by intersectionality.

WHITE RACIAL SOCIALIZATION IN COUNSELING AND PSYCHOTHERAPY TRAINING PROGRAMS

Moving from superficial acknowledgement of White privileges to meaningful critical consciousness requires sustained intentional strategies implemented at individual, program, and institutional levels (Sue, 2010). While the next section will describe individual training strategies, this section highlights possible program and institutional strategies. Training programs are primary socializing agents both through the content of what they teach students and through the processes, policies, and values to which they expose students while in the program. In this light, programs should have a clear mission statement that outlines a dedication to social justice based on an analysis of systemic oppression as a central organizing principle. Program goals and objectives should then relate to the overarching mission and intentionally incorporate social justice skill building. In order to facilitate critical consciousness around WRS, social justice issues should be infused in all courses, inform recruitment and retention, be introduced as foundational at new student orientations, and be an integral part of faculty clinical and research endeavors. Furthermore, programs should offer advocacy/social justice based courses or concentrations, emphasizing a systemic analysis of health and justice, as well as training on the specific skills necessary to promote individual and community change.

As mentioned above, programs operating within and from a mostly White lens embrace approaches that are geared toward teaching White students how to work with racial and ethnic minorities, thus perpetuating othering, marginalization, microaggressions, and systemic silence about the ways in which one participates or benefits from institutional racism (Sue, 2010). Counseling and psychotherapy training programs that purport to advocate for marginalized racial minorities by focusing habitually on POC, inadvertently (or sometimes intentionally) perpetuate the racial status quo by ignoring or minimizing the meaning and impact of Whiteness. Systemic collusion unfolds when Whiteness is made invisible or non-central to the counseling process, issues of race are relegated to faculty or students of Color, or supervisors don't investigate how WRS impacts the work between a White counselor and a White client.

Furthermore, programs that don't actively work to name and develop skills to disrupt systemic racism in the classroom, educational institution, clinical placements, or the community, reinforce ineffective WRS messages. Rudimentary content knowledge about Whiteness does not translate into discernable skills, whereby White students are empowered to acknowledge, name, and disrupt individual and systemic manifestations of racism. However, similar to individual avoidance tactics, programs may focus on clinical issues (e.g., anxiety, where the problem is located exclusively within the client) to the detriment of nurturing critical consciousness (e.g., anxiety as a normal response to systemic racism) and the strategies needed to respond to injustice or empower individuals and communities to change oppressive systems. In other words, the dialogue about race within counseling and psychotherapy training programs must extend beyond basic multicultural knowledge and ask student to become change agents and social justice advocates combating racism on individual and systemic levels (Naples & Bojar, 2002; Toporek & McNalley, 2006). Thus, consistent with feminist lenses, we make a call for programs to intentionally strive to foster critical consciousness by placing WRS and social justice skill development in the spotlight.

The invisibility of White privilege also permeates the systems within which counseling and psychotherapy training programs must function, such as the guidelines, and sometimes confines, of licensing boards, accreditation bodies, and institutional politics. Instructors, clinicians, and students with heightened critical consciousness must be able to negotiate with systems that perpetuate the racial status quo and further racial marginalization, and recognize the ways in which White privileges are actually perpetuated within their settings. For instance, faculty of Color are often assigned to teach diversity courses despite a bulk of research that indicates that faculty of Color addressing issues of skin color privileges are frequently rated lower on course evaluations than their White counterparts (e.g., Pittman, 2010). White faculty need to not only develop racial consciousness, but also step up to name and address systemic barriers for instructors and students of Color, such as rates of tenure, promotion, access, equal representation in faculty and student of Color, success rate, graduation, retention, and the like. This functions not only to counteract institutional racism, but also provides constructive and implicit WRS by modeling advocacy skills for students.

WHITE RACIAL SOCIALIZATION OF WHITE PSYCHOTHERAPISTS

In this last section, we describe a comprehensive racial socialization strategy for White psychotherapists encompassing three areas: racial messages, content knowledge, and skills. Accurate racial messages provide an overarching framework for effective racial socialization, and thus an opportunity to challenge the potentially less effective racial socialization messages received by students before entering graduate school. However, even accurate racial messages are not sufficient to provide White students with the tools needed to engage in conversations about race with peers or clients. For that to occur, knowledge about racial concepts and dynamics and how they impact interpersonal relationships and functioning, as well as confidence in one's ability to contribute to or intervene in conversations or interactions about race, are of paramount importance. In other words, racial consciousness doesn't challenge inaccurate information nor tells us how to act in ways that may disrupt the status quo. Skill training is especially important for White students since, as mentioned above, Whites tend to receive primarily *implicit* messages about race and only clear mandates about what *not* to do (Hamm, 2001; Thandeka, 2000).

Messages About Race

TALKING ABOUT RACE IS NOT RACIST

Color-blindness often teaches Whites that simply noticing differences in phenotypic characteristics is a sign of racism. Many White students enter graduate programs not only with little experience in conversing about race, but often with an aversion to naming race as a topic or to verbally identifying racial groups. Exploring the impact of race with clients or challenging the (racial) status quo in any given setting can only occur through open dialogue (Ridley, 2005). Such dialogue requires one's ability to comfortably name race to either empower our clients to enter a potentially uncomfortable conversation, or indicate to clients that we are open to that conversation.

RACE AS A RICH SOURCE OF IDENTITY

Conversations about race, especially in White households, tend to arise around negative racial incidents (whether occurring in one's community or portrayed by the media) or when race becomes "a problem" (Bartoli et al., 2014). However, race contributes meaningfully to a variety of experiences (e.g., racist incidents as much as cross-racial friendships and community), and for POC is a valued part of one's identity and a source of pride. In this context, it is essential for White psychotherapists to embrace a fuller view of race in order to assist White clients to build more authentic relationships with POC, and to assist clients of Color to question internalized racist messages (Enns & Williams, 2012).

Being white does have meaning for you and your clients

Many White students enter graduate school with little awareness of themselves as a racial being. However, being White in a racist society holds meaning and implications whether we acknowledge it or not (Sue, 2004; McInstosh, 1997). Our clients' lives and interactions are in fact shaped by their own or others' Whiteness (Harris, 1993; Kendall, 2006). White clients might be unaware that some of their interpersonal struggles may be due to racial dynamics (e.g., they keep being passed for a promotion because of their inability to interact effectively with their co-workers of Color), while others might hesitate to express the challenges they experience with peers of Color with their White therapist for fear that the therapist may not understand or engage appropriately. Just like we wouldn't hesitate to speak about gender with a client struggling with body image issues, we must be able to recognize where racial dynamics are at play without colluding with our clients by viewing their interpersonal problems as exclusively intrapsychically determined, rather than a consequence of their racial training or scripts.

Learning about and developing a positive white identity

Historically, identification or pride as a White person was reflective of a White supremacist stance. More recently, White identity is most often associated with colorblindness, ignorance, or racist attitudes (Tatum, 2003). As Tatum (2003) suggests, none of these are identities White students will be inspired to develop further as they become more racially aware. We must offer Whites the vision of an anti-racist White identity, through which they can begin identifying both as Whites with unearned privileges as well as Whites that can use their privileges to subvert the status quo. Here is where the progression from basic multicultural competence to advocacy and social justice training can take place. White psychotherapists should be called to act as agents of social change, both at institutional (e.g., recognizing and intervening within a racist power structure preventing adequate treatment to be delivered to communities of Color) and individual levels (e.g., fostering effective racial socialization when racist comments are made by clients; Bartoli & Pyati, 2009).

Content Knowledge

Race is both a fictional and meaningful category

While race is not a biological phenomenon (as humans' evolution on earth is too recent for genetic variance to have developed), its socially constructed nature has very real/tangible consequences for all of us (e.g., economics, geographical, educational). White students will be able to view themselves accurately as racial beings only after they learn the history of Whiteness, how it was constructed, and how it is maintained at institutional/structural levels (Adelman, 2003).

Racism is systemic

Just like understanding that "the personal is political" in feminist thought was revolutionary in women's ability to accurately identify and fight systems of oppressions that directly affected the quality of their lives, it is essential for White students to understand that racism operates within structures and systems, not simply at the individual level (Enns & Williams, 2012). Such a broader and more comprehensive view of racism allows for a clear understanding of the absurdity of the term "reverse racism," of the impact of exclusionary practices in primarily White institutions (who then "struggle" to diversify their campuses), and of the continued segregation of the educational system.

The costs of racism

Racism doesn't simply impact POC; it is rather the driving force behind everyone's history. The history of Whites and POC are inextricably connected and should be taught as such. Racism gave all of us a legacy to contend with that has a tangible impact on psychosocial functioning (Spanierman, Poteat, Wang, & Oh, 2008) and health (Mays, Cochran, & Barnes, 2007). Within this context, it is essential that White students learn about their ancestors' roles in perpetuating an unjust system as well as the role of anti-racist Whites in joining with POC and forming meaningful and effective alliances (Pheterson, 1986). Without such knowledge, it will be difficult for White students to know both how to resist participating in systems that systematically disadvantage POC (i.e., what *not* to do), while also know how to actively intervene to disrupt unjust practices and develop authentic relationships and alliances with POC (i.e., what *to* do).

Identifying stereotypes and acquiring accurate information

We are all exposed to inaccurate or distorted images and information about POC, some of which we are aware of (whether we actually believe them to be true or not) and some of which we have so fully internalized that are simply reified. Stereotypical narratives are longstanding, pervasive, readily available, well-rehearsed, and expertly interconnected. This means that a concerted effort must be made to assist students not only in identifying such misinformation, but also in developing clear, powerful, and nuanced counter-narratives reflecting the richness and diversity of the lives of both Whites and POC (Ponterotto, Utsey, & Pedersen, 2006).

Skills

ONGOING SELF-AWARENESS

White students must understand that it is not in fact possible for them to develop a non-racist consciousness or to extricate themselves from a system of oppression that advantages them. However, in order to use one's privilege in the service of social justice (e.g., using one's position of power to facilitate the development of more just policies or connecting a client of Color to helpful resources) and in order to avoid perpetuating acts of racism (e.g., by colluding with White clients' racist views or invalidating the experience of a client of Color), *ongoing* self-awareness is key. White students must commit to exploring their mainstream and marginalized identities (embedded in an understanding of intersectionality, rather than an additive multicultural model), recognize their internalized biases, and become aware of the ways in which they perpetuate, benefit, and collude with the status quo (assuming that all three occur on a regular basis).

Feminists have long used self-reflexivity as a "minimum requirement" to carefully scrutinize what we bring to our relationships (Sholock, 2012). Lorde (1984) refers to this process as identifying and confronting the oppressor in us. This level of continuous interrogation is necessary on both individual and social levels. Reflexivity is a particular approach to antiracist work that helps us manage what is perhaps most difficult, i.e., the dysphoria of guilt and anxiety, as well as a tool for cultural self-awareness (Kowal, Franklin, & Paradies, 2013). Here feminism is an especially useful framework as it pairs self-knowledge with social action.

However, because of our very racial biases and scripts, self-exploration is impossible without appropriate support and mirroring. Therefore, White students must also learn to seek and develop relationship with White allies who can provide them with opportunities for peer supervision and accountability, and to whom they can provide feedback as well (Kivel, 2002). White students must develop the ability to support both empathetically and with honesty White peers in the learning process, while also seeking the feedback of other Whites with whom they can explore their biases without harming colleagues of Color in the process. Further, because Whites don't have a direct experience of racism, they must develop alliances with peers of Color, (1) with whom they can collaborate to maximize impact because of their different positionalities (e.g., a faculty of Color may be able to provide additional mentoring/mirroring to an advisee of Color of a White faculty when professional development concerns are discussed, or a White faculty can support the racial identity development of a White student in a multicultural course taught by a faculty of Color); and (2) to whom they can be accountable for, or seek input from, about decisions or actions aimed at disrupting racist dynamics. In other words, the development of an anti-racist community in all of one's spheres (personal, academic, professional) are essential in empowering individuals to sustain both the vision and process needed for systemic change.

Analysis of racial scripts

The media and social norms are primary sources of racial messages, which then provide us with highly reinforced scripts prescribing the "right" way to understand or approach racial situations or conversations. A critical analysis of such messages is key so that both the delivery methods and content can be understood and questioned (Avery, Richeson, Hebl, & Ambady, 2009). In this process, it is also essential for White students to develop, or at least experiment with, alternative scripts (e.g., race talk is allowed in a comical context or when negative events may occur; an alternative script would be to name race when it's not "warranted" and engage the expanded perspective that the new dialogue provides), as well as practice questioning out loud the narrower/biased scripts. This is especially important given that gender and race have interdependent and interactive scripts that reinforce both privilege and the ignorance of privilege (Gillman, 2007).

Social justice action

Most Whites become extremely anxious and use the flight or fight reaction when they encounter racist incidents – whether they are the perpetrators, a witness, or otherwise involved. Silence, forcefully providing a non-racial explanation, or simply moving away from the situation, are often the only strategies they know. Therefore, it is crucial for them to learn effective and safe ways of becoming agents of social change. This involves recognizing if the situation warrants an immediate versus deferred action, an individual intervention or a collaborative one, or a combination of any of the above (depending on effectiveness and safety). This also involves learning specific language they can employ in that process that is both firm and empathetic. A helpful model in this process is "Name It, Claim It, Stop It" by Berrill and Cummings-Wilson (n.d.). See also Ridley (2005) for a behavioral analysis of racism and how to respond to it.

Managing racial stress

Even though White students will become more comfortable naming race and discussing racial topics, their privileged position paired with often lifelong colorblindness training makes them especially prone to experience guilt and anxiety when racial topics or conflict arise (Spanierman et al., 2008). In order to sustain the process needed to develop authentic relationships and disrupt the status quo (which involves remaining present and open to be transformed by others), they must learn how to withstand their own anxiety, confusion, and uncertainty (Stevenson, 2013). Mindfulness training can be useful in this context (Lillis & Hayes, 2007).

Recognize, respect, and facilitate affinity spaces for colleagues or clients of color

Affinity spaces for POC in predominantly White spaces allow for safety, growth, and camaraderie especially in the face of stereotype threat (Steele, 1997). It is important for White allies to respect and support such spaces without feeling threatened or excluded, and to recognize their positive impact on healthy cross-racial interactions. White students should also learn to identify when such spaces are needed, so that they might facilitate appropriate referrals for clients of Color to affinity groups, psychotherapists of similar ethnic backgrounds, or additional resources outside of treatment. This skill implies recognizing the potential limitations (via self-awareness) of White psychotherapists to offer support to clients of Color because of White psychotherapists' very sociopolitical standing—which, again, cannot be escaped regardless of sophistication in critical consciousness. However, White psychotherapists *can* use their understanding and privileged position to support meaningful safe spaces for their clients of Color in primarily White institutions. Furthermore, White allies can serve as educators and agents of social change by helping other Whites to listen more critically to their own voices as well as the voices of peers of Color (Smith & Redington, 2010; Lorde, 1984).

Recognizing one's racist and anti-racist identities

Students must be able to acknowledge the "both/and" possibility of being racist and anti-racist at the same time (Raby, 2004; Thompson, 2003). Also called "multiple subjectivities" (Yon, 2000) or "ambivalence theory" (Katz & Hass, 1988), this is the idea that White Americans may simultaneously project both a sense of welcome or friendliness and rejection towards POC. Acknowledging this seemingly contradictory state of being can be critical to breaking down the binary in which people are always either "racist" or "not racist." This expanded perspective creates the space to receive important critical feedback that may challenge one's self-image as anti-racist, while it also offers the possibility of growing in one's anti-racism. In fact, it assists students in becoming allies to other White students in supportive and constructive ways.

CONCLUSIONS

In this article we have argued for the necessity of moving beyond an additive model of multicultural training towards one that recognizes the reality of intersectionality. We have also argued for counseling and psychotherapy programs to offer training that doesn't simply target self-awareness, but also a clear understanding of the unavoidable impact of systemic racism and consequently of the roles and scripts embedded in our socio-political positionalities. These considerations propel Whiteness to the center of the conversation, rather than as the unquestioned vantage point from which "others" are analyzed. It also necessitate that programs demonstrate a commitment to social justice in their policies and practices, and provide avenues for WRS in their curricula. In these context, skill development becomes essential as it lies at the core of what allows for the social justice mission inherent in feminist therapy to move beyond an aspirational proposition and become at least an option, if not a reality.

REFERENCES

Adelman, L. (Creator, & Executive Producer). (2003). *Race: The power of an illusion* [Documentary]. San Francisco, CA: California Newsreel.

American Counseling Association. (2005). *ACA code of ethics*. Alexandria, VA: Author.

American Psychological Association. (2010). *Ethical principles of psychologists and code of conduct*. Washington, DC: American Psychological Association.

Arredondo, P., Tovar-Blank, Z. G., & Parham, T. A. (2008). Challenges and promises of becoming a culturally competent counselor in a sociopolitical era of change and empowerment. *Journal of Counseling & Development, 86*, 261–268. doi:10.1002/j.1556-6678.2008.tb00508.x

Avery, D. R., Richeson, J. A., Hebl, M. R., & Ambady, N. (2009). It does not have to be uncomfortable: The role of behavioral scripts in Black–White interracial interactions. *Journal of Applied Psychology, 94*(6), 1382–1393. doi:10.1037/a0016208

Bartoli, E., Michael, A., Bentley-Edwards, K. L., Stevenson, H. C., Shor, R., & McClain, S. (2015). Chasing colorblindness: White racial and ethnic socialization. Manuscript submitted for publication.

Bartoli, E., & Pyati, A. (2009). Addressing clients' racism and racial prejudice in individual psychotherapy: Therapeutic considerations. *Psychotherapy Theory, Research, Practice, Training, 46*(2), 145–157. doi:10.1037/a0016023

Bentley, K. L., Adams, V. N., & Stevenson, H. C. (2009). Racial socialization: Roots, processes, and outcomes. In H. A. Neville, B. M. Tynes, & S. O. Utsey (Eds.), *Handbook of African American psychology* (pp. 255–267). Thousand Oaks, CA: Sage Publications, Inc.

Berrill, K., & Cummins-Wilson, D. (n.d.). *Name it, claim it, stop it* [Handout]. Retrieved from http://englishmakesmesmarter.weebly.com/uploads/5/2/0/0/5200949/name_it.pdf

Brown, D. L., Blackmon, S. K., Schumacher, K., & Urbanski, B. (2013). Exploring clinicians attitudes toward the incorporation of racial socialization in psychotherapy. *Journal of Black Psychology, 39*(6), 507–531. doi:10.1177/0095798412461806

Collins, P. H. (1990). *Black feminist thought: Knowledge, consciousness, and the politics of empowerment*. Boston, MA: Unwin Hyman.

Crenshaw, K. (1993). Mapping the margins: Intersectionality, identity politics, and violence against women of color. *Stanford University Law Review, 43*(124), 1241–1299. doi:10.2307/1229039

D'Andrea, M., & Heckman, E. F. (2008). A 40-year review of multicultural counseling outcome research: Outlining a future research agenda for the multicultural counseling movement. *Journal of Counseling & Development, 86,* 356–363. doi:10.1002/j.1556-6678.2008.tb00520.x

Enns, C., & Williams, E. (2012). *The Oxford handbook of feminist multicultural counseling psychology.* New York, NY: Oxford University Press.

Fawcett, M., & Evans, K. (2013). *Experiential approach for developing multicultural counseling competencies.* Thousand Oaks, CA: Sage Publishing.

Fine, M. (2004). Witnessing whiteness/gathering intelligence. In M. Fine, L. Weis, L. Powell Pruitt, & A. Burns (Eds.), *Off White: Readings on power, privilege and resistance* (pp. 245–256). New York, NY: Routledge.

Gillman, L. (2007). Beyond the shadow: Re-scripting race in women's studies. *Meridians: Feminism, Race, Transnationalism, 7*(2), 117–141. doi:10.2979/mer.2007.7.2.117

Gushue, G. V., Constantine, M. G., & Sciarra, D. T. (2008). The influence of culture, self-reported multicultural counseling competence, and shifting standards of judgment on perceptions of family functioning of white family counselors. *Journal of Counseling & Development, 86*(1), 85–94. doi:10.1002/j.1556-6678.2008.tb00629.x

Hamm, J. V. (2001). Barriers and bridges to positive cross-ethnic relations: African American and White parent socialization beliefs and practices. *Youth and Society 33*(1), 62–98. doi:10.1177/0044118x01033001003

Hare-Mustin, R. T. (1978). A feminist approach to family therapy. *Family Process, 17*(2), 181–194. doi:10.1111/j.1545-5300.1978.00181.x

Harris, C. I. (1993). Whiteness as property. *Harvard Law Review, 106*(8), 1707–1791. doi:10.2307/1341787

Helms, J. E. (1993). *Black and White racial identity: Theory, research, and practice.* New York: Greenwood Press.

Inman, A. G., & DeBoer Kreider, E. (2013). Multicultural competence: Psychotherapy practice and supervision. *Psychotherapy, 50*(3), 346–350. doi:10.1037/a0032029

Katz, P., & Hass, G. R. (1988). Racial ambivalence and American value conflict: Correlational and priming studies of dual cognitive structures. *Journal of Personality and Social Psychology, 55*(6), 893–905. doi:10.1037/0022-3514.55.6.893

Kendall, F. E. (2006). *Understanding white privilege: Creating pathways to authentic relationships across race.* New York, NY: Routledge.

Kivel, P. (2002). *Uprooting racism: How White people can work for racial justice.* Gabriola Island, BC: New Society Publishers.

Kowal, E., Franklin, H., & Paradies, Y. (2013). Reflexive antiracism: A novel approach to diversity training. *Ethnicities, 13,* 316–337. doi:10.1177/1468796812472885

Kryzanowski, E., & Stewin, L. (1985). Developmental implications in youth counselling: Gender socialization. *International Journal for the Advancement of Counselling, 8*(4), 265–278.

Lillis, J., & Hayes, S. C. (2007). Applying acceptance, mindfulness, and values to the reduction of prejudice: A pilot study. *Behavior Modification, 31*(4), 389–411. doi:10.1177/0145445506298413

Lorde, A. (1984). *Sister outsider: Essays and speeches.* Trumansburg, NY: Crossing Press.

Mays, V. M., Cochran, S. D., & Barnes, N. W. (2007). Race, race-based discrimination, and health outcomes among African Americans. *Annual Review of Psychology, 58*, 201–225.

McCreary, M. L., Cunningham, J. N., Ingram, K. M., & Fife, J. E. (2006). *Stress, culture, and racial socialization: Making an impact*. Dallas, TX: Spring Publications.

McInstosh, P. (1997). White privilege and male privilege: A personal account of coming to see correspondences through work in women's studies. In R. Delgado & J. Stefancic (Eds.), *Critical White studies* (pp. 291–299). Philadelphia, PA: Temple University Press.

Naples, A., & Bojar, K. (2002). *Teaching feminist activism: Strategies from the field*. New York: Routledge.

Pahlke, E., Bigler, R. S., & Suizzo, M.-A. (2012). Relations between colorblind socialization and children's racial bias: Evidence from European American mothers and their preschool children. *Child Development, 83*(4), 1164–1179. doi:10.1111/j.1467-8624.2012.01770.x

Pheterson, G. (1986). Alliances between women: Overcoming internalized oppression and internalized domination. *Signs, 12*(1), 146–160. doi:10.2307/3174362

Pinderhughes, E. (1989). *Understanding race, ethnicity and power: The key to efficacy in clinical practice*. New York, NY: Free Press.

Pittman, C. (2010). Race and gender oppression in the classroom: The experiences of women faculty of Color with White male students. *Teaching Sociology, 38*, 183–196. doi:10.1177/0092055x10370120

Ponterotto, J. G., Gretchen, D., Utsey, S. O., Rieger, B. P., & Austin, R. (2002). A revision of the multicultural counseling awareness scale. *Journal of Multicultural Counseling and Development, 30*(3), 153–180. doi:10.1002/j.2161-1912.2002.tb00489.x

Ponterotto, J. G., Utsey, S. O., & Pedersen, P. B. (2006). *Preventing prejudice: A guide for counselors, educators, and parents*, (2nd ed.). Thousand Oaks, CA: SAGE Publications.

Raby, R. (2004). 'There's no racism at my school, it's just joking around': Ramifications for anti-racist education. *Race, Ethnicity and Education, 7*(4), 367–383. doi:10.1080/1361332042000303388

Ridley, A. R. (2005). *Overcoming unintentional racism in counseling and therapy*, (2nd ed.). Thousand Oaks, CA: Sage Publications.

Rowe, W., Bennett, S. K., & Atkinson, D. R. (1994). White racial identity models: A critique and alternative proposal. *Counseling Psychologist, 22*(1), 129–146. doi:10.1177/0011000094221009

Sholock, A. (2012). Methodology of the privileged: White anti-racist feminism, systematic ignorance, and epistemic uncertainty. *Hypatia, 27*(4), 701–714. doi:10.1111/j.1527-2001.2012.01275.x

Smith, L., & Redington, R. (2010). Lessons from the experiences of White antiracist activists. *Professional Psychology: Research and Practice, 41*(6), 541–549. doi:10.1037/a0021793

Spanierman, L. B., Poteat, V. P., Wang, Y.-F., & Oh, E. (2008). Psychosocial costs of racism to white counselors: Predicting various dimensions of multicultural counseling competence. *Journal of Counseling Psychology, 55*(1), 75–88. doi:10.1037/0022-0167.55.1.75

Steele, C. M. (1997). A Threat in the air: How stereotypes shape intellectual identity and performance. *American Psychologist, 52*, 613–629. doi:10.1037//0003-066x.52.6.613

Stevenson, H. C. (2013). *Promoting racial literacy in schools: Differences that make a difference.* New York, NY: Teachers College Press.

Sue, D. (2010). *Microaggressions in everyday life: Race, gender and sexual orientation.* Hoboken, NJ: John Wiley & Sons.

Sue, D. W. (2004). Whiteness and ethnocentric monoculturalism: Making the "invisible" visible. *American Psychologist, 59*(8), 761–770. doi:10.1037/0003-066x.59.8.761

Sue, D. W., Arredondo, P., & McDavis, R. J. (1992). Multicultural counseling competencies and standards: A call to the profession. *Journal of Multicultural Counseling & Development, 20*, 64–88. doi:10.1002/j.2161-1912.1992.tb00563.x

Sue, D. W., & Sue, D. (2012). *Counseling the culturally diverse: Theory and practice,* (6th ed.). Hoboken, NJ: John Wiley & Sons.

Tatum, B. D. (2003). *Why are all the Black kids sitting together in the cafeteria?* New York: Basic Books.

Thandeka. (2000). *Learning to be White.* New York, NY: Continuum.

Thompson, A. (2003). Tiffany, friend of people of color: White investments in antiracism. *International Journal of Qualitative Studies in Education, 16*(1), 7–29. doi:10.1080/0951839032000033509

Thornton Dill, B., & Kohlman, M. (2012). Intersectionality: A transformative paradigm in feminist theory and social justice. In J. Spade & C. Valentine (Eds.), *The kaleidoscope of gender: Prisms, patterns and possibilities.* Thousand Oaks, CA: Sage.

Toporek, R., & McNalley, C. (2006). Social justice training in counseling psychology: Needs and innovations. In R. Toporek, L. Gerstein, N. Fouad, G. Roysircar, & T. Israel (Eds.), *Handbook for social justice in counseling psychology: Leadership, vision, and action* (pp. 37–43). Thousand Oaks, CA: Sage Publishing.

Wei, M., Chao, R. C.-L., Tsai, P.-C., & Botello-Zamarron, R. (2012). The concerns about counseling racial minority clients scale. *Journal of Counseling Psychology, 59*(1), 107–119. doi:10.1037/a0026239

Yon, D. A. (2000). *Elusive culture: Schooling, race and identities in global times.* New York, NY: SUNY Press.

White Practitioners in Therapeutic Ally-ance: An Intersectional Privilege Awareness Training Model

KIM A. CASE

Department of Psychology and Women's Studies, University of Houston-Clear Lake, Houston, Texas

Among White[1] licensed psychologists, social workers, marriage and family therapists, and counselors, research has documented a severe lack of awareness of unconscious stereotyping, systemic racism, white privilege, and white racial identity. This article introduces a privilege awareness pedagogical model as a framework for White students in clinical training programs learning about white privilege, enhancing multicultural competencies, and developing as effective allies in the therapeutic relationship, or therapeutic ally-ance. The model emphasizes intersectional privilege studies to address white privilege along with a wide variety of oppressions often neglected in the curriculum, involves personal reflection on biases and assumptions to enhance multicultural competencies, and promotes student learning through social action to dismantle privilege. The pedagogical benefits of the following activities and assignments are described: 1) group analysis of therapeutic scenarios, 2) photo voice identity assignment, 3) white privilege reflection paper, and 4) identities education project.

In the years since clinical training programs originally began incorporating curricular content to enhance multicultural competencies (Helms, 1990; Parker, 1988; Pedersen, 1988; Sabnani, Pomterotto, & Borodovsky, 1991), faculty in social work, clinical psychology, family therapy, and counseling programs introduced curricula to address the potential impact of race on the therapeutic relationship (Ancis & Syzmanski, 2001; Gushue & Constantine, 2007; Hays, Chang, & Havice, 2008; Mindrup, Spray, & Lamberghini-West, 2011; Sabnani et al., 1991; Sue et al., 2010; Utsey, Gernat, & Hammar, 2005). For White[1] counseling trainees, awareness and reflection on racism, white racial identity, and white privilege are essential to working effectively with clients of color (Hays, 1996; Hays et al., 2008; Mindrup et al., 2011; Pewewardy, 2004; Tummala-Narra & Kaschak, 2013). In fact, speaking specifically to the field of family therapy, Pewewardy (2004) describes trainees as possessing "incomplete white consciousness" (p. 60) that prevents them from recognizing invisible white privilege and working as allies for racial justice.

To address the gaps within that incomplete consciousness, this article presents a pedagogical model of privilege studies (Case, 2013a) that emphasizes intersectionality (Cole, 2009; Collins, 1990; Crenshaw, 1989; Dill & Zambrana, 2009) as a framework for White trainees learning about white privilege, enhancing multicultural competencies, and developing as effective allies in the therapeutic relationship, or what I call *therapeutic ally-ance*. The pedagogical model of privilege studies (Case, 2013a) emphasizes an intersectional privilege studies to address white privilege along with a wide variety of oppressions often neglected in the curriculum, involves personal reflection on biases and assumptions, and promotes student learning through social action as allies to dismantle privilege and racism. Given the resistance and denial that often present obstacles to learning for White students (Ancis & Syzmanski, 2001; Case, 2013b; Case & Cole, 2013; Case & Hemmings, 2005; Hays, Chang, & Dean, 2004; Sue et al., 2010; Tatum, 1994; Utsey et al., 2005; Wise & Case, 2013), effective pedagogical approaches offer faculty, as supervisors of White trainees, strategies for maximizing student engagement, learning, and professional development.

INCOMPLETE WHITE CONSCIOUSNESS: CONSEQUENCES FOR CLIENTS OF COLOR

Privilege refers to automatic unearned benefits bestowed upon perceived members of dominant groups based on social identity (Case, Iuzzini, & Hopkins, 2012; McIntosh, 1988, 2012). As described by McIntosh (1988), privilege functions as "an invisible weightless knapsack of special provisions, assurances, tools, maps, guides, codebooks, passports, visas, clothes, compass, emergency gear, and blank checks" (pp. 1–2). Among White licensed psychologists, social workers, marriage and family therapists, and counselors, research has documented a severe lack of awareness of unconscious stereotyping, systemic racism, white privilege, and white racial identity (Ancis & Syzmanski, 2001; Constantine, Juby, & Liang, 2001; Fuertes, Mueller, Chauhan, Walker, & Ladany, 2002; Gushue & Constantine, 2007;

Hays et al., 2004; Mindrup et al., 2011; Richardson & Molinaro, 1996; Sabnani et al., 1991; Sue et al., 2010). Due to this incomplete white consciousness (Pewewardy, 2004), gaps in knowledge among current and future White practitioners translate into serious gaps in clinical skills that lead to concrete negative consequences for cross-racial and cross-cultural therapist-client relationships (Ancis & Syzmanski, 2001; Cardemil & Battle, 2003; Hays et al., 2008; Sue et al., 2010; Utsey et al., 2005). For example, lack of awareness and gaps in knowledge often result in White therapists avoiding discussions of race and racism when working with individuals from marginalized and oppressed racial groups (Cardemil & Battle, 2003; Sue et al., 2010; Utsey et al., 2005). In fact, practitioners may direct the conversation away from race due to fear of offending or in an effort to escape personal discomfort, guilt, and insecurities (Cardemil & Battle, 2003; Utsey et al., 2005). Research also documented the tendency of White therapists to endorse a color-blind viewpoint that prevents acknowledgement of differences in life experience among people from various racial and ethnic backgrounds (Gushue & Constantine, 2007; Sue et al., 2010; Utsey et al., 2005). Viewing clients of color through unconscious stereotypes (Gushue & Constantine, 2007; Hays et al., 2008; Nelson et al., 2001; Pewewardy, 2004), these practitioners may over-pathologize and more specifically, invalidate race discrimination experiences by attributing them to client pathology (Ancis & Syzmanski, 2001; Fuertes et al., 2002; Hays et al., 2004; Maxie, Arnold, & Stephenson, 2006; Utsey et al., 2005). White therapists lacking appropriate multicultural training tend to perpetuate white cultural norms, thus creating an ethnocentric environment that serves to alienate clients of color (Ancis & Syzmanski, 2001; Hays, Chang, & Dean, 2008; Mindrup et al., 2011; Richardson & Molinaro, 1996).

The lack of multicultural competencies to address client needs harms the therapeutic relationship by failing to provide a safe space, often resulting in distrust from the client's perspective (Hays et al., 2004; Nelson et al., 2001; Richardson & Molinaro, 1996). Clients of color may also become avoidant of attending therapy and detach from the process (Hays et al., 2008), potentially leading to early termination and decreased use of mental health services (Cardemil & Battle, 2003; Maxie et al., 2006; Nelson et al., 2001; Richardson & Molinaro 1996). However, with proper training and supervision, White counselors and therapists can work toward ethical practices (Hays et al., 2004; Hays et al., 2008) through deeper understanding of the pervasiveness of white privilege and its impact on both Whites and people of color (Ancis & Syzmanski, 2001).

WHITE PRIVILEGE AWARENESS: OPPORTUNITIES FOR THERAPEUTIC "ALLY-ANCE"

As White practitioners gain awareness of systemic racism, their own racial identity, and especially white privilege, they become better skilled at engaging in racial dialogues, empathizing with racism experienced by clients, using culturally-relevant therapeutic approaches, and working as allies for social justice (Ancis & Syzmanski, 2001; Hays, 1996; Utsey et al., 2005). Within a therapy setting, the multiculturally competent counselor will be well-equipped to handle topics such as racial identity and instances of race discrimination as they arise, rather than purposely avoiding the issues at hand (Cardemil & Battle, 2003; Fuertes et al., 2002; Utsey et al., 2005). In addition, proper training helps promote empathy and validation of client experiences with racism (Ancis & Syzmanski, 2001; Fuertes et al., 2002), as well as reflecting on a client's presenting problems from a systemic perspective (Hays et al., 2008). Better hypotheses and questions devised by the therapist may potentially develop due to deeper understanding of racism, culture, and privilege (Hays, 1996). As White practitioners become better skilled at recognizing the complexity of the individual client (Cardemil & Battle, 2003), rather than relying on stereotypes, they seek personal knowledge about not only the individual client, but also culturally relevant approaches to the client's needs (Hays, 1996; Richardson & Molinaro, 1996). These competencies speak to establishing a stronger therapeutic alliance to better serve the needs of diverse clients (Cardemil & Battle, 2003; Gushue & Constantine, 2007; Mindrup et al., 2011). As White trainees increase their awareness of white privilege, they can begin to work toward effective *therapeutic ally-ances*, taking action to dismantle racism and privilege for social justice (Ancis & Syzmanski, 2001; Pewewardy, 2004).

Since McIntosh's (1988) groundbreaking essay on white, male, and heterosexual privilege, scholarly research on privilege and pedagogical strategies to help students think critically about systems of privilege increased dramatically (Case, 2013a; Case et al., 2012; McIntosh, 2012, 2013). Within my own research on diversity course effectiveness, greater white privilege awareness correlated with increased awareness of racism and support for affirmative action, as well as lower levels of race prejudice (Case, 2007). In their study of social work and clinical psychology trainees, Mindrup and colleagues (2011) found white privilege awareness correlated positively with greater multicultural knowledge and awareness. In classroom settings and counseling training programs, White students cannot achieve comprehension of systemic racism and oppression without examining white privilege (Case, 2013a, 2013b; Case et al., 2012; McIntosh, 2012, 2013; Pewewardy, 2004). White clinical students need a guided exploration for ongoing self-assessment and reflection on white privilege and personal biases within the curriculum (Hays, 1996; Hays et al., 2008; Mindrup et al., 2011; Pewewardy, 2004). In fact, programs that aim to prepare competent White therapists would benefit from infusion of privilege content throughout the curriculum (Case, 2013a; Case et al., 2012; McIntosh, 2012, 2013; Mindrup et al., 2011). The intersectional privilege studies training model described below provides pedagogical strategies for incorporating white privilege across the curriculum.

INTERSECTIONAL THEORY: EXPLORING WHITE PRIVILEGE VIA COMPLEX IDENTITIES

In an effort to challenge typical categorical generalizations about social groups, Crenshaw (1989) introduced the term "intersectionality" which highlighted the vast, yet unrecognized, complexity of identities (based on race, gender, sexuality, class, age, and more). Patricia Hill Collins' (1990) framework of the "matrix of domination" also provides an intersectional conceptual structure to advance understanding of the various social locations that result from complex privileged and marginalized identities. Intersectional scholarship highlighting interwoven complexities of social identity informs not only theoretical advances with regard to privilege and oppression (Cole, 2009; Collins, 1990; Crenshaw, 1989; Dill & Zambrana, 2009; Dottolo & Stewart, 2008), but also pedagogical implications. Using this intersectional approach pedagogically, instructors provide students with a sophisticated critical framework for examining the complexity of identity (Case, 2013a, 2013b; Case & Lewis, 2012; Case et al., 2012; Dill & Zambrana, 2009). In contrast to intersectional theory, many training programs addressed gaps in multicultural competencies by developing distinct courses to address either gender or culture (i.e., race), and less often sexuality or other social identity categories. These courses enriched therapist and counselor training and promoted multicultural awareness and knowledge (Ancis & Syzmanski, 2001; Constantine et al., 2001; Gushue & Constantine, 2007; Mindrup et al., 2011; Sue et al., 2010), but also treated social identities and various forms of oppression as mutually exclusive. What happens when faculty challenge future therapists to think in more complex and comprehensive ways about how social identities interact to affect lived experiences? What happens when supervisors offer them the opportunity to consider both privileged and oppressed identities within themselves and others? How can faculty facilitate deeper understanding of intersecting identities among White students training to work in therapeutic settings?

Liu, Pickett, and Ivey (2007) argue that integration of an intersectional framework for understanding race, culture, and privilege is an essential component of multicultural competency among counselor trainees. As Utsey and colleagues (2005) argue, White trainees learning about racism and the impact of their own privilege are sometimes resistant to feedback about improving their multicultural competencies and may even consider race discussions socially taboo. In a qualitative study of White counselors (Hays et al., 2004), participants found it difficult to discuss non-racial oppressed identities, such as low socioeconomic status, due to the salience of their own whiteness. This invisibility and concealability of various identities calls for an intersectional approach to learning that allows students to more fully explore complexities and interconnections, rather than feeling invalidated in terms of their non-privileged experiences. Given common reactions of fear, guilt, shame, and defensiveness among White students learning about race and privilege (Case & Cole, 2013; Case & Hemmings, 2005; Tatum, 1994; Wise & Case, 2013), an intersectional pedagogy that facilitates students' explorations of not only their own oppressor roles in racism, but also their personal experiences with systemic disadvantage and discrimination due to non-racial identities. Incorporation of intersectional learning about privilege and oppressed social identities and ways those various social locations interact to affect an individual's lived experiences ultimately helps minimize student resistance and psychological barriers to learning. By utilizing an intersectional lens, White students can draw connections between their complex personal social identities, and therefore strengthen learning about racism and white privilege (Ancis & Syzmanski, 2001).

A PEDAGOGICAL MODEL FOR INTERSECTIONAL PRIVILEGE STUDIES

For faculty working with future therapists, the privilege studies pedagogical model (Case, 2013a) facilitates transformative learning with a focus on intersectionality to aid Whites' self-reflection and analysis of their own invisible privilege. White students in counseling or family therapy graduate programs may encounter the concept of white privilege for the first time and face difficulty in processing privilege (Ancis & Syzmanski, 2001; Hays et al., 2004; Sue et al., 2010). In fact, students may exhibit resistance behaviors and avoid readings, class discussions, and self-reflection on white privilege, preferring to focus on their own status outside the privileged group, for example, in terms of patriarchal systems or sexuality (Ancis & Syzmanski, 2001; Case & Cole, 2013; Case & Hemmings, 2005; Sue et al., 2010; Utsey et al., 2005; Wise & Case, 2013). Classroom analysis of white privilege and power in teaching about privilege pushes the boundaries of teaching multiculturalism, diversity, or oppression and discrimination and provides spaces for professional growth among White practitioners. The model extends learning goals to consistently include privileged identities and how white privilege operates to maintain oppression. Although the full 10-point model (Case, 2013a) provides valuable pedagogical strategies for effective privilege studies, the following four aspects of the model facilitate multicultural competencies among White trainees in the classroom and supervision:

- includes various forms of privilege;
- frames privilege studies through an intersectional lens;
- encourages critical analysis through student reflection; and
- promotes social action to dismantle white privilege.

To facilitate teaching and learning about white privilege, the description below of these four key points of the model elaborates on pedagogical benefits for faculty and students.

Inclusive Privilege Studies: White Privilege and Beyond

Most existing scholarship on privilege focuses on white privilege (Ancis & Syzmanski, 2001; Case, 2007, 2012; Case & Hemmings, 2005; Gushue & Constantine, 2007; Hays et al., 2004; Mindrup et al., 2011; Tatum, 1994) while neglecting additional forms of privilege. Although McIntosh's (1988) famous essay integrates white, male, and heterosexual privilege, references to the work rarely acknowledge male or heterosexual privilege. This trend of emphasizing her points about white privilege renders her discussion of two other forms of privilege invisible. With a strict focus on white privilege, instructors may end up neglecting other forms of privilege, thereby weakening student ability to learn about privilege as both a theoretical and practical concept that spans all forms of oppression. Student learning focused on white privilege must also acknowledge and encourage exploration of privilege that results from non-racial social identities, such as sex, ability, social class, sexuality, citizenship, religion, and gender identity (Case, 2013a). Within therapist training programs, inclusion of privilege across a wide variety of oppressions that are often neglected in the curriculum will better prepare White trainees for their roles in practice. By opening up privilege studies to address multiple forms of privilege, White students may feel less targeted as dominant group members learning about their own biases, assumptions, and unearned advantage. Engaging students in activities that focus on not only white privilege, but also forms of privilege that students typically find less threatening, helps reduce resistance as they begin to explore the concept.

By incorporating various forms and beginning with a more visible form of privilege, instructors build student understanding of the concept while working toward white privilege as a taboo and uncomfortable topic for many White students. One way to initially introduce White students to critical thinking and deconstruction of therapist privilege is through group work analyses of counseling scenarios involving. With peer support working through the "Counseling Privilege Scenarios Group Assignment," students can identify and analyze stereotypes, norms, assumptions, and invisible privilege(s) at play between therapist and client. By using fictional accounts, this approach offers a less threatening learning experience in comparison to immediately asking students to eventually analyze their own white privilege. In addition, this group project incorporates critical thinking and analysis that depends on peer support to do the difficult work of making privilege visible. However, planned phases of scenarios that introduce carefully chosen types of privilege may aid student learning about white privilege.

When students first learn about privilege, the concept seems very foreign and abstract. In fact, White students exhibiting difficulty and resistance behaviors in the context of learning about white privilege are often much more capable of analyzing a more visible form such as able-bodied privilege (Wise & Case, 2013). As described by Tim Wise (Wise & Case, 2013), he often introduces White students to privilege by asking them to consider how they arrived in the room, if they had to call ahead for special accommodations, if they had any difficult getting to the seat, etc. Students understand fairly quickly that being able-bodied provides certain privileges that are typically invisible to them. This newfound awareness opens the door to more challenging conversations about white privilege.

Beginning the group scenarios activity with two client scenarios involving disability and able-bodied privilege, such as a client dealing with social isolation because friends are unsure of how to address her mobility challenges, should allow students the chance to analyze privilege in a less threatening context. Following that with two scenarios about another form of privilege, such as living in poverty versus middle-class privilege, will present a more challenging analysis that prepares students for deconstructing white privilege. When introducing the white privilege group scenarios, it may help to conduct a critical analysis of the scenario with the full class before giving them more white privilege scenarios to work on in small groups. Group analyses of therapist privilege within case studies allows student trainees to explore privilege in professional scenarios without personal defensiveness or feeling like the direct and focused target of an attack, therefore reducing the fear, guilt, and resistance to learning.

Complicating Privileged Identities Through Intersectional Learning

By incorporating intersectional analyses into coursework, faculty challenge "traditional disciplinary boundaries and the compartmentalization and fixity of ideas" (Dill & Zambrana, 2009, p. 2) that dominate learning environments. Framing learning about white privilege through an intersectional theory perspective allows White students to develop a deeper understanding of the matrix of oppression and privilege (Collins, 1990). When white students are able to simultaneously consider their own oppressed identities while learning about white privilege, it relieves some of the anxiety, fear, and guilt often associated with being the dominant group focus of the classroom discussion. An intersectional learning paradigm supports student reflections on their own lived experiences with oppression and how that can inform a deeper understanding of their invisible privilege (Case, 2013a). When students feel validated in terms of their personal discrimination experiences, they are often more open to developing connections and parallels that make their white privilege visible.

As clinical faculty encourage White trainees to consider their own multiple and interconnected social locations, the intersectional photo-voice project (Case & Lewis, 2012; Case, Miller, & Jackson, 2012) offers an avenue for moving from the fictional case study analyses to a more personal assignment. The "Intersectional Photo-voice Assignment" invites students to use photos taken specifically for this project, and sometimes photos from childhood, to explore and present on their privileged and marginalized social identities with special attention to where and how these intersect. At this second stage, students turning attention to themselves for a comprehensive inventory of their social identities begin to make visible their own social locations, interactions of identity, and collective impact on their lived experiences. The following instructions were provided to students in my graduate-level course:

- This approach, known as photovoice, has been used for several decades by social scientists, educators, and counselors to work with people and provide a space for individualized expression (Chio & Fandt, 2007; Wang, 1999). When used as a methodological approach to working with marginalized communities, it can be a powerful way to gather perspectives from people that are traditionally silenced. For example, a psychology professor once gave cameras to women immigrants from Taiwan living in a domestic violence shelter. She asked them to take pictures that represented who they were and their experiences as immigrant women.
- Your charge will be to take pictures over the next few weeks that capture your voice with regard to intersectionality, including privileged and oppressed identities, while addressing each bullet:
- Photos that represent the intersections of your own various identities, including those that are associated with privilege and oppression
- Photos that attempt to illustrate privilege and intersectionality as a concept. You might take pictures of items, locations, and abstract images that would help others understand intersectional theory and the matrix of oppression and privilege.
- Each student will display and explain the photos taken as part of an in-class presentation. Powerpoint is the recommended format, but more creative solutions (such as a website) are welcome.

This project builds on previous learning via critical analyses of fictional scenarios while challenging white women students to consider personal privilege and oppression. Presenting these to the full class of peers provides intersectional identity awareness for classmates, further complicating student conceptualizations of identity as distinctly categorical. In the next stage of the model, students call white privilege into sharper focus for deeper reflection on the influence of privilege within therapist-client interactions and relationships.

Student Personal Reflection on White Privilege

Taking their own intersecting privileged and oppressed identities into consideration provides a path to reflection on social location. This aspect of the pedagogical model (Case, 2013a) emphasizes White students' reflections on the ways their own white privilege may affect how clients view them, how they see clients, and how they may approach therapy due to blind spots caused by privilege. For White individuals training to work in therapeutic settings, reflection on preconceptions and acknowledgement of the ways power and privilege may affect therapy are essential components of multicultural competency (Cardemil & Battle, 2003). Future practitioners must gain awareness that their own worldviews, values, and opportunities are not universal (Richardson & Molinar, 1996; Tummala-Narra & Kaschak, 2013).

At this stage, the "White Privilege Reflections Paper" encourages students to critically analyze how invisible white privilege results in real benefits, as well as consequences, in both personal and professional contexts. White students now apply what they have learned about privilege in therapeutic settings, intersectionality, and social location to the privileged self. Bringing the impact of invisible white privilege into focus, each student identifies and analyzes examples from their own lives that illustrate unearned group advantage, how privilege affects their perceptions of people of color and vice versa, and how privilege has altered behavioral interactions between the student and people of color. Lastly, students identify specific roles privilege may play in clinical practice, such as the impact on therapeutic hypotheses, questions, and diagnoses, client comfort and possible early termination, and the ability to establish a successful therapeutic ally-ance. More specifically, the following questions may be posed as prompts for White students writing this reflective paper:

- What is white privilege? How is white privilege related to systematic/institutional racism, power, and racial discrimination? In other words, describe how these various parts work together & support each other.
- Identify **five specific** examples of white privilege from **your life** and describe them. This may be something you have experienced or something you saw a friend experience, but they should be real examples from your life. And you should be describing white privilege rather than instances of discrimination.
- Give an example (not already used above) of white privilege in **each** of the following social institutions: education; the workforce/corporate world; government; media; language; religion. Your answer should illustrate your recognition of how these institutions perpetuate privilege.
- How would your life be different if your race privilege were taken away? Really think about this before you write. What if you woke up tomorrow and discovered everything was reversed and people of color had all of the power and privilege?

- How does white privilege affect, alter, shape, change you psychologically? How does it shape how you view race, people of color, white people, and your perceptions of discrimination (such as when a person of color says they have been discriminated against, for example)?
- How does white privilege impact, influence, alter, shape your interactions with white people versus people of color? Think about your own beliefs, attitudes, stereotypes, and behaviors as a dominant group member when interacting with members of your in-group versus members of your out-group. What is the impact? Think about how whites' and people of color's views of you might impact the interaction.
- Reflecting on the client-therapeutic relationship, how might white privilege impact clinical practice, therapeutic hypotheses, questions, and diagnoses, client comfort and possible early termination, and the ability to establish a successful therapeutic ally-ance?
- What specific actions can you take within your own sphere of influence to challenge or deconstruct white privilege? Spheres of influence include areas where you have any power or influence—self, family, friends, acquaintances, coworkers, community members, etc.

Students of color may also be provided questions altered to fit their social identity or choose to write a reflective paper on an area where they do experience privilege (e.g., male, heterosexual). For all questions above, students are instructed to cite readings from the course as well as outside academic sources.

Student Engagement Through Social Action

The pedagogical model for intersectional privilege studies (Case, 2013a) promotes social action to dismantle white privilege through student learning that extends beyond the classroom walls. This social action could materialize in the form of service learning, community research projects, public education projects, community engagement assignments, and ally action for social change. By providing White students with avenues for taking action to challenge racism and white privilege, instructors can help reduce resistance to learning. Ancis and Syzmanski (2001) suggest incorporating action for change within the curriculum as students need productive avenues for directing the negative feelings that often come with learning about oppression and personal privilege. White counseling trainees need guided practice with evaluating their own eurocentric values and assumptions, responding appropriately to client discussions of experiences with racism, identifying culturally relevant solutions to presenting problems, and especially using their own sphere of influence to engage in social action (Pewewardy, 2004).

The "Intersecting Identities Practitioner Education Project" requires students to utilize their newfound knowledge of privilege and intersectionality for further training and education among current and future counselors across various disciplines (Case & Lewis, 2012; Case, Miller, & Jackson, 2012). In other words, students transform their learning into social action by creating and delivering products to benefit the professional community and promote intersectional privilege awareness. For example, students might create videos, brochures, documentaries, workshops designed to prepare White counselors for effective therapeutic ally-ance with clients of color. The assignment provides avenues for students to learn through application of intersectionality to their own whiteness and privilege while sharing knowledge with peers and the wider community. The following instructions provide students with a roadmap for developing their own innovative ways to contribute to the profession via social action and education of current and future counselors and therapists:

- This project has two main goals:
- Focus on privilege via intersectionality (concept or some specific intersection)
- Educating current and/or future practitioners to raise awareness about intersectional privilege
- Creativity and organized planning are essential to an effective and successful project. The two main decisions are 1) what will I focus on for the project? And 2) how will I educate the profession?
- Possible projects in final form: website, Youtube channel with videos, mini-documentary, art show, informational brochures for social service agencies, training for educators or counselors, Facebook page.
- Community Partners – You will need to think very carefully about partners with in the community to gain access to current or future professionals for educating about privilege and intersectionality.
- For example, if you create a website or Facebook page, how will you get practitioners to the sites? This must be done as part of your project. By the due date, you will need to show that some group of practitioners in your profession has been educated in some way or that you have made these connections so that the target audience is being reached. In other words, a summary of how you would hypothetically go about reaching the audience means your project is incomplete.
- Another example – if you create brochures on a particular intersectional privilege issue, you will need to partner with agencies, clinics, professional organizations, schools, or whatever appropriate institutions to gain access to your target audience of practitioners. You will need to convince your partnering agencies that the information you plan to provide is something they need and will commit to sharing with the audience you seek.
- Reflection Paper – You will also turn in an American Psychological Association (APA)-style reflection paper about your project. This paper will be 4–5 pages in length and will explain why you chose your topic,

how it relates to privilege and intersectionality theory and other theories covered in the course, your rationale for effective practitioner education, and how you are getting the information to your target audience.
- Research Support – You may cite readings from the course, but should have a minimum of six journal articles (peer-reviewed) as part of your reflection piece.

In my own Psychology of Gender, Race, and Sexuality course, Master's students in both clinical psychology and family therapy developed: a) workshops on intersectional approaches to masculinity and homophobia for juvenile detention case workers; b) a Youtube video series on white, male, heterosexual, and religious privilege, with the final video focusing on intersectionality; and c) an interactive art sculpture and display on campus that challenged visitors to reflect on privilege intersections and record their thoughts on a community dialogue poster. Students expressed their enthusiasm as the public audiences responded with curiosity and new awareness as a direct result of their projects. They recognized the possibilities for applying their learning to real world problems, identifying concrete avenues for raising awareness about intersections of privilege and oppression, and taking social actions as allies to raise awareness.

IMPLICATIONS FOR TRAINING WHITE PRACTITIONER ALLIES

In her article considering future directions for privilege studies, McIntosh (2012) calls for an intersectional privilege studies that spans the curriculum. By infusing white privilege and a broader intersectional privilege studies throughout practitioner training programs in social work, family therapy, clinical psychology, and counseling, White trainees will enter practice with greater awareness and skills for an effective therapeutic ally-ance (Mindrup et al., 2011) As Constantine and colleagues (2001) point out, White trainees may be unlikely to request the support in supervision to address race discussions that arise in therapy settings. Therefore, taboo topics such as racism, white privilege, and racial identity must be imbedded into the curriculum and practicum experiences of trainees. As training programs expand intersectional white privilege studies, White counselors will benefit from enhanced multicultural competencies for serving communities of color (Ancis & Syzmanski, 2001; Hays, 1996; Hays et al., 2008; Mindrup et al., 2011; Pewewardy, 2004).

NOTE

1. When referring to individuals or a group of people, "White" is capitalized in accordance with APA style guidelines. However, references to concepts such as whiteness and white privilege, guilt, and identity are not capitalized.

REFERENCES

Ancis, J. R., & Syzmanski, D. M. (2001). Awareness of white privilege among white counseling trainees. *The Counseling Psychologist, 2*(4), 548–569. doi:10.1177/0011000001294005

Cardemil, E. V., & Battle, C. L. (2003). Guess who's coming to therapy? Getting comfortable with conversations about race and ethnicity in psychotherapy. *Professional Psychology: Research and Practice, 34*(3), 278–286. doi:10.1037/0735-7028.34.3.278

Case, K. A. (2012). Discovering the privilege of whiteness: White women's reflections on anti-racist identity and ally behavior. *Journal of Social Issues, 68,* 78–96. doi:10.1111/j.1540-4560.2011.01737.x

Case, K. (2013a). Beyond diversity and whiteness: Developing a transformative and intersectional privilege studies pedagogy. In K. Case (Ed.), *Deconstructing privilege: Teaching and learning as allies in the classroom,* (pp. 1–14). New York, NY: Routledge.

Case, K. A. (2007). Raising white privilege awareness and reducing racial prejudice: Assessing diversity course effectiveness. *Teaching of Psychology, 34,* 231–235. doi:10.1080/00986280701700250

Case, K. A., & Cole, E. R. (2013). Deconstructing privilege when students resist: The journey back into the community of engaged learners. In K. A. Case (Ed.), *Deconstructing privilege: Teaching and learning as allies in the classroom* (pp. 34–48). New York, NY: Routledge.

Case, K. A., & Hemmings, A. (2005). Distancing strategies: White women preservice teachers and anti-racist curriculum. *Urban Education, 40*(6), 606–626. doi:10.1177/0042085905281396

Case, K. A., Iuzzini, J., & Hopkins, M. (2012). Systems of privilege: Intersections, awareness, and applications. *Journal of Social Issues, 68,* 1–10. doi:10.1111/j.1540-4560.2011.01732.x

Case, K. A., & Lewis, M. K. (2012). Teaching intersectional LGBT psychology: Reflections from historically Black and Hispanic serving universities. *Psychology and Sexuality, 3*(3), 260–276. doi:10.1080/19419899.2012.700030

Case, K. A., Miller, A., & Jackson, S. B. (2012). "We talk about race too much in this class!" Complicating the essentialized woman through intersectional pedagogy. In S. Pliner & C. Banks (Eds.), *Teaching, learning, and intersecting identities in higher education* (pp. 32–48). New York, NY: Peter Lang.

Chio, V. C. M., & Fandt, P. M. (2007). Photovoice in the diversity classroom: Engagement, voice, and the 'eye/I' of the camera. *Journal of Management Education, 31,* 484–504. doi:10.1177/1052562906288124

Cole, E. R. (2009). Intersectionality and research in psychology. *American Psychologist, 64*(3), 170–180. doi:10.1037/a0014564

Collins, P. H. (1990). *Black feminist thought: Knowledge, consciousness, and the politics of empowerment.* New York, NY: Routledge.

Constantine, M. G., Juby, H. L., & Liang, J. J.-C. (2001). Examining multicultural counseling competence and race-related attitudes among white marital and family therapists. *Journal of Marital and Family Therapy, 27*(3), 353–362. doi:10.1111/j.1752-0606.2001.tb00330.x

Crenshaw, K. (1989). Demarginalizing the intersection of race and sex: A Black feminist critique of antidiscrimination doctrine, feminist theory, and antiracist politics. *University of Chicago Legal Forum, 1989*, 139–167.

Dill, B. T., & Zambrana, R. E. (2009). Critical thinking about inequality: An emerging lens. In B. T. Dill & R. E. Zambrana (Eds.), *Emerging intersections: Race, class, and gender in theory, policy, and practice* (pp. 1–21). New Brunswick, NJ: Rutgers University Press.

Dottolo, A. L., & Stewart, A. J. (2008). "Don't ever forget now, You're a Black man in America:" Intersections of race, class and gender in encounters with the police. *Sex Roles, 59*, 350–364. doi:10.1007/s11199-007-9387-x

Fuertes, J. N., Mueller, L. N., Chauhan, R. V., Walker, J. A., & Ladany, N. (2002). An investigation of European American therapists' approach to counseling African American clients. *The Counseling Psychologist, 30*(5), 763–788. doi:10.1177/0011000002305007

Gushue, G. V., & Constantine, M. G. (2007). Color-blind racial attitudes and white racial identity attitudes in psychology trainees. *Professional Psychology: Research and Practice, 38*(3), 321–328. doi:10.1037/0735-7028.38.3.321

Hays, P. A. (1996). Cultural considerations in couples therapy. *Women & Therapy, 19*(3), 13–23. doi:10.1300/j015v19n03_03

Hays, D. G., Chang, C. Y., & Dean, J. K. (2004). White counselors' conceptualization of privilege and oppression: Implications for counselor training. *Counselor Education & Supervision, 43*, 242–257. doi:10.1002/j.1556-6978.2004.tb01850.x

Hays, D. G., Chang, C. Y., & Havice, P. (2008). White racial identity statuses as predictors of white privilege awareness. *The Journal of Humanistic Counseling, Education and Development, 47*, 234–246. doi:10.1002/j.2161-1939.2008.tb00060.x

Helms, J. E. (Eds.). (1990). *Black and white racial identity: Theory, research, and practice*. Westport, CT: Praeger Publishers.

Liu, W. M., Pickett, T., Jr., & Ivey, A. E. (2007). White middle-class privilege: Social class bias and implications for training and practice. *Journal of Multicultural Counseling and Development, 35*, 194–206. doi:10.1002/j.2161-1912.2007.tb00060.x

Maxie, A. C., Arnold, D. H., & Stephenson, M. (2006). Do therapists address ethnic and racial differences in cross-cultural psychotherapy? *Psychotherapy: Theory, Research, Practice, Training, 43*(1), 85–98. doi:10.1037/0033-3204.43.1.85

McIntosh, P. (1988). *White privilege and male privilege: A personal account of coming to see correspondences through work in women's studies* (Working Paper No. 189). Wellesley, MA: Wellesley Centers for Women.

McIntosh, P. (2012). Reflections and future directions for privilege studies. *Journal of Social Issues, 68*(1), 194–206. doi:10.1111/j.1540-4560.2011.01744.x

McIntosh, P. (2013). Teaching about privilege: Transforming learned ignorance into usable knowledge. In K. A. Case (Ed.), *Deconstructing privilege: Teaching and learning as allies in the classroom* (pp. xi–xvi). New York, NY: Routledge.

Mindrup, R., Spray, B., & Lamberghini-West, A. (2011). White privilege and multicultural counseling competence: The influence of field of study, sex, and racial/ethnic exposure. *Journal of Ethnic and Cultural Diversity in Social Work, 20*(1), 20–38. doi:10.1080/15313204.2011.545942

Nelson, K. W., Brendel, J. M., Mize, L. K., Lad, K., Hancock, C. C., & Pinjala, A. (2001). Therapists' perceptions of ethnicity issues in family therapy: A qualitative inquiry. *Journal of Marital and Family Therapy, 27,* 363–373. doi:10.1111/j.1752-0606.2001.tb00331.x

Parker, W. M. (1988). *Consciousness-raising: A primer for multicultural counseling.* Springfield, IL: Charles C Thomas.

Pedersen, P. B. (1988). *A handbook for developing multicultural awareness.* Alexandria, VA: American Association for Counseling and Development.

Pewewardy, N. (2004). The political is personal: The essential obligation of White feminist family therapists to deconstruct white privilege. *Journal of Feminist Family Therapy, 16,* 53–67. doi:10.1300/J086v16n01_05

Richardson, T. Q., & Molinaro, K. L. (1996). White counselor self-awareness: A prerequisite for developing multicultural competence. *Journal of Counseling & Development, 74,* 238–242. doi:10.1002/j.1556-6676.1996.tb01859.x

Sabnani, H. B., Ponterotto, J. G., & Borodovsky, L. G. (1991). White racial identity development and cross-cultural counselor training: A stage model. *The Counseling Psychologist, 19*(1), 76–102. doi:10.1177/0011000091191007

Sue, D. W., Rivera, D. P., Capodilupo, C. M., Lin, A. I., & Torino, G. C. (2010). Racial dialogues and White trainee fears: Implications for education and training. *Cultural Diversity and Ethnic Minority Psychology, 16*(2), 206–214. doi:10.1037/a0016112

Tatum, B. D. (1994). Teaching White students about racism: The search for White allies and the restoration of hope. *Teachers College Record, 95,* 462–476.

Tummala-Narra, P., & Kaschak, E. (2013). Women and immigration: Feminist and multicultural perspectives on identity, acculturation, and implications for clinical practice. *Women & Therapy, 36,* 139–142. doi:10.1080/02703149.2013.797755

Utsey, S. O., Gernat, C. A., & Hammar, L. (2005). Examining White counselor trainees' reactions to racial issues in counseling and supervision dyads. *The Counseling Psychologist, 33*(4), 449–478. doi:10.1177/0011000004269058

Wang, C. C. (1999). Photovoice: A participatory action research strategy applied to women's health. *Journal of Women's Health, 8,* 185–192. doi:10.1089/jwh.1999.8.185

Wise, T., & Case, K. A. (2013). Pedagogy for the privileged: Addressing inequality and injustice without shame or blame. In K. A. Case (Ed.), *Deconstructing privilege: Teaching and learning as allies in the classroom,* (pp. 17–33). New York, NY: Routledge.

I Don't See Color, All People Are the Same: Whiteness and Color-Blindness as Training and Supervisory Issues

MICHI FU

California School of Professional Psychology, Alliant International University, Los Angeles, California

This article describes cultural responsiveness training, with a particular emphasis to working with white students. Training methods, which have been effective in examining issues of power and privilege, will be described. Excerpts from previous trainees' correspondences will be shared to demonstrate how they may have been influenced by such exercises. I will share how reflections of this work have helped to shape who I am. Recommendations for others who wish to pursue cultural sensitivity training will be offered.

I started teaching about cultural diversity early in my career, without knowing that was what I was doing. One of the first classes I taught as a new professor was a clinical interviewing course for substance abuse counselors that were specifically working with the underserved in the most impoverished section of Oahu, Hawai'i. As I incorporated these concepts into practice, many interesting discussions emerged of whether or not the same skills would work with culturally diverse populations. For example, the conventional ways that graduate programs encouraged use of eye contact to convey interest may not have the same effect with those who consider direct eye contact to be inappropriate or rude (such as Native Hawaiians).

I have been teaching one of the most controversial graduate-level, diversity courses that emphasize examining the impact of one's own culture, biases, and assumptions on the therapeutic relationship. The course is considered controversial since many students do not consider themselves racist and have a difficult time accepting their privileges. The majority of my students and trainees (from here on out I will refer to both groups interchangeably) tend to be White despite the demographics of the growing minority-majority state of California. Non-White trainees benefit from the approaches I utilize because it helps them to examine the impact of power and privilege on their professional identities.

Training about power and privilege has its limitations. There are times when the trainer has a perspective different from the trainees that may be for them to relate. For example, women should contribute to the majority of the housework. Therefore, I have learned to appreciate the power of experiential exercises in diversity-related work. Ice-breaker activities can be powerful opportunities to set the stage for awareness enhancing, such as the power walk (an exercise intended to highlight power and privilege). In-depth immersion activities can be effective tools for students to explore how their socialization process has impacted their current ways of interacting with others. One type of immersion activity is to spend the day with a culturally different trainee and his or her family.

The purpose of this article is to describe some training methods illustrated by case vignettes. The vignettes will help to witness the impact of such teaching tools, personal reflections of how this work has affected me, and recommendations for others who choose to embark upon this journey with others.

WHAT DOES WHITENESS HAVE TO DO WITH IT?

My philosophy is that the training of culturally responsive therapists should include awareness-raising, opportunities to explore one's own racial anxieties, and helping therapists address racial dynamics in order to be more culturally sensitive to their clients (Chang & Yoon, 2011). McIntyre and Lykes (1998) discussed the importance of being aware of mentoring supervisory relationship and power dynamics. My approach to teaching others is to acknowledge power and try to equalize the relationship through self-disclosure and role-modeling when appropriate. Rose and Paisley (2012) suggested that experiential education could be used as a process to talk about race. My teaching approach requires reflexivity to explore values being transmitted and who is being empowered or disempowered by employing those values. One of my challenges in teaching diversity courses is to help my White students become aware of how their Whiteness is an important force—at times at the expense of enduring critiques for teaching one of the more controversial mandatory courses. According to Puchner and Roseboro (2011), a critical step in White student's identity development is to have dialog regarding their White privilege. Hays and Chang (2003) discuss the importance of openly exploring concepts such as white privilege, racism, and oppression in supervision to help supervisees understand various oppressive and privileged systems. It is difficult to openly explore these concepts with trainees when engaging trainees in these types of activities for their first times.

There are a few things I employ that help with these processes. In order to work with others who are exploring their racial identity, it is important for the trainer to be clear in his or her own racial identity status (Blitz, 2006). In addition, it is important to remember that racial identity development is considered a lifelong process. I have often revisited my own development and how it impacts my work. For example, my understanding regarding gender identity has shifted from a binary model to be more fluid.

Some White students have difficulty accepting their White privilege. On the first class session some may say, "I don't see color, all people are the same." Others have difficulty accepting that they may experience privileges that are not a possibility for their non-White peers. For example, a White student didn't believe that her African American female or Latino male classmates were oftentimes pulled over by law enforcement and treated disrespectfully for no apparent reason. One possibility may be that they are "color-blind" to their privilege. Perhaps this is a defense mechanism. One of my trainee's description of her own process of becoming more aware is telling. Jennifer (Jennifer, personal communication, 2014) describes how she used to be color-blind and gained an understanding of how this may be a disservice to others who wish to have their differences recognized and respected. Jennifer shared her experience:

> I thought it was interesting that someone brought up that maybe it is best not to bring up these depressing disadvantages and stay "color-blind." I used to consider myself "color-blind." I thought I was so admirable in that I did not see my friends as Chinese, Japanese, Black, or White. However, I now realize that by not seeing their individual races as a part of who they are, I was seeing them as white, through my own perspectives and value systems, and was doing them a disservice. Race is an important part of how people identify and by not recognizing their different races I am not seeing all aspects of the individual. This is something I definitely need to keep in mind when conducting therapy … It would be detrimental to my clients if I was "color-blind."

Neville, Awad, Brooks, Flores, and Bluemet (2013) argue that racial color-blindness is not just unattainable but it also reinforces racial prejudices and inequality. It is a representation of modern racism known as covert racism (Neville et al., 2013). Yeung, Spanierman, and Landrum-Brown (2013) argue that society has programmed White individuals to be ignorant about structural racism. Therefore, I use an approach that increases awareness before imparting knowledge or skills (Sue & Sue, 2013).

It can be problematic to disregard differences. Nilsson and Duan (2007) found that "unexamined white privilege can result in … disregard for the experience of individuals from other cultural and racial backgrounds." Hurd and McIntyre (1996) encourage us to "de-privilege the historical legacy of sameness in psychology and work toward acknowledging the complexities inherent in all feminist research."

At times, my White female trainees have a difficult time embracing their privilege due to the complications of their intersection of identities. Since "gender is always raced and race is always gendered," the intersectional approach is required to explain the problems of inequality (Levine-Rasky, 2011). Certainly, scholars such as Landrine (1995) describe inequities that occur when one experiences multiple levels of oppression. Examining one's intersection of identities may highlight areas where one simultaneously enjoys privileges or experiences discrimination based on varying aspects of one's identity. For example, I am an Asian American female which is considered a double minority status. If I were a transgendered individual, this would be an additional minority status that I would have to negotiate. Therefore, it is important to consider how Whiteness is experienced by men and women differently. Sometimes my white female students are easily grasp the concept of privileges they enjoy for being born White after we review the privileges they usually do not experience due to being female.

While helping my White female trainees to explore ways in which they are privileged or lack power, many inevitably find it easier to gravitate towards being oppressed as a woman than acknowledging privileges they enjoy for being born white. "In feminist therapy—as compared to traditional modes —emphasis is on helping women change [the] balance of power, rather than continue to make adjustments to it" (Brody, 1987). Therefore, one of my main challenges is helping my students to see all aspects of power dynamics, including how their gender and race may impact their work. At times, the results can be very rewarding, as in the case of the trainee below who made discoveries about racism and privilege. After wrestling with concepts such a racial privilege, this white female student eventually came to an understanding that avoiding "the truth" was actually a disservice. She later comes to the realization that she can be a useful ally after facing the truth:

> White privilege is not something that I think about on a normal basis. It is just something that I have lived with. I have never had to think about how my race may affect a situation positively or negatively. Essentially, I have closed myself off to the fact that others get put down. My whole life I have been telling myself that everyone is equal and those types of injustices do not have this day in age anymore. I have cast myself into a bubble to hide from the hate crimes that still exist in our world. Now after reading the ... article and the ... book, I can no longer hide from the truth. I am now held accountable for my actions as well as holding others accountable for their actions and thoughts. I do understand that I have to be strong in order to put up for this fight ... Thus, now knowing about white privilege and racism better, I can no longer hide and tell myself that the world is one happy place.

DEVELOPING AN INTEGRATIVE MODEL OF TEACHING CROSS-CULTURAL PSYCHOLOGY

Over the years, I've tried many different training exercises with varying degrees of success. Some cohorts found the activities to be extremely beneficial while others offered opportunities for improvement. Along the way, I've continued to refine my teaching methods as my philosophy towards this subject is that cultural responsiveness training is a lifelong endeavor that can never truly be perfected since this is an ideal to strive towards. To prevent my participants from becoming discouraged, I liken the process to physical activity – something to be maintained and dynamic depending on where the person is at. This section offers some examples of activities which seem to have produced the most awareness-raising results in an efficient manner.

Story of My Name

The first impression is of upmost importance in setting the stage for the remainder of teaching, supervision or training. Therefore, one of the curricula that I've helped to develop has all-day culturally responsive trainings starting with simple exercises, such as "Story of My Name." (http://www.creativeyouthideas.com) Usually an ice-breaking activity such as this requires some level of self-disclosure. This means that I need to role model for others the level of depth that I am hoping for when they engage in this exercise. For example, my family name is rare and therefore it's relatively easy to guess which part of the world my ancestors might have come from. My middle name was assigned to all the females of my generation even before I was born. My unique identifying given name was given to me by my paternal grandfather as his wish for characteristics he hoped I would embody. This activity typically results in participants reflecting back on their family of origin. Some may even disclose that their family name had been changed generations ago when they immigrated to where they currently reside now, which results in people being aware that they are linked to another country of origin. Aside from being entertaining, this has demonstrated to be a non-threatening way for participants to learn about one another.

Addressing Model

Hays' (2013) ADDRESSING model is something I incorporate on the first day of a graduate-level, year-long diversity training course as I have students interview then introduce one another. I spell out for my students what the acronym stands for A: Age; D: Developmental Disability; D: Acquired Disability; R: Religion and Spiritual Orientation; E: Ethnicity; S: Socioeconomic Status; S: Sexual Orientation; I: Indigenous Heritage; N: National Origin; G: Gender (Hays, 2013). I usually tell my students that I will not ask them to engage in activities that I myself am not willing to in order to increase trust and class participation. Therefore, my students learn lots about me during the first few minutes together when I self-disclose by role-modeling the amount of thoughtfulness and depth that I expect of each of them. It's a model that I incorporate into an "Introduce Your Partner" exercise so that they learn lots of demographic information that may challenge some of the assumptions they have of one another based on phenotype. It is oftentimes an exercise that they will refer back to time and time again when writing their papers throughout the year.

Difficult Dialogues

National Multicultural Conference Summit (NMCS) is composed of four APA divisions that come together biyearly to share knowledge on culturally diverse issues. One of my favorite aspects of the NMCS is the difficult dialogue programming, which explores controversial issues (e.g., racism in the workplace), led by a facilitator who is attuned to examining such sensitive topics. I take this approach to my diversity courses and trainings. I recall an instance when leading a debriefing of a mandatory field trip to the Simon Wiesenthal Museum of Tolerance (dedicated to remembering the Holocaust and other civil rights issues). During course discussion, two students (one who identified as being white and the other who identified as being black) engaged in a heated debate, which resulted in one student storming out of the classroom, leaving the others speechless. One of the exhibits polled museum visitors who deserved to experience violence more: (1) Rodney King or (2) Reginald Denny. The white student offered that Rodney King deserved to be beat for being under the influence of an uncontrolled substance and not complying with police requests, while Reginald Denny did not deserve to be beat because he was a white man who naively drove through the wrong neighborhood when the LA Riots broke out. The black student shared her perspective that neither of them deserved to be beat—that even if one of them were breaking the law, this did not justify the level of police brutality that was suffered. This led to a heated discussion of personal experiences of unprovoked encounters with the police (e.g., the perception of being constantly pulled over while driving simply for being the wrong color) and the white woman repeatedly discounting that such occurrences could happen unless the reasons were founded (e.g., perhaps a traffic violation had occurred). I recall the other students' stunned expressions as I allowed the two to engage in such a lively discussion. The two students were eventually able to understand one another's perspectives, feel heard, and one of them even changed her opinion on such matters. Years later, I would be told by one of them that that volatile class discussion was one of the most powerful learning opportunities of her graduate school experience. It is for this reason, that I have my students agree upon a list of ground rules at the beginning of the class, which I then refer back to time and time again. It is my belief that difficult dialogues need a safe space (hence the mutually agreed upon ground rules) and are delicate (it's not unusual for people to cry or leave the classroom when upset) but necessary for genuine exploration of sensitive topics. Here are excerpts of actual ground rules that one of the groups I am currently working with co-created:

a) Confidentiality.
b) Honesty. Openness of expression.
c) Being open-minded. Keeping as much of an open mind as possible. Open-mindedness to new categories of thought, new concepts, etc.
d) Non-judgmental: Do not speak judgmental words (only constructive).
e) Be supportive & understanding.
f) Taking personal responsibility for your experience and reactions.
g) Notifying others of emergency situations.
h) Think before reacting.
i) Respectful dialogue. Don't talk over people. No talking over others.
j) Constructive criticism. If you are going to criticize, offer a solution or a suggestion.
k) Moderate cell phone usage (emergencies, maybe some texting in important situation without disturbing others, etc.). Cells on vibrate.
l) To be respectful of others—but allow for explicit language as long as it's not directed towards others. Being tolerant of (any kind of) non-aggressive communication (e.g., ability to use non-targeted profanity).

Knapsack of Privileges

I am grateful to McIntosh (1988) and her writings about white privilege. Her work as a white ally oftentimes mean that my white students will be able to hear her voice with less defensiveness and examine whether or not some of her statements might also apply to them. In her seminal article, she acknowledges some of the privileges that she enjoys by being born white. For example, growing up with role models that look like her or having a higher likelihood of being able to find the right shade of makeup for her skin tone. The first time I assigned her reading was over 15 years since it had been published, yet the content remains relevant to this day. The year I initially assigned her article for my students' consumption, one of my students spontaneously wrote about all the privileges she enjoyed by being a white woman. This demonstrated to me that she truly understood the concepts. The next few years of teaching the diversity course, resulted in occasional spontaneous lists from other white students. I decided one year to encourage students to create their own list of privileges during their journal assignments. Some had to challenge themselves while others wrote freely about the privileges that they inherited by virtue of being born white. It's an exercise that my trainees have referred back to months later. Below are excerpts from a student who created her own list of privileges and reflected upon the process afterwards. One can see how creating a list of privileges can create some discomfort that the supervisor should be ready to discuss:

> This got me thinking of all the times in my life that I have been given privilege over others due to the fact that I am a white woman. People don't single me out for cutting in line, I am not questioned when I walk into nice stores, I have access to many networks of people though family connections, I enjoy pastimes such as meditation and travel, my sexuality is never questioned, I have access to higher education, I have no debt, and I live in a nice two bedroom apartment with my boyfriend. It has been hard for me to come to terms with these privileges...I don't consider myself a "racist" person, but I am now able to recognize the power structures that exist across racial, socioeconomic, and religious lines... This is a hard concept to acknowledge because it means accepting that I have power over others simply because I was born a white female.

BARNGA

While developing curricula for cultural responsiveness training, my colleagues and I integrated BARNGA, a simulation game involving culture clashes. This is a card game that highlights the importance of not making assumptions when engaging in nonverbal communication. Traveling across the state, my team of trainers and I have witnessed full-grown adults become agitated when their assumptions interfere with their ability to play well with others. During the critical debriefing period, participants typically develop empathy for those who immigrate to a host culture without understanding the social norms. Trainees usually come to understand how their usual methods of communicating with one another may not translate well into other cultures. It's an eye-opening exercise that leads to awareness-raising. The debriefing portion of the activity helps to solidify the learning objective of how cross-cultural norms may impact perceptions of one another.

Drawing Difference

Harrell (personal communication, October 21, 2013) developed an exercise which usually helps even the most guarded student to develop empathy for others who experience difference on a daily basis. The activity requests that participants silently recall and draw an experience of difference that they had. They are then asked to reflect upon the details of the event – Where were they? Who else was present? What do they remember seeing/hearing/etc.? How did they feel? Participants are asked in a non-judgmental way to share their recollections, particularly focusing in on their feelings. Objective observations are then shared aloud by the facilitator of common themes that may have emerged (e.g., shame, confusion, anger, embarrassment, disappointment, etc.). I had the privilege of observing Harrell execute the activity to my own students and noted that even some of the white students who typically had difficulty seeing the relevance of focusing on differences (rather than using a color-blind approach which ignores the diversity among people), were able to move beyond white guilt and find an experience that helped them to understand what others might go through based on their race. It's a powerful exercise that I recently used in a meeting of peers that produced the same results—people emailing after the training to tell me how moved they were by the experience. For example, I've heard participates share about being the last to be picked for an elementary school team of Dodge Ball and what it felt like to be different. More importantly some of the individuals who often have difficulty understanding the plight of those less fortunate are then able to see how they have a shared human experience of feeling different in a non-shaming way. Indeed, Anne-Jorunn (2008) encourages use of memory work to assuage the inevitable feelings of white guilt that emerge when once confronts issues related to whiteness.

WORLDVIEW GENOGRAM

Since the cultural backgrounds of both supervisors and supervisees can influence the content, process, and outcome of supervision, the Worldview Genogram is an example of a tool that can serve as a mechanism for discussing values from one's cultural backgrounds (Nilsson & Duan, 2007). During internship, the interns at our community health center are encouraged to examine the impact of their family history on their professional development, especially how this relates to them as a supervisor/supervisee and therapist. The Worldview Genogram (Chege & Fu, 2013) utilizes the typical family genogram (McGoldrick, Gerson, & Shellenberger, 1999) as a foundation to build upon. There is an emphasis for participants to reflect upon family dynamics, sources of pride/shame, values, etc. Powerful themes emerge (e.g., family sources of pride for a history of supporting higher education vs. sources of shame for intergenerational patterns of infidelity) that allow the supervisor and supervisee to discuss how this influences professional identity, ways of conducting therapy, etc.

For the first few years as an intern supervisor that my trainees were being asked to engage in this exercise during their group supervision (facilitated by my colleague), when they took turns presenting their Worldview Genograms to one another. One year, my intern expressed disappointment that I wasn't able to observe her presentation to her intern cohort (something that wasn't typical for supervisors to participate in) since she believed it would help us to work on her countertransference issues. We agreed that she would present her Worldview Genogram to me during our individual supervision. The following year, I informed my intern that the previous year's intern had expressed a wish for me to observe their worldview genogram, so I offered to attend her presentation during group supervision or the alternative to present to me in private. She sheepishly requested that we present our genograms to one another during individual supervision. Our supervision lasted well beyond the normal allotted amount of time and the sharing of our genograms seemed to facilitate our rapport-building. From then on, I've always presented the same opportunities to my interns to share our genograms with one another.

CULTURAL IMMERSION ACTIVITY

Another powerful learning opportunity involves having trainees immerse themselves in a foreign culture/activity. This is another activity where I disclose when I've done something similarly outside of my comfort zone and the lessons I've learned from engaging in such an activity (e.g., attending a wedding of another culture). For the purposes of my class, students would be paired off and required to engage in the other's culture for a half-day at minimum. For example, attend a religious service of another that is unfamiliar to you. Or, accompany someone to a holistic healing experience (e.g., acupuncture). The writing assignments and discussions that result showed that much-learning would have occurred because people's assumptions of one another were challenged. For example, two white students who were paired together realized very quickly that one's veteran background and the other's polyamorous lifestyle meant that the two led very different lives despite phenotypically having more in common in relation to the other students in the classroom. This may be the reason why I ultimately decided to lead a cultural immersion class to Asia, challenging students to step outside their comfort zones for over a week. Many often complain about how time-consuming such activities can be, but some have exclaimed that such experiences were life-changing.

CASE VIGNETTES

Perhaps the best way to demonstrate the effectiveness of some of these training methods would be consider some of the thoughts of former students who have experienced some of the exercises mentioned above. In the first case vignette, the reader can see how "Gina's" first impressions of African Americans are challenged and how gaining awareness has been a powerful step for her. In the second case vignette, "Christina" describes how avoiding the plight of others was a luxury that she could engage in as a white woman until she developed an awareness of what others may experience. "Carrie," from the third vignette, shared about the concept of intersectionality that was covered earlier in this chapter. Later on, the reader can see that she stated: "I am privileged and oppressed simultaneously and I unconsciously accept this as the way it is."

Case Vignette 1: Gina

My biggest fear when I meet an African American is that they think I'm superficial, that I have the luxury of naiveté by virtue of being white, that I'm a lightweight human being, that I haven't suffered, that I'm not as deep or savvy as they are, or as intuitive or honest. And for this, I feel deep shame ... I am now aware how I've projected my shame and insecurity onto African Americans. ... My parents never engaged me in conversations about what was going on in the world. They never engaged in conversations about racism between themselves for me to witness ... This attitude, combined with the rhetoric that we were all one and that everyone was equal and the same, fed my blindness ... Going through this class, taking a community counseling course last summer, and reading the articles for this class, has allowed me to finally talk about these issues and think about them on a deeper level. The pain I have experienced and the experience of aging has helped me to open up my perspective. To acknowledge that we ARE different and have had different experiences has been liberating for me. But I didn't realize how trapped I felt until now. I'm very grateful for the experience. I no longer assume that African Americans have specific thoughts about my lack of depth, and I don't feel like I'm actively trying to wear blinders anymore.

Case Vignette 2: Christina

I have already been discovering what it means to be White in this society, and that there is actually a meaning, so beginning to read actual studies and literature on it is pretty exciting.

I believe what underlies my thoughts and feelings while going through this experience is a sign that I am on the road towards developing a healthy White identity.

Being a Caucasian person in America, I am not often challenged to think about my race or my place in the world. This can make it hard to be able to understand where people of other ethnicities are coming from when they talk about what it means to them to be of a minority group ... This is something that I have become aware of in myself, and it is something I have decided I want to work on. I have always come from a good place in my desire for the world to be a more peaceful place, and for everyone to be treated equally, but it may have contributed to some of my ignorance. It is important for me to be able to understand where people are coming from, so that I do not devalue it when I am a practicing clinician. I have not experienced a great deal of racism or discrimination, but I want to be able to put myself in the shoes of those who have ... This is exactly what I want to be able to do, because it has become more apparent to me that people of minority groups feel very strongly about their history, what has happened to them or their ancestors, and these experiences stick with them. I wish that the world could let go of the things that have happened in the past, and that everyone could get along and be equal, but that is a wish that I don't see coming true. I have begun to face the harsh reality that I have not wanted to have to accept. This is the reality that the world is not what I thought it was, and people really do experience racism and oppression more than I was aware of ... The cruelty that mankind has inflicted upon each other, and that continues on today makes me very sad. I think as a Caucasian person it has been easier to ignore a lot of these truths, but now I cannot and do not want to.

Case Vignette 3: Carrie

I know, and have always known, that being white has afforded my family and myself certain things that other people have not always been afforded. At the same time, I also know that because I am a woman, I am not always given opportunities that men are. So, while knowing that I am part of a "privileged group," I also have felt repressed within this group ... We all seemed to easily fall into our unspoken roles and assumed the responsibilities attached to these roles with no question or adversity. I saw our group as being a microcosm of the bigger world that we all live in and, in a way; we constructed our own social reality based on what we know to be familiar and safe. I liked the exercise because it did cause so many feelings in me. At times I felt comfortable with the assignment, at other times I felt awkward and disadvantaged because I felt a sense of hopelessness at our efforts, and still at other times I felt frustration because I didn't like the role I assumed in the group, and I felt that others (and myself) put me in this role due to assumptions of how it should be ... There is a way in which the oppressed 'collude' with their own oppression and accept that this is normalcy, however unjust it may be ... I am privileged and oppressed simultaneously and I unconsciously accept this as the way it is ... I am grateful for the experience, and for the deeper level of understanding it took me to realize the importance of the exercise. Regardless of my feelings at the time, my feelings now are such that I can look back on it with a greater sense of appreciation for seeing things now a little differently then I did then.

What stood out for me too after our class discussions surrounding these issues is my own 'unconsciousness' about white people not talking about themselves as being white, they are just simply 'human beings'. This is a stark realization of my own perceptions about being white. I know I am white, I check that I am white on documents that ask for my ethnicity but I don't *think* about being white, I just simply am. I think about being white when I am told to think about it, which generally occurs when I am with someone who is not white. I don't like that this is the case. I didn't ask for it to be this way and I certainly don't want it to define who I am. I too have been socialized like everyone else, to be what society tells us we are. Society never tells me I'm white, at least not like it tells black people they are black. Being told you are white happens when you are given things from society that you assume are normal. I think it is very different for those who are not white. They are told that they are black, or brown by having things taken away or never given to them in the first place. I don't like that our society has created our world this way, and regardless of being the recipient of things I have never asked for, I feel the disparity for those who have not been afforded equal opportunities. Through my own personal deliberation and thought processes, I hope that at a minimum I can garner enough insight about my own feelings of oppression, persecution and privilege to make my own personal strides toward understanding.

REFLECTIONS

Although it's not always easy, I accept that practicing culturally-responsible training principles includes understanding and incorporating one's cultural identity into the supervisory relationship (Barker, 2011). As such, I've sometimes discussed my own family's ways of dealing with mental illness from a cultural perspective. For example, I have sometimes commented that when pathology has been spiritualized in my family and home remedies include making offerings to the temple. I also have come to accept that the traditional power distribution between supervisor and supervisee sometimes have to be reexamined in order for trust to develop more quickly. Therefore, interns see a glimpse of the impact of intergenerational relationship patterns in my Worldview Genogram.

GUIDELINES AND SUGGESTIONS FOR CULTURALLY RESPONSIVE TRAINING

1. It's important to be self-aware. Therapy must always be viewed in the context of one's own perspective, attitudes, and biases, while care must be taken to know and respect those of the client (Brody, 1987). This self-awareness will also be useful in the supervisory context.
2. Since the issues related to racial and ethnic differences between the therapist and client are usually discussed in the first two sessions (Brody, 1987), I also dive in immediately to discussing similar dynamics with my supervisees. In fact, I usually bring up that I am Taiwanese American early on in the relationship and invite my potential supervisees to share

any reactions they may have towards such a disclosure so that they know ours is a space where exploring one's own reactions is expected.
3. Use appropriate levels of self-disclosure. This is a delicate balance of being able to role model for others what I wish to see from them, without being inappropriate. Oftentimes, my trainees will share their appreciation for my willingness to take the first step.
4. Build a foundation built on trust. It's important for supervisors to set an environment of safety by helping to eliminate emotional and cognitive barriers that are present when discussing race (Hays & Chang, 2003). Encouraging an open and safe environment for the supervisee growth and development could enhance the process for all involved. In the spirit of this, I encourage my participants to co-create a list of groundrules needed in order for them to explore sensitive issues together. I ask everyone to sign these and we revisit them as often as needed throughout our time together.
5. Utilize experiential activities rather than relying on theories or didactic approaches. I encourage my students to attend one another's family dinners or religious ceremonies. When appropriate, I'll share of something that I learned by immersing myself in another's culture. As such, my students have learned of assumptions that I've made while traveling abroad and how I was able to challenge some of my stereotypes.
6. Enlist the aid of allies when possible. These can be in the form of textbooks and articles as well as guest speakers. Sometimes my trainees are able to "get it" once they have been assigned reading or hear from a colleague who is already out in the field doing the work that we discuss.
7. Be understanding when supervisees are in a different racial identity status that prevents them from processing an event the way that others might. They may appreciate the space and explore in a safe environment, rather than potentially becoming defensive – a space where learning is less likely to occur.
8. The foundation of culturally responsiveness training is awareness-raising. I usually review a diagram emphasizing that the danger-zone is when people don't know what they don't know. I use this approach to disarm people so that they may be more open to learning about the aspects of diversity training that they are not aware of yet.
9. Make sure you have a good support system for this work. I've been fortunate to have excellent supervision, even by informal mentors. I've also been glad for a peer network of colleagues who engage in similar work to consult with when I'm unsure of how to proceed with sensitive topics or students that offer a particular challenge for me.
10. Be mindful that this is a lifelong learning process. Reaching cultural competency is an ideal to strive towards, but the outcome is less important than the journey. Instead, striving for culturally responsive allows for a more dynamic response. Enjoy the journey.

ACKNOWLEDGMENTS

The author wishes to express appreciation towards the editors of this special issue: Andrea L. Dottolo and Ellyn Kaschak for their patience and guidance throughout the writing process. The views expressed in this article are solely those of the author and do not necessarily reflect the opinions of the publishers and editors.

REFERENCES

Anne-Jorunn, B. (2008). Silence and articulation – Whiteness, racialization and feminist memory work. *Nordic Journal of Feminist and Gender Research, 16* (4), 213–227. doi:10.1080/08038740802446492

Barker, M. (2011). Racial context, currency and connections: Black doctoral student and White advisor perspectives on cross-race advising. *Innovations in Education and Teaching International, 48*(4), 387–400.

Blitz, L. V. (2006). Owning whiteness: The reinvention of self and practice. *Journal of Emotional Abuse, 6*, 241–263. doi:10.1300/J135v06n02_15

Brody, C. M. (1987). White therapist and female minority clients: Gender and culture issues. *Psychotherapy: Theory, Research, Practice, Training, 24*(1), 108–113. doi:10.1037/h0085678

Chang, D., & Yoon, P. (2011). Ethnic minority clients' perceptions of the significance of race in cross-racial therapy relationships. *Psychotherapy Research, 21*(5), 567–582.

Chege, C., & Fu, M. (2013). Walking the talk: Clinical supervisors modeling diversity competency. *The California Psychologist, 46*(4), 9–11.

Hays, D. G., & Chang, C. Y. (2003). White privilege, oppression, and racial identity development: Implications for supervision. *Counselor Education and Supervision Journal, 43*, 134–145. doi:10.1002/j.1556–6978.2003.tb01837.x

Hays, P. A. (2013). *Connecting across cultures: The helper's toolkit* (pp. 15–16). Thousand Oaks, CA: SAGE.

Hurd, T. L., & McIntyre, A. (1996). The seduction of sameness: Similarity and representing the other. In S. Wilkinson & C. Kitzinger (Eds.), *Representing the other: A feminism & psychology reader*, (pp 78–82). Thousand Oaks, CA: Sage Publications Inc.

Landrine, H. (1995). *Bringing cultural diversity to feminist psychology: Theory, research, and practice*. Washington, DC: American Psychological Association.

Levine-Rasky, C. (2011). Intersectionality theory applied to whiteness and middle-classness. *Social Identities, 17*(2), 239–253. doi:10.1080/13504630.2011.558377

McGoldrick, M., Gerson, R., & Shellenberger, S. (1999). *Genograms: Assessment and intervention*, (2nd ed.). New York, NY: W. W. Norton & Co, Inc.

McIntosh, P. (1998). White privilege and male privilege: A personal account of coming to see correspondences through work in Women's Studies. In M. Andersen & P. H. Collins (Eds.), *Race, class, and gender: An anthology* (3rd ed., pp. 94–105). Belmont, CA: Wadsworth.

McIntyre, A., & Lykes, M. B. (1998). Who's the boss? Confronting whiteness and power differences within a feminist mentoring relationship in participatory action research. *Feminism & Psychology*, *8*(4), 427–444. doi:10.1177/0959353598084003

Neville, H. A., Awad, G. H., Brooks, J. E., Flores, M. P., & Bluemet, J. (2013). Color-blind racial ideology: Theory, training, and measurement implications in psychology. *American Psychologist*, *68*(6), 455–466. doi:10.1037/a0033282

Nilsson, J., & Duan, C. (2007). Experiences of prejudice, role difficulties, and counseling self-efficacy among U.S. racial and ethnic minority supervisees working with White supervisors. *Journal of Multicultural Counseling and Development*, *35*(4), 219–229.

Puchner, L., & Roseboro, D. L. (2011). Speaking of whiteness: Compromise as a purposeful pedagogical strategy toward white students' learning about race. *Teaching in Higher Education*, *16*(4), 377–387. doi:10.1080/13562517.2010.546528

Rose, J., & Paisley, K. (2012). White privilege in experiential education: A critical reflection. *Leisure Sciences*, *34*, 136–154. doi:10.1080/01490400.2012.652505

Sue, D. W., & Sue, D. (2013). *Counseling the culturally diverse: Theory and practice*, (6th ed.). New York, NY: John Wiley & Sons.

Examining Biases and White Privilege: Classroom Teaching Strategies That Promote Cultural Competence

GINA C. TORINO

Human Development and Educational Studies, SUNY Empire State College, New York, New York

This article will discuss in-depth how a variety of effective classroom teaching strategies have been employed to assist White counseling trainees in developing a non-racist White racial identity (i.e., by examining biases and exploring privilege) thereby increasing cultural competence. Specifically, this article will address the utility of implementing classroom teaching strategies that promote both cognitive understanding and affective processing of biases and White privilege for White trainees. It will outline the efficacy of specific didactic (e.g., lecture, videos, discussions, readings) and experiential (e.g., small group interviews, journaling, autobiographies, modeling) in creating a non-racist White racial identity, thereby promoting cultural competence.

Mental health professionals have been charged with providing competent and ethical mental health care to individuals from a variety of racial cultural groups (American Psychological Association, 2003; Brown, 2013; Kapoor, Dike, Burns, Carvalho, & Griffith, 2013). In response to this charge, training programs have steadily increased the number and improved the quality of multicultural courses taught in their curricula. While cultural competency integration has been largely met with openness, some White trainees exhibit resistance to learning about topics such as race and racism (Carter, 2005).

Oftentimes, an examination of biases and White privilege is frequently accompanied by feelings of guilt, anxiety, shame, and anger (Sue, Lin, Torino, Capodilupo & Rivera, 2009; Sue, 2013). However, over the past 30 years, scholars and researchers have developed sophisticated didactic and experiential teaching strategies that have assisted White students in working through personal and collective racism. This article will discuss the challenges faced by White trainees in developing cultural competence as well as the effective classroom teaching strategies that have been shown to promote the examination of biases and White privilege, thereby increasing cultural competency.

OVERVIEW: CULTURAL COMPETENCY DEVELOPMENT FOR WHITE STUDENTS

The development of cultural competency allows for clinicians to effectively counsel individuals from all racial-cultural groups. Briefly, cultural competency focuses on three general areas that include the clinicians' awareness, knowledge, and skills (Sue et al., 1982, 1998; Sue, Arredondo, & McDavis, 1992). Awareness encompasses psychologists' cultural and racial self-awareness, which includes the clinicians' understanding of cultural or racial beliefs and attitudes about themselves and others (Sue & Sue, 2013; Sue & Torino, 2005). Knowledge primarily focuses on the understanding of clients' beliefs, sociopolitical experiences, worldviews, cultural values, influences, and how all of these guide the clinicians' ability to conceptualize cases and plan treatments for clients. Skills refer to the clinicians' ability to effectively use interventions that are sensitive to the clients' contextual and cultural factors such as the clients' spiritual beliefs and cultural traditions.

With respect to developing cultural competency, scholars agree that the examination of what it means to be White is particularly challenging to White student trainees (Carter, 2005; Sue & Sue, 2013). Many White individuals have never thought about what it means to be White prior to encountering this question through coursework (Sue, 2010). According to Sue (2005), White trainees fear that they harbor unconscious biases and prejudices toward people of color. Research on aversive racism and implicit bias supports the contention that all White individuals have internalized racial biases and prejudices (Dovidio, Kawakami, & Gaertner, 2002; Jones, 1997). These implicit biases are extremely resistant to change as they operate unconsciously and manifest in subtle ways (e.g., microaggressions) (Sue, 2010). Most White people conceive of themselves as non-racist individuals and, as such, developing self-awareness of one's own biases can be threatening to one's ego (Sue, 2013).

Along with the examination of what it means to be White, confronting White privilege is essential to the development of cultural competency. White privilege has been defined as the unearned advantages of being White in a racially stratified society and has been characterized as an expression of institutional power that is largely unacknowledged by most White individuals (Neville, Worthington, & Spanierman, 2001; Qureshi & Eiroa-Orosa, 2013). In her seminal piece, Peggy McIntosh (1988) describes the ways in which she has gained unearned privileges in society just by the virtue of being White. Thinking about White privilege means confronting the myth of meritocracy by acknowledging that Whites have not attained success in life purely by their own individual efforts and that Whites have in fact benefitted from historical and contemporary forms or racism that have disadvantaged people of color (Sue, 2013).

In response to learning about White privilege, many White individuals experience fear, guilt, and anger (Sue et al., 2009; Sue, 2013). Scholars speculate that fear may be linked to downward mobility and potential loss of material benefits as well as the absence of race-based advantages, and, ultimately, fear of losing power (Neville et al., 2001). In addition, Whites may fear losing relationships and/or being rejected by people of color (Spanierman, Oh, et al., 2008).

Guilt and shame are also common reactions of White individuals to societal inequity and White privilege (Iyer, Leach, & Crosby, 2003). Scholars have found that higher levels of White privilege awareness lead to greater levels of White guilt as well as to increased support for affirmative action (Swim, Becker, Lee, & Pruitt, 2010).

In addition to affective reactions, trainees may experience cognitive defense mechanisms such as denial, rationalization and/or minimization (Sue et al., 2009; Sue & Sue, 2013). Among counseling trainees, qualitative response to Peggy McIntosh's (1988) list of White privileges ranges from a denial to an awareness of the systemic nature of privilege (Ancis & Szymanski, 2001). Behavioral reactions to White privilege range from avoidance or unwillingness to discuss its existence (Rains, 1998).

To facilitate this racial self-exploration among White trainees, educators encourage them to contemplate, write about and discuss their Whiteness as they learn about pervasive social inequities (Todd, Spanierman, & Aber, 2010). Generally, topics associated with race tend to be emotionally charged, so instructors must attend to affective responses (Hogan & Mallott, 2005).

Scholars and educators emphasize the particular importance of White trainees' emotional responses to learning about race, racism and White privilege (Bonilla-Silva, 2010; Carter, 2005). Racism is deeply embedded in the psyche and cannot be brought out into the open without experiences that challenge the invalid assumptions and beliefs of trainees (Sue, 2003). Scholars suggest a strong anti-racist component must be a part of counselor training programs. Coursework and experiential activities related to understanding oneself as a racial being are important facets of becoming culturally competent. A useful starting point is the assumption that everyone possesses biases, prejudices and racist attitudes. However, this assumption seems especially difficult for Whites to acknowledge (Sue & Torino, 2005). In order to provide competent and ethical care, White trainees need to understand White privilege and how it functions in an unjust system of White supremacy (Sue & Sue, 2013; Tatum, 1992). However, this is no easy undertaking, as society's institutions socialize White individuals to be ignorant about structural and cultural racism (Mills, 2007; Bonilla-Silva, 2010; Yeung, Spanierman, & Landrum-Brown, 2013). As educators have argued, to move White trainees from ignorance perpetuated by the White racial frame to an alternative frame that enhances their understanding of power, privilege and oppression, addressing Whiteness explicitly in coursework is crucial (Carter, 2005; Monture, 2009; Sue & Sue, 2013). Some maintain that the task of instructors is to help trainees move from a detached, cognitive understanding of course content to a more personal affective understanding (Carter, 2003). Carter (2003) states that it is essential for White trainees to examine their affective experiences in conjunction with their cognitive understanding if they are to develop cultural competency. It is recommended that instructors combine both didactic and experiential activities within one course given the affectively evocative nature of race for White trainees (Carter, 2005; Sue, Rivera, Capodilupo, Lin, & Torino, 2010).

Didactic Teaching Strategies

To increase the knowledge and awareness of what it means to be White, it is essential for any course related to cultural competency development to include didactic teaching strategies such as lectures, readings, discussions, and videos. These teaching strategies are essential because they provide trainees with knowledge (e.g., historical laws regarding the creation of Whiteness; statistics on structural inequality, etc.) that can ground racial-cultural exploration. The ultimate goal of such didactic components is to increase trainees' knowledge about race and racism as well as the sociopolitical forces that create racial disparities (Carter, 2005). In addition, these components can be useful in educating White trainees about the theories underlying White racial identity development, clinical research regarding cross-racial dyads, and White privilege. In other words, didactic teaching strategies should be focused on increasing cognitive awareness and knowledge about the *self* and *others*.

It is essential for trainees to develop a cognitive understanding of, for example, White racial identity development as well as White racial consciousness prior to undertaking an affective exploration of the meaning of Whiteness (Helms, 1995; Leach, Behrens, & LaFleur, 2002). Recommended readings include: *Counseling the Culturally Diverse: Theory and Practice* (Sue & Sue, 2013); *Microaggressions in Everyday Life: Race, Gender, & Sexual Orientation* (Sue, 2010); *Handbook of Prejudice, Stereotyping, and Discrimination* (Nelson, 2009); *A Race is a Nice Thing to Have* (2nd ed.) (Helms,

2007); *Overcoming our Racism: A Journey to Liberation* (Sue, 2003); *White by Law: The Legal Construction of Race* (Lopez, 1996); *Off White: Readings on Race, Power, and Society* (Fine, Weis, Powell, Mun Wong, 1997); *The Influence of Race and Racial Identity in Psychotherapy: Toward a Racially Inclusive Model* (Carter, 1995), and *Unpacking the Invisible Knapsack* (McIntosh, 1988) (Please see references for full citations).

Videos that document and provide illustrations of racial/cultural issues are highly recommended. The utilization of videos can supplement lectures and engage trainees by presenting thought-provoking narratives or documentaries. One video, *The Color of Fear* (Stir Fry Productions, 1994), features a racially diverse group of men who explore their life experiences as racial-cultural beings and their resulting attitudes. Another video, *A Class Divided* (Frontline, 1985) demonstrates the psychological impact of discrimination and highlights the role of socialization in the learning, or "unlearning," of bias. Other noteworthy videos include: *Mirrors of Privilege: Making Whiteness Visible* (World Trust Films), which highlights interviews with leading researchers on privilege; *True Colors* (MTI Film & Video), which investigates the experiences of two college men (one Black and one White) as they explore levels of prejudice solely based on race; and *Crash* (2004), a fiction film based on racial tensions in Los Angeles, California.

After any lecture and/or video presentation, it is important for the instructor to facilitate a discussion with the class. Scholars indicate that cognitive understanding of societal racism can lead to thoughts about personal racism and biases (Sue, 2010). As mentioned earlier, graduate training courses may be the first opportunities trainees have had to begin to think about what it means for them to be White (Jones, Sander, & Booker, 2013). Furthermore, as trainees begin to think about White privilege and how it operates in their lives, they many begin to experience such emotions as fear, anger, guilt, shame, and frustration (Sue et al., 2010). Thus, it is important that as these discussions are facilitated, the instructor attends to emotions brought out in the classroom. It is imperative that the instructor not only validate the feelings that arise for trainees but also encourage the trainees to further process such emotions in the experiential activities associated with the course.

Experiential Teaching Strategies

Experiential learning involves trainees personally and affectively examining their own reactions, assumptions, beliefs, attitudes, values, standards of normality, prejudices, stereotypes, biases, privileges, and goals (Sue & Sue, 2013). Experiential learning is particularly well-suited to raising multicultural awareness of trainees, calling assumptions into question and cultivating cultural empathy and openness (Pope-Davis, Ottavi, & Ottavi, 1994). This learning approach also involves examining how cultural factors form and direct trainees' own attitudes, behavior and beliefs (Arthur & Achenbach,

2002). Experiences that challenge a White trainee can help him or her to confront sometimes difficult and emotional aspects of his or her own racial experience. Moreover, in the classroom setting, affective learning can be experienced with lower potential negative outcomes than when trainees undergo similar experiences in the more unguided situation of actual counseling (Fowler, 1994).

In his Racial-Cultural Counseling Laboratory, Carter (2005) eloquently describes many effective experiential teaching strategies. One well-documented strategy that can assist White trainees in working through biases and White privilege is the small group interview (Carter, 2005). This interview includes prepared questions about such things as stereotypes or personal development with regard to reference groups (Carter, 2005). As one student is interviewed, other trainees are asked to take the perspective of the interviewee. Trainees in the small groups are asked to understand their various emotional and behavioral responses.

More specifically, the interview occurs in assigned small groups, which consist of approximately five to seven members that convene in a space that is separate from the large group classroom. Group selection is determined by the instructor and the teaching assistants in an effort to promote a racially diverse composition. Preferably doctoral level or advanced master's level trainees facilitate these small group interviews, which take place over the duration of the semester. The interview protocol is developed for the purposes that the trainees gain an in-depth understanding of Whiteness and of what it means to belong to that specific reference group (Carter, 2005). During the interviews, each student is provided with the opportunity to explore him or herself as a racial-cultural being. While the process of facilitating the interview may vary depending on the style and experience of the teaching assistant, each student in the group answers questions to assist in the self-reflective exploration of personal racial-cultural issues along several domains of awareness. Each student's interview lasts approximately four hours, which is usually distributed over two or three class periods. Examples of interview questions can include: "What is your earliest recollection about becoming aware of racial issues? What does being White mean to you? What do you think others might think about you as a White person? What are some of the biases, prejudices and stereotypes that you possess?"

During this interview process, difficult emotions often arise. It is important that a skilled facilitator be able to process emotions experienced by all group members. For example, White trainees, as the dominant group, may become defensive and resist fully exploring their own values, assumptions, and beliefs, if they sense that the facilitators or others are blaming them for the historical oppression of other cultures (Mio & Barker-Hackett, 2003). In many instances, a White trainees who is asked to explore what it means to be White may resist this task by denying that race is a salient factor in his or her life for fear of being labeled a racist (Sue, 2003). Furthermore, some have observed individual psychological resistance to training, including intellectualization, projection, and denial (Carter, 2003). In a similar way, trainees may resist when racism is not part of their self-concept and they perceive that racist attitudes or beliefs are being attributed to them. Other trainees may feel guilty upon realizing that they hold racist assumptions, beliefs, and attitudes (Mio & Barker-Hackett, 2003). Trainees may also be afraid of how their classroom peers will respond to their admission of socially undesirable characteristics, such as racism. They may not want to be labeled or to be judged negatively (Sue, 2010).

Trainees have found small group interviews to be highly valuable to their learning about biases and White privilege (Carter, 2005). One female trainee who underwent the Racial-Cultural Counseling Laboratory at Teachers College, Columbia University, stated that she learned *"...that I have biases very deep down...I learned through my classmates challenging me in the small group... "*(Torino, 2010).

Some educators suggest explicitly directing trainees to attend to their personal feelings, thoughts, and behavior during the experiential activities and recommend discussions that expose trainees to conflicting cultural perspectives (Arthur & Achenbach, 2002). Similarly valuable is explicitly asking trainees to reflect on potential counseling approaches based on the experience and to become a reflective practitioner in their counseling. The process of reflective practice is a goal of many professional training programs beyond counseling (Schön, 1987).

After each small group interview, trainees are asked to write in their weekly personal journals, which provide an opportunity to process their reactions, thoughts, feelings, and questions that arise from each class session (Carter, 2003). Carter (2003) recommends two journal sections: a cognitive factual section and an affective/reactive section. Trainees are prompted to discuss cognitive/factual information raised during the small group interaction and are then asked to process and make sense of their affective reactions. Teaching assistants, who have also taken the course, are trained to provide feedback that is helpful, challenging, and critical; the professor reviews the feedback to ensure that it is both appropriate and of high quality (Carter, 2003). The feedback provided is aimed at facilitating students' development and self-exploration with respect to further cultural issues. It is then mandatory for the trainees to respond to this feedback in the subsequent week's journal. This is seen to be an important outlet, apart from peers, for trainees to express their responses to class and small group experiences (including interactions with their peers). The journals essentially become ongoing dialogues between trainees and their respective teaching assistants.

One successful way to provide feedback is through "sober" factual information which addresses trainees' affective responses (Mio & Barker-Hackett, 2003). For example, a White male student wrote in a journal that he was upset that a multicultural author cites himself in his own work, a text used in the course (Sue, 2013). Perceiving this to be a form of racist resistance to personal reflection about the content of the text, the instructor pointed out in responding to the journal entry that the text's author was perhaps the most cited scholar in the field, and it would be a less thorough and helpful text if the author were to omit his own previous work (Sue, 2013). Asking trainees to reflect on such cognitive information can help them to raise awareness of their own biases, prejudices and racism.

Moreover, it seems helpful if instructors refrain from directly confronting White trainees who deny in their journals that they hold racist beliefs or have any complicity in the oppression of people of color (Garmon, 1998). Rather, an instructor can focus on having trainees explore their thoughts further, thereby placing the onus of exploration on them. Research suggests that resistance to cultural competency training is somewhat alleviated through journal writing (Mio & Barker-Hackett, 2003). Additional studies have found that journal writing promotes student self-reflection, enhances self-knowledge and improves student learning overall in multicultural courses (Garmon, 1998; Mio & Barker-Hackett, 2003; Jones, Sander, & Booker, 2013).

Furthermore, experts assert that an autobiography can be especially effective for developing the competencies involving awareness of values, biases, attitudes and beliefs (Arredondo & Arciniega, 2001). This technique often involves trainees' writing about personal experiences that are related to their cultural group. The autobiographical sketch, a variation of this type of assignment, involves trainees discussing how an event influenced their development and knowledge in each of several reference groups: gender, race, religion, social class, and ethnicity (Carter, 2003). This assignment helps trainees understand themselves as racial-cultural human beings and to deepen this understanding. The autobiography is also an opportunity for trainees to document their development by citing recollections from their childhood, and by considering influences from their families, education, and the media with regard to their racial and cultural identities. Trainees are also encouraged to explore the messages they have received about race from various sources (e.g., family, school, media, etc.) and how these messages have shaped and continue to shape their own personal role in promoting or maintaining racism.

The autobiography assignment might also involve asking trainees to focus on a particular type of opportunity or lack of opportunity, such as education (Arredondo & Arciniega, 2001). Trainees focus on how these experiences have influenced them as individuals and as a member of a cultural group. The expectations of others and of the trainees themselves can be made explicit as well as elaborated on. Advantages and disadvantages of group membership can also be explored. Making these autobiographical pieces available to others (whether facilitators or other trainees) can open up the possibility of questioning the presuppositions of the trainees. The autobiographies can also help in comparing one group's experience to another's.

Finally, a pedagogical approach that can be used in all instructional activities is that of modeling (Ponterotto, 1998). Instructors and other facilitators can provide an example in themselves of how to be open about their multicultural identities, attitudes, values, and beliefs. Instructors can talk about their own racial identity development, including negative and positive experiences and emotions. They can also talk about their concerns at the moment and their plans for continuing to develop their cultural competence. If the instructor and/or small group facilitator is White, it may be helpful to use judicious self-disclosure in admitting to holding biases against people of color as well as the ways in which he or she benefits from White privilege. It can be helpful for trainees to understand that the instructor continues to uncover the meaning of race and that he or she experiences personal challenges in the process of developing a non-racist White identity.

CONCLUSION

Examining biases and White privilege in graduate level racial-cultural counseling courses is a complex endeavor. With a combination of both didactic and experiential teaching strategies, White trainees have an opportunity to cognitively understand the construction of Whiteness as well as how racism operates in society along with underlying emotions associated with new-found knowledge and awareness. This is crucial for developing cultural competency in working with clients from all racial groups. It would be to the advantage of the fields of counseling and clinical psychology as well as social work to continue to conduct research into the efficacy of varied classroom teaching techniques in order to ensure that graduates develop the capacity to provide the highest quality mental healthcare to all individuals.

REFERENCES

American Psychological Association. (2003). Guidelines on multicultural education, training, research, practice, and organizational change for psychologist. *American Psychologist, 58*(5), 377–402. doi:10.1037/0003-066x.58.5.377

Ancis, J. R., & Szymanski, D. M. (2001). Awareness of White privilege among White counseling trainees. *The Counseling Psychologist, 29*, 548–569. doi:10.1177/0011000001294005

Arredondo, P., & Arciniega, G. M. (2001). Strategies and techniques for counselor training based on the multicultural counseling competencies. *Journal of Multicultural Counseling and Development, 29*, 263–273. doi:10.1002/j.2161-1912.2001.tb00469.x

Arthur, N., & Achenbach, K. (2002). Developing multicultural counseling competencies through experiential learning. *Counselor Education & Supervision, 42*(1), 2–14. doi:10.1002/j.1556-6978.2002.tb01299.x

Bonilla-Silva, E. (2010). *Racism without racists: Color-blind racism and the persistence of racial inequality in the United States* (3rd ed.). Boulder, CO: Rowman & Littlefield.

Brown, L. S. (2013). Compassion amidst oppression: Increasing cultural competence for managing difficult dialogues in psychotherapy. In A. W. Wolf, M. R. Goldfried, & J. Muran (Eds.), *Transforming negative reactions to clients: From frustration to compassion* (pp. 139–158). Washington, DC: American Psychological Association.

Carter, R. T. (1995). *The influence of race and racial identity in psychotherapy: toward a racially inclusive model.* Oxford, England: John Wiley & Sons.

Carter, R. T. (2003). Becoming racially and culturally competent: The racial-cultural counseling laboratory. *Journal of Multicultural Counseling and Development, 31,* 20–30. doi:10.1002/j.2161-1912.2003.tb00527.x

Carter, R. T. (2005). Teaching racial-cultural counseling competence: A racially inclusive model. In R. T. Carter (Ed.), *Handbook of racial-cultural psychology and counseling: Training and practice* (Vol. 2, pp. 36–56). Hoboken, NJ: Wiley.

Dovidio, J. F., Kawakami, K., & Gaertner, S. L. (2002). Implicit and explicit prejudice and interracial interaction. *Journal of Personality and Social Psychology, 82,* 62–68. doi:10.1037/0022-3514.82.1.62

Elliott, J., Yale University, WGBH (Television station: Boston, MA), & PBS DVD (Film). (2003). *A class divided* [Motion picture]. New Haven, CT: Yale University Films.

Fine, M., Weis, L., Powell, L. C., & Mun Wong, L. (Eds.). (1997). *Off white: Readings on race, power, and society.* New York, NY: Routledge.

Fowler, S. M. (1994). Two decades of using simulation games for cross-cultural training. *Simulation & Gaming, 25,* 464–476. doi:10.1177/1046878194254004

Garmon, M. A. (1998). Using dialogue journals to promote student learning in a multicultural teacher education course. *Remedial and Special Education, 19*(1), 32–45. doi:10.1177/074193259801900104

Haggis, P., & Yari, B. (2004). *Crash* [Motion picture]. United States: Lions Gate Films.

Helms, J. E. (2008). *A race is a nice thing to have: A guide to being a White person or understanding the White persons in your life* (2nd ed.). Hanover, MA: Microtraining Associates.

Helms, J. E. (1995). An update of the Helm's White and POC racial identity models. In J. G. Ponterotto, J. M. Casas, L. A. Suzuki, & C. M. Alexander (Eds.), *Handbook of multicultural counseling* (pp. 181–198). Thousand Oaks, CA: Sage Publications.

Hogan, D. E., & Mallott, M. (2005). Changing racial prejudice through diversity education. *Journal of College Student Development, 46,* 115–125. doi:10.1353/csd.2005.0015

Iyer, A., Leach, C. W., & Crosby, F. J. (2003). White guilt and racial compensation: The benefits and limits of self-focus. *Personality and Social Psychology Bulletin, 29*(1), 117–129. doi:10.1177/0146167202238377

Jones, J. M. (1997). *Prejudice and racism.* New York, NY: McGraw-Hill.

Jones, J. M., Sander, J. B., & Booker, K. W. (2013). Multicultural competency building: Practical solutions for training and evaluating student progress. *Training and Education in Professional Psychology, 7,* 12–22. doi:10.1037/a0030880

Kapoor, R., Dike, C., Burns, C., Carvalho, V., & Griffith, E. E. H. (2013). Cultural competence in correctional mental health. *International Journal of Law and Psychiatry, 36*(3–4), 273–280. doi:10.1016/j.ijlp.2013.04.016

Leach, M. M., Behrens, J. T., & LaFleur, N. K. (2002). White racial identity and white racial consciousness: Similarities, differences, and recommendations. *Journal of Multicultural Counseling and Development, 30*(2), 66–80. doi:10.1002/j.2161-1912.2002.tb00480.x

Lee, M. W., Hunter, M., Goss, R., & Bock, R. C., Stir-Fry Productions., & Stir-Fry Seminars & Consulting. (2000). *The color of fear: A film* [Motion picture]. Oakland, CA: Stir-Fry Seminars & Consulting.

Lopez, I. F. H. (1996). *White by law: The legal construction of race.* New York, NY: New York University Press.

McIntosh, P. (1988). White privilege: Unpacking the invisible knapsack. In V. Cyrus (Ed.), *Experiencing race, class, and gender in the United States* (pp. 209–213). Mountain View, CA: Mayfield Publishing.

Mills, C. W. (2007). White ignorance. In S. Sullivan & N. Tuana (Eds.), *Race and epistemologies of ignorance* (pp. 13–38). Albany, NY: SUNY Press.

Mio, J. S., & Barker-Hackett, L. (2003). Reaction papers and journal writing as techniques for assessing resistance in multicultural courses. *Journal of Multicultural Counseling and Development, 31,* 12–19. doi:10.1002/j.2161-1912.2003.tb00526.x

Monture, P. (2009). Doing academia differently: Confronting "whiteness" in the university. In F. Henry & C. Tator (Eds.), *Racism in the Canadian university: Demanding social justice, inclusion, and equity* (pp. 76–105). Toronto, ON: University of Toronto Press.

Nelson, T. D. (2009). *Handbook of prejudice, stereotyping, and discrimination.* New York: Psychology Press.

Neville, H. A., Worthington, R. L., & Spanierman, L. B. (2001). Race, power, and multicultural counseling psychology: Understanding White privilege and color-blind racial attitudes. In J. Ponterotto J. M. Casas, L. A. Suzuki, & C. M. Alexander (Eds.), *Handbook of multicultural counseling* (pp. 257–288). Thousand Oaks, CA: Sage.

Ponterotto, J. G. (1998). Charting a course for research in multicultural counseling training. *The Counseling Psychologist, 26*(1), 43–68. doi:10.1177/0011000098261004

Pope-Davis, D. B., Ottavi, T. M., & Ottavi, T. M. (1994). Examining the association between self-expressed multicultural counseling competencies and demographic variables among counselors. *Journal of Counseling & Development, 72,* 651–654. doi:10.1002/j.1556-6676.1994.tb01697.x

Qureshi, A., & Eiroa-Orosa, F. (2013). Training for overcoming health disparities in mental health care: Interpretive-relational cultural competence. In S. Barnow, & N. Balkir (Eds.), *Cultural variations in psychopathology: From research to practice* (pp. 248–269). Cambridge, MA: Hogrefe Publishing.

Rains, F. (1998). Is the benign really harmless? Deconstructing some "benign" manifestations of operationalized White privilege. In J. L. Kincheloe, S. R. Steinberg, N. M. Rodriguez, & R. E. Chennault (Eds.), *White reign: Deploying whiteness in America* (pp. 76–101). New York, NY: St. Martin's Press.

Schön, D. A. (1987). *Educating the reflective practitioner: Toward a new design for teaching and learning in the professions.* San Francisco, CA: Jossey-Bass.
Spanierman, L. B., Oh, E., Poteat, V. P., Hund, A. R., McClair, V. L., Beer, A. M., & Clarke, A. M. (2008). White university students' responses to societal racism: A qualitative investigation. *The Counseling Psychologist, 36*(6), 839–870.
Sue, D. W. (2003). *Overcoming our racism: The journey to liberation.* San Francisco, CA: Jossey-Bass.
Sue, D. W. (2005). Racism and the conspiracy of silence: Presidential Address. *The Counseling Psychologist, 33*(1), 100–114. doi:10.1177/0011000004270686
Sue, D. W. (2010). *Microaggressions in everyday life: Race, gender, and sexual orientation.* Hoboken, NJ: John Wiley & Sons.
Sue, D. W. (2013). Race talk: The psychology of racial dialogues. *American Psychologist, 68*(8), 663–672.
Sue, D. W., Arredondo, P., & McDavis, R. J. (1992). Multicultural counseling competencies and standards: A call to the profession. *Journal of Counseling & Development, 70,* 477–486. doi:10.1002/j.1556-6676.1992.tb01642.x
Sue, D. W., Bernier, J. E., Duran, A., Feinberg, L., Pedersen, P., Smith, E. J., & Vasquez Nuttall, E. (1982). Position paper: Cross-cultural counseling competencies. *The Counseling Psychologist, 10,* 45–52. doi:10.1177/0011000082102008
Sue, D. W., Carter, R. T., Casas, J., Fouad, N. A., Ivey, A. E., Jensen, M., LaFromboise, T., Manese, J. E., Ponterotto, J. G., & Vazquez-Nutall, E. (1998). *Multicultural counseling competencies: Individual and organizational development.* Thousand Oaks, CA: Sage Publications.
Sue, D. W., Lin, A. I., Torino, G. C., Capodilupo, C. M., & Rivera, D. P. (2009). Racial microaggressions and difficult dialogues on race in the classroom. *Cultural Diversity and Ethnic Minority Psychology, 15,* 183–190. doi:10.1037/a0014191
Sue, D. W., Rivera, D. P., Capodilupo, C. M., Lin, A. I., & Torino, G. C. (2010). Racial dialogues and white trainee fears: Implications for education and training. *Cultural Diversity and Ethnic Minority Psychology, 16*(2), 206–214. doi:10.1037/a0016112
Sue, D. W., & Sue, D. (2013). *Counseling the culturally diverse* (6th ed.). Thousand Oaks, CA: Sage Publications.
Sue, D. W., & Torino, G. C. (2005). Racial-cultural competence: Awareness, knowledge, and skills. In R. T. Carter (Ed.), *Handbook of racial-cultural psychology and counseling: Training and practice* (Vol. 2, pp. 3–18). Hoboken, NJ: Wiley.
Swim, J. K., Becker, J. C., Lee, E., & Pruitt, E. R. (2010). Sexism reloaded: Worldwide evidence for its endorsement, expression, and emergence in multiple contexts. In H. Landrine & N. F. Russon (Eds.), *Handbook of diversity in feminist thought* (pp. 137–171). New York, NY: Springer.
Tatum, B. (1992). Talking about race, learning about racism: The application of racial identity development theory in the classroom. *Harvard Educational Review, 62,* 1–25. doi:10.17763/haer.62.1.146k5v980r703023
Todd, N. R., Spanierman, L. B., & Aber, M. S. (2010). White students reflecting on whiteness: Understanding emotional responses. *Journal of Diversity in Higher Education, 3*(2), 97–110. doi:10.1037/a0019299

Torino, G. C. (2010). White counselor trainee experiences in the Racial-Cultural Counseling Laboratory (Dissertation Abstracts International: Section B: The Sciences and Engineering, Vol 71(2-B)). Teachers College, Columbia University, New York, NY.

Yeung, J. G., Spanierman, L. B., & Landrum-Brown, J. (2013). "Being white in a multicultural society": Critical whiteness pedagogy in a dialogue course. *Journal of Diversity in Higher Education*, *6*(1), 17–32. doi:10.1037/a0031632

Racial Microaggressions, Whiteness, and Feminist Therapy

SILVIA L. MAZZULA and KEVIN L. NADAL

*Department of Psychology, John Jay College of Criminal Justice,
City University of New York, New York, New York*

Over the last decade, several authors have described the role of racial microaggressions in the lives of historically marginalized populations. However, the exact mechanisms in which racial microaggressions manifest in psychotherapy remain an area in need of further exploration. Drawing from research and scholarship on Feminist therapy and microaggressions, we use a case vignette of a 40-year-old African-American woman in treatment for depression with a White female therapist to demonstrate how microaggressions may unwittingly occur in a clinician–client dyad. We underscore the challenges that White therapists may encounter and provide suggestions and recommendations for culturally responsive therapy.

Numerous initiatives, ethical standards and guidelines have been implemented over the past several decades to ensure mental health therapists provide culturally sensitive services inclusive of client worldviews and historical-political realities. Research shows that treatment services devoid of contextual racial-cultural factors explain poor treatment engagement (Chow, Jaffee, & Snowden, 2003), failed appointments (Atdjian & Vega, 2005), cultural mistrust (Bell & Tracey, 2006), and high rates of premature termination (Sue & Sue, 2012). Practitioners of all backgrounds are socialized within historical, political and social-cultural systems (e.g., cultural group, ethnic group, racial group, etc.), and therefore hold values, assumptions and beliefs about themselves, the therapeutic relationship and psychological wellbeing

(American Psychological Association, 2002; Carter, 1995; Mazzula & Rangel, 2011).

In recognition of understanding the context in which human behaviors occur, the American Psychological Association (2002) *Guidelines on Multicultural Education, Training, Research, Practice and Organizational Change for Psychologists* outlined skills and knowledge needed for the field to competently service diverse populations in the United States. These included the importance of having knowledge about ethnically and racially diverse individuals and clinical skills that are culturally congruent with diverse clients. The importance of culturally appropriate practice was recently highlighted with the *Diagnostic and Statistical Manual of Mental Disorders* (*DSM*-V)'s inclusion of a cultural formulation interview guide providing clinicians with the tools to assess to cultural, historical and cultural contexts that may impact treatment and service (American Psychiatric Association, 2014).

However, perhaps the most challenging aspect of culturally sensitive treatment is the call for mental health practitioners to provide culturally appropriate treatment for their clients, while also recognizing their cultural selves in context. APA guidelines encourage psychologists to "... recognize that, as cultural beings, they may hold attitudes and beliefs that can detrimentally influence their perceptions of and interactions with individuals who are ethnically and racially different from themselves" (American Psychological Association, 2002, p. 17). The notion that we, as psychologists, may hold attitudes and beliefs that are detrimental to our clients may be, for many, inconsistent with knowing our "self" as an agent of change. This may be particularly relevant for feminist therapists who are inherently committed to social justice and client empowerment (Hurtado & Stewart, 2004).

From a feminist theoretical framework, practitioners understand that mental health problems may develop as a result of negative systemic discrimination and subsequent socialized experiences- including encounters with discrimination, gender role conflicts, social class issues, or struggles with sexual orientation identity development (Enns, 2004; Worrell & Remer, 2002). As a result, feminist therapists are encouraged to conceptualize their clients through this lens, while guiding their clients toward empowerment, collaboration and shared-power (Worrell & Remer, 2002). Feminist therapists, female or male, are also encouraged to explore how they themselves have been socialized, which may influence their worldviews, their everyday problems, and their own mental health. As a result, feminist therapists are encouraged to engage in this level of self-reflection, particularly in exploring how power and privilege may influence their everyday lives, as well as their therapeutic relationships with clients. While feminist therapists may be more able to understand how their lives are affected by identities in which they have less power and privilege (e.g., a female therapist may be very cognizant of how sexism influences her life), at times they may also be less able to recognize ways that their lives are affected by identities in which they have more power or privilege (e.g., a White therapist may not recognize how her race affords her benefits and advantages in her life).

Perhaps one of the primary reasons why it may be difficult to recognize power and privilege is because of the invisibility of Whiteness (Hurtado & Stewart, 2004; McIntosh, 2003; Smith & Redington, 2010). In a seminal article in the *American Psychologist,* Sue (2004) describes how White individuals may not view themselves as White and rather declare themselves to be colorblind; as a result, many may develop the worldview that the world is fair and just and that racism no longer exists in our society. Sue continues to describe how American society is embedded in a subtle, often invisible, ethnocentric monoculturalism or "the strong belief in the superiority of one group's cultural heritage, history, values, language, beliefs, religion, traditions, and arts and crafts" (Sue, 2004, p. 764). Because Whites are the historically dominant group in the U.S., they have the power to establish the cultural norms, standards, beliefs and practices in the US; however, because racism has become socially unacceptable in the U.S., Whites may not admit that the U.S. is an ethnocentric country, nor that they may have power and privilege that is afforded as a result (Sue, 2004).

There has been increasing scholarship and studies on Whiteness as access to resources and power beyond that which is granted to other groups (McIntosh, 2003; Smith & Redington, 2010). From a social justice framework, Whiteness is a component of dominance characterized by unearned power to define normalcy, which in turn hides under invisibility. Whiteness has received considerable attention in colorblindness research (e.g., Neville, Lilly, Duran, Lee, & Browne, 2000). Given the invisibility of Whiteness, scholars have noted the lack of attention to issues of race among White Americans (see McIntosh; Smith & Redington). Mainly because, as Gill Tuckwell noted in *Racial Identity, White Counsellors and Therapists* Tuckwell (2002)

> The dominant group seldom needs to speak its name: it is defined in contrast to the more explicit naming of marginal and subordinated subjects. Historically the silence about white representation and white identity was part of the internalised assumption that white values, customs, traditions and characteristics were the exclusive standards against which other peoples and world orders must be evaluated and perceived. (p. 71)

This lack of attention to Whiteness and White people was addressed by Janet Helm's seminal work on white racial identity development (1990); the psychological process that White individuals undertake in developing a non-racist identity. In recent years, scholars have initiated research on White antiracists—or White individuals who are committed to combatting racism in their everyday lives. In one qualitative study, participants noted the difficulties that may arise in being White antiracists (Smith & Redington, 2010). One commonly reported theme was "Interpersonal conflicts"; White participants described that when they became committed to issues of racial advocacy, both their personal and public relationships were affected. The study also found the importance of continuing self-reflection and awareness of racism. One participant, for example, noted that irrespective of their personal commitment to antiracism "I still forget I'm White" (p. 564). Smith and Redington's study supports the first, and perhaps most important, guideline of the APA Multicultural Guidelines (2002)—the importance of continuing self-awareness, particularly in working with clients that are racially or culturally different.

White Feminist therapists must uncover, and fights against, deep seeded biases engendered within such social structure and history. Uncovering personal biases and prejudices can generate difficult and conflicting feelings for all therapists (Mazzula & Rangel, 2011), particularly when called to challenge power and privilege (Smith & Redington, 2010). Yet, deliberate self-discovery and awareness of social power and status are perhaps the main methods to ensure we prevent manifesting oppressive acts in treatment (Jacobs, 2000). Relatively little, however, has focused on managing race-based power and privilege in psychotherapy. Yet, given that U.S. culture has been historically organized around notions of inferior and superior peoples based on the social construction of race, power differentials within the treatment room are likely to occur (Carter, 1995).

Historical and current events of discrimination also engender feelings of mistrust and discomfort (Shim, Compton, Rust, Druss, & Kaslow, 2009) among marginalized populations engaging in treatment with clinicians whose characteristics may resemble that of those who have historically been the oppressor (e.g., male or White). In studies examining perceptions of psychotherapists, Thompson, Bazile, and Akbar (2004) found that African-American clients described perceptions of therapists as older, male, and White who were uncaring, unavailable, and out of touch with the reality of African-American communities to provide competent treatment. Others have found that African-American clients may fear misdiagnosis or "brainwashing" (Thompson, Bazile, & Akbar) and may mistrust mental health services (Bell & Tracey, 2006). Perceived discrimination based on sexism and racism has also shown to impact help-seeking behaviors and treatment engagement (Gary, 2005). Similar trends have also been found for lesbian, gay, bisexual, and transgender (LGBT) people of color who may mistrust clinicians due to the historical mistreatment and discrimination of both LGBT people and people of color (Greene, 1997; Nadal, 2013).

Recent studies on treatment engagement also show that racial and ethnic minorities are not as unwilling to seek mental health treatment as previously thought. For example, Shim et al. (2009) found that African Americans were more likely than both Hispanics and non-Hispanic Whites to indicate they would engage in services and were also less likely to feel embarrassed about their help-seeking. Among immigrant Hispanic women, Nadeem and colleagues (2007) also found that Hispanics were more likely to want mental health services compared with U.S.-born White women. The findings of both Nadeem and colleagues and Shim and colleagues contradict the notion that racial-ethnic minorities are less likely to want professional help. Instead, these studies highlight the potential role of perceived discrimination or mistrust in therapists' ability to fully engage and understand the experiences of racial-ethnic minority clients.

Over the last decade, there has been an increasing attention to the unique role of experiences with microaggressions in the lives of marginalized communities (Nadal, 2011, 2013; Nadal, Mazzula, Rivera, & Fujii-Doe, 2014; Sue et al., 2007). Racial microaggressions are "brief and commonplace daily verbal, behavioral, and environmental indignities, whether intentional or unintentional, that communicate hostile, derogatory, or negative racial slights and insults to the target person or group" (Sue et al., p. 273). These insidious acts of discrimination have been found to be pervasive in the lives of marginalized communities, particularly in the lives of Latinas/os, Asian Americans, and African Americans (Nadal, 2011; Nadal, Escobar, Prado, David, & Haynes, 2012; Rivera, Forquer, & Rangel, 2010; Sue, Bucceri, Lin, Nadal, & Torino, 2010; Sue et al., 2008). Microaggressions have been found to influence negative mental health symptoms (Nadal, Griffin, Wong, Hamit, & Rasmus, 2014), binge drinking (Blume, Lovato, Thyken, & Denny, 2012), and negative emotional intensity (Wang, Leu, & Shoda, 2011).

Despite this increase in literature, the exact mechanisms in which racial microaggressions may manifest in treatment remain an area in need of further exploration. Given racial microaggressions are brief exchanges that, while sending denigrating messages, may be out of the perpetrator's awareness (Nadal, Griffin, et al., 2014) it becomes of grave importance for therapists to be self-aware and able to identify their own race-based biases, assumptions and prejudices. Self-awareness of microaggressive acts are particularly important when racial microaggressions transpire in the context of power differentials – in this case that of a client and of a therapist. Although processing issues of race may create feelings of discomfort in therapists, creating a safe environment in which these can be discussed is essential for clients of color who continue to experience racist encounters that cause psychological distress, at times rising to levels of trauma (Carter et al., 2013).

RACIAL MICROAGGRESSIONS AND WHITE FEMINIST THERAPISTS

Given the previous literature on racial microaggressions, as well as our overview of how Whiteness may manifest in feminist therapy, we propose that there are several types of racial microaggressions that may occur in dynamics between White Feminist therapists and clients of color. Although there is a dearth of research concerning this specific topic, we draw from theoretical works on racial microaggressions (Sue et al., 2007), as well as qualitative and quantitative research regarding microaggressions and people of color (Nadal et al., 2012; Nadal, Mazzula, et al., 2014; Rivera et al., 2010; Sue et al., 2010; Sue, Bucceri, Lin, Nadal, & Torino, 2010; Watkins, LaBarrie, & Appio, 2010). We also conceptualize our research from the few known studies that examine racial microaggressions in therapy (Owen, Tao, Leach, & Rodolfa, 2011) and sexual orientation microaggressions in therapy (Shelton & Delgado-Romero, 2011).

In this section, we will provide four types of racial microaggressions that may occur in therapy with White, feminist therapists: (a) Assumptions of White Cultural Values, (b) Colorblindness/ Unwillingness to Discuss Race, (c) Denial of Individual Racism, and (d) Assumptions of Stereotypes. To assist in illustrating these themes, we discuss examples from previous literature, while also using a case vignette as way to demonstrate how these microaggressions may unwittingly occur in a therapist–client relationship.

Assumptions of White Cultural Values

Because of the invisible nature of Whiteness (McIntosh, 2003), many therapists may not recognize the ways that race may manifest in therapeutic dyads. For White feminist therapists specifically, Whiteness may be even more difficult to recognize or address for two main reasons. First, because the therapist is committed to feminism and social justice issues, she/he may believe that she/he is incapable of discriminating against her/his clients on any level. Second, because the therapist may be committed to empowerment of her/his clients, she or he may not recognize how her/his own racial biases may influence how or when she/he empowers her/his clients, and how these instances may be based on her or his own White cultural values.

There are many ways that therapists may inadvertently promote White cultural values in therapy sessions. First, a therapist who is not aware of her/his biases may assume that her or his experiences and worldviews are normalized and that all others are incorrect. For instance, if a therapist insists that all of her/his clients communicate in a certain way, she/he is not considering the various cultural communication styles that may exist. One way that this can manifest is if a therapist were to strongly encourage an Asian-American client to be more assertive and confrontational with her parents. While well intentioned, the therapist may not recognize that some Asian-American clients may be uncomfortable with direct communication, or that being assertive is not acceptable in many Asian-American families (Sue et al., 2010). Second, a therapist may view certain behaviors that are exhibited by her/his clients of color as being pathological or deviant. For instance, if a therapist diagnoses an African-American client with paranoia for always thinking of race, she/he may not realize that to be conscious of race on a daily basis is actually considered a healthy behavior (Sue et al., 2008). Fear of misdiagnosis in treatment has been noted among African-American clients (Sanders Thompson et al., 2004) and also shown to cause mistrust in mental health services (Bell & Tracey, 2006). Yet, according to Hansen et al. (2006), psychologists rarely incorporate racial or cultural issues in their clinical formulations. Given most theories of psychology are grounded within Western White cultural values, without a deliberate commitment to understanding clients' own cultural worldviews therapists may inadvertently promote them in therapy sessions.

Color-Blindess/Unwillingness to Discuss Race

In general, theories on racism purport that people often present themselves as unbiased and fair (Dovidio & Gaertner, 1986; Sue, 2004) and therefore may endorse color-blindness as a way to ensure, albeit potentially harmful, that all clients are treated equally. Sue et al. (2007) define color-blindness microaggressions as "statements that indicate that a White person does not want to acknowledge race" (p. 276). While therapists who claim to be color-blind have good intentions (i.e., they purport that they view everyone as equals), they may leave clients to feel misunderstood or invalidated. That is, the client is essentially told that her or his race does not matter. Furthermore, researchers have suggested that it is very unlikely for individuals to be color-blind, due to the inherent nature of stereotyping, racial socialization, and racism (Carter, 1995; Dovidio & Gaertner, 1986; Neville et al., 2000). So, while therapists may desire to be color-blind (and inform clients of this wish), it is not only invalidating to a client but is also based on a false belief. Given that all individuals are socialized within a racist society (Carter, 1995), it is virtually impossible to hold no biases or prejudices. Owning that we may have such biases is the first step toward competent feminist therapy.

There are several ways that color-blindness may manifest in therapy. Sue and colleagues (2007) share an example of a therapist telling a client: "I think you are being too paranoid. We should emphasize similarities, not people's differences" (p. 282). In this instance, a covert message is communicated that (a) race and culture are not salient aspects of people's lives and (b) clients who think about racial issues are overly sensitive or unreasonable. Another example of color-blindness may include a client of color who brings up a race-related stressor in a therapy session and continues to describe how race affects her everyday life; after listening to her story, the therapist interjects with, "It's interesting that you experience all of this, because when I see you, I don't see color." In this case, an indirect message is communicated that the client's perceptions about race are not valid. Although the therapist may have attempted to purport that she was not racist, the therapist may have inadvertently damaged their therapeutic rapport.

Denial of Individual Racism

Sue and colleagues (2007) define racial microaggressions that fit under the category "Denial of Individual Racism" as "A statement made when Whites renounce their racial biases" (p. 276). These types of microaggressions can manifest in therapy in a couple of ways. First, a client can confront her/his therapist on a microaggression that may have occurred in therapy; in response, the therapist might tell the client that she or he is not racist or may vehemently deny that the interaction was a microaggression. Second, a therapist may preemptively describe her or himself as a non-racist person, perhaps in an attempt to connect with the client or present her or himself as someone fair and unbiased (Dovidio & Gaertner, 1986; Sue, 2004). However, in doing so, the client may view the therapist as insincere and incapable of recognizing her or his racial biases. These types of microaggressions are likely well intentioned, in that the therapist truly believes that they are incapable of committing racially biased acts. However, in not being able to own her or his potential prejudice or bias, clients may feel an array of emotions, including frustration, doubt, or mistrust.

There are many ways that microaggressions based on denial of individual racism may occur in therapy settings. For instance, a client of color may bring up that she feels uncomfortable talking about race with her therapist because she is White, in which the therapist replies, "race does not affect the way I treat you." Again, while well intentioned, the therapist invalidates the racial reality of the client who may have difficulty in discussing race with White people. Scholars have shown that clients of color may have previous experiences with discrimination that create general feelings of mistrust when in treatment with therapists that represent those that have been oppressive, whether historically or in their day-to-day lives (Shim et al., 2009). Therefore, it is likely that clients may feel discomfort talking about race and therefore important for the therapist to validate the client's experience. This leads to a second way in which "Denial of Individual Racism" microaggressions may occur in therapy; a therapist failing to acknowledge that there may indeed be a racial dynamic that is affecting the client's experience in therapy. Finally, the therapist's claim that race doesn't affect her/his treatment of the client negates any individual responsibility, but instead places the fault or responsibility on the client.

Another way in which a therapist may deny any potential racism in a therapy session may be when she or he turns to another marginalized identity to either negate the client's experience or in an attempt to bond with the client. For example, Sue and colleagues (2007) describe a situation in which a male client of color expresses uncertainty in discussing racial issues with his White female therapist; in response, she states, "I understand. As a woman, I face discrimination also" (Sue et al., 2007, p. 282). In this case, the therapist has the best intentions and perhaps wants to relate to the client in some way; however, the client may actually have the opposite response and may be offended or upset by her attempts. First, in bringing up her experiences with sexism, the therapist is equating racism and sexism, while claiming to understand how her male client experiences racism in the world. Despite this, she, as a White woman, would never fully understand what it means for him to be a man of color in this country. In fact, in making such a statement, she is also communicating that she does not recognize how her Whiteness affords her power and privilege. While sexism is still rampant on systemic, institutional, and interpersonal levels, the therapist's White identity places her into the dominant group, which has historically defined the cultural norms, standards, and beliefs in the U.S. (Bennett & Stewart, 2005).

When an individual is oppressed in one identity but privileged in another, it may be even more difficult for them to recognize the advantages and privileges that they do have (Nadal, 2013). For instance, imagine a White gay male therapist who experiences discrimination regularly, based on his sexual orientation. As a result of these experiences, he may become very cognizant of the many ways that heterosexism has negatively impacted his life (e.g., he recognizes homophobic language, he notices when people stare at him if he holds his husband's hand, etc.). However, it may be challenging for him to identify the ways that he has privilege because of his race or his gender. As a result, he may operate in subtly racist and sexist ways because he does not believe that he could possibly discriminate against others in the same ways that he has been. If a client confronted him on the ways that he may have racial or gender biases, he may be defensive and incapable of hearing or validating the client's reality. As a result, it would be crucial for him (and others) to recognize how power and privilege manifest in all of their identities.

Assumptions of Stereotypes

All individuals, including therapists, have been socialized in an environment in which stereotypes are formed about certain groups. The psychological study of race suggests that racial attitudes, biases, and prejudices are subconscious processes (see Carter, 1995; Helms, 1990) and that implicit biases often result in racial stereotyping (Amodio & Devine, 2006). Therefore, it is possible for stereotypes to result in microaggressions in therapy without conscious malicious intent from therapists. For instance, Sue and colleagues (2007) share an example of a Black client who is accused of stealing from work, and how her therapist does not believe her. Because the therapist would have no reason to believe that the client would engage in such behavior, such an assumption could be interpreted as being based on the therapist's racial biases against African Americans. In studies with African Americans (e.g., Sue et al., 2008), participants describe an array of microaggressions including "Assumptions of Criminal Status" (i.e., microaggressions in which African Americans are presumed to be violent, deviant, or likely to engage in illegal behaviors) and "Assumptions of Inferiority" (i.e., microaggressions in which African Americans are presumed to be less intellectual). For example, if a therapist presumed that an African American would be less intelligent (e.g., assuming a client did not go to college or that she did not have a high-status job), the therapist would be committing a microaggression based on her/his own stereotypes.

Microaggressions towards Latinas/os or Asian Americans may result from stereotypes as well. For instance, in studies with Latinas/os (Rivera et al., 2010) and Asian Americans (Sue et al., 2010), participants describe being treated as perpetual foreigners or "Aliens in their own Land" (i.e., individuals assume that they would not be American-born or would not speak English well). These types of microaggressions can be especially daunting for individuals who were raised in the United States or whose families have been in the United States for generations. When individuals commit these types of microaggressions, they indirectly communicate that Latina/os or Asian Americans are not "American enough," primarily because they equate "American" with being "Anglo-White," Other scholars have found microaggressions manifest differently when considering within group factors. For example, a recent study found Puerto Ricans are more likely to be treated as criminals (i.e., perceived to be deviant or prone to crime) or as "Second-Class Citizens" (i.e., receive subordinate treatment) compared to other Latino sub-ethnic groups (Nadal, Mazzula, et al., 2014). Similarly, Filipino Americans were found to experience microaggressions that were similar to those experienced by other Asian Americans (e.g., being exoticized or viewed as "perpetual foreigners"), but they also encountered microaggressions that were not as typical for other Asian Americans (e.g., being viewed as criminal or intellectually inferior; Nadal et al., 2012).

In a therapy session, assumptions of stereotypes can occur in an array of ways. For instance, in an intake session, a therapist may ask a male Asian American client "Where you from?" and when the client answers "New Jersey," the therapist may ask further clarification by asking "I mean, where are you *really* from?" Although the therapist may have been well intentioned in an effort to gather background information, the client may feel offended as an individual who was born and raised in New Jersey. If the therapist is interested in knowing about the client's ethnic heritage, microaggressions based on stereotypes can be prevented, for example, by asking more direct questions (e.g., "How do you identify ethnically? What is your family's ethnic background?" or "What is your family's immigration history?").

Microaggressions based on stereotypes can also manifest through clinical diagnoses. For instance, Sue and colleagues (2007) describe an instance in which a therapist takes great care to ask substance abuse questions during an intake with a Native American client, and is skeptical of the client's absent history with substances (Sue et al., 2007). Similar types of overgeneralizations can be made for non-diagnostic clinical conceptualizations. For example, therapists may assume that all Latino male clients are macho and would be incapable of expressing emotion; that all Black women clients are aggressive or have anger issues; or that all Asian male clients are emotionally inept or exhibit symptoms of alexithymia.

Finally, stereotypes may result in microaggressions when therapists make presumptions that race would be a central factor in every aspect of a client's life. In Shelton and Delgado-Romero's (2011) study with lesbian, gay, and bisexual (LGB) clients' experiences of microaggressions, one common theme was therapists' assumption that sexual orientation was the cause of all of their presenting issues. Although it is important for therapists to recognize how individuals' identities and experiences can be salient and integral parts of their lives, it is also important to recognize that such identities may not be central in every case. Sometimes, making these assumptions may be due to therapists' desires, whether conscious or subconscious, to overidentify with a client or compensate for their recognition of social injustices in the world. Recent studies show that, for some minority clients, cultural issues are not an integral part of psychotherapy (Chang & Berk, 2009). Therefore, making broad generalizations can also be viewed as microaggressions because clients are not viewed as individuals, but rather treated based on preconceived stereotypes, which may or may not reflect the client's life or life experiences.

CASE STUDY

Drawing from feminist theory and research on racial microaggressions, we present the case of a 40-year-old African-American woman who is in treatment for depression. We demonstrate how challenging it may be to note racial microaggressions in the moment, the reality of their existence, and the importance of validating client's experiences and engaging in meaningful discussions. The conceptualization of the client's problem and engagement in treatment is contextualized within microaggressions scholarship (Sue et al., 2007) and studies with people of color (Nadal et al., 2012; Rivera et al., 2010; Sue et al., 2008), as well as our own clinical experiences in working diverse clients.

The Case of Nicole

Nicole is a 40-year-old African-American woman who seeks therapy to help overcome her symptoms of depression. While she has worked as an attorney for the past 10 years, she has overcome a spectrum of difficulties in recent years—including a tumultuous divorce, work stressors, and obstacles in raising her 8-year-old daughter, Sophia. Because Nicole has been experiencing chronic feelings of sadness, hopelessness, and worthlessness, one of her close friends suggested that she seek therapy at a local community mental health agency. The agency is in the heart of a predominantly working-class Black and Latino neighborhood in a Northeastern metropolitan city. Most of the agency's clients (including Nicole and her daughter) live in the community.

Two weeks after signing up for therapy, Nicole was assigned to Linda, a fifth-year psychology intern from a local clinical doctoral program. Linda is a 28-year-old White American, who identifies as middle-class. She has completed most of her coursework and has worked at the agency for the past year. Linda grew up in a small rural town, several thousand miles away, and moved to the metropolitan city as a result of her doctoral program. She views herself as "a liberal feminist" and reports that she "does not see race and treats everyone the same."

When Nicole attends her first meeting, she is a "bit" surprised when she sees that Linda would be her therapist. Having grown up in the neighborhood (and knowing that many of the agency's clients were people of color), Nicole falsely assumed that the clinicians would be mostly people of color too. Nicole wanted to work with a person of color, particularly a woman of color, because she thought it would be easier to relate. However, she decided that she wanted to remain open-minded in her first meeting with Linda.

At their first meeting, Nicole perceived Linda to be a warm therapist. She was friendly, pleasant and comforting as Nicole started to talk about the various issues in her life. Nicole discussed how she felt "stressed out" about being a single mother most of the time (i.e., her ex-husband had custody every other weekend) and about how hard it was to pay bills and keep the household afloat. The first meeting was a good "venting session" for Nicole, and after a few similar sessions, Nicole was optimistic that therapy could actually be helpful for her.

In their fifth session together, Nicole decided to open up about her failed marriage with her ex-husband, David. She described how she and David had been together since college and how they married after dating for ten years because "it was the next logical step." She explained how they were married for an additional 10 years and how hard it was to divorce after being with someone for twenty years. When telling the story, Nicole noticed that Linda's facial expression was one of surprise; in fact, Linda even responded, "Oh, I didn't realize you had been together for that long. I just assumed that you...." Linda paused and then finished her statement with "Wait, let me just clarify... Did you get married before or after your daughter was born?" Nicole answered her but was very annoyed by this interaction; however, she was unsure what made her annoyed and decided to let it go.

When Nicole arrived to their sixth session, she appeared to be very rushed and anxious. She began to talk about some of the stressors at work including how she felt very overwhelmed because she perceived her colleagues to have high expectations for her. Nicole described how she felt even more burdened because she was the only Black woman in her office and felt that she had to outperform everyone else. After realizing that she had never explicitly brought up race in the room, Nicole intently looked up to notice Linda's reaction. Although Linda seemed comfortable and empathic, Nicole recognized that Linda did not directly address the topic of race or validate Nicole's experiences of being the only Black woman in the office. Disappointed by this, Nicole continued the session, but was emotionally checked out for the rest of the session.

For their seventh session, Nicole decided that she needed to share how she felt about therapy. She began by sharing how disappointed she was with the previous session; she shared that she wanted to be comfortable in talking about the topic of race in her therapy sessions. Linda replied, "Why do you think you are fixated on race?" Nicole immediately became angry and hesitatingly replied: "Because it is an important of my life." Linda replied, "Well, maybe that is a problem. By fixating on race so much, you won't be able to recognize the potential you have." Nicole felt stunned, annoyed, and invalidated, but remained silent. She decided to not to return to therapy.

Case Study Discussion

In this vignette, we see many ways in which racial microaggressions manifested in the therapeutic dyad between Linda and Nicole. Let's begin with the four types of microaggressions that we highlighted (e.g., Assumptions of White Cultural Values, Colorblindness/ Unwillingness to Discuss Race, Denial of Individual Racism, and Assumptions of Stereotypes) and discuss how those materialized in the therapy sessions.

First, it was clear that Linda assumed many White cultural values that impeded her ability to work with Nicole. During the first meeting, Nicole discussed stressors related to single parenting, finances and maintaining her household. While seemingly innocuous, the value of balancing of multiple roles is a common trait for women of color; studies on African-American women show some women are expected, and expect of themselves, to have the ability to manage multiple roles (e.g., that of a mother, employee, etc.) on their own without asking others for help (see Speight, Isom, & Thomas, 2013). If Linda endorses White American cultural values of autonomy and democracy, she may (1) have a difficult time understanding that the management of multi-tasks for Nicole indicates a culturally sanctioned worldview that differs from her own, and (2) intervene at one point incorrectly assuming that Nicole is doing this on her own (e.g., pathologizing Nicole's need to hold this role as head of household). Second, from the outset, it was clear that Linda tried to maintain a colorblind attitude, as demonstrated by her belief that she "does not see race and treats everyone the same." However, race and racial dynamics will become evident in the therapeutic dyad whether or not the therapist is able to engage the conversation (Carter, 1995). For example, after meeting with

Linda several times, Nicole described feeling burdened by being the only Black woman in her office. While Linda was emphatic, she did not address Nicole's experience directly. She did not acknowledge that race is a salient part of Nicole's life or that racism (and sexism and other forms of discrimination) may be a regular experience in Nicole's life. Perhaps if Linda was aware of research studies that have demonstrated this phenomenon (see Carter et al., 2013), she may have recognized that Nicole's experiences were quite common.

Further, it appears that Linda had been somewhat successful in establishing a trusting relationship with Nicole, as indicated by the notion that Nicole did initially feel safe in discussing her experience as a Black woman. Yet, perhaps due to the invisibility of Whiteness, Linda was unable to see this as an opportunity to further engage the client around issues of race. It is possible that Linda was uncomfortable about issues of race or did not want to bring up race because she believes race to be a socially taboo topic. However, in doing so, she unintentionally dismissed the client's reality, as well as the opportunity to develop a stronger therapeutic bond. Scholars and researchers note clients' perceptions of their therapists' ability to value the salience of racial and cultural issues in clients lives are related to better therapeutic rapport and client-therapist relationship (see Owen et al., 2011).

When Nicole expressed disappointment with therapy, Linda's response was that Nicole was too focused on race. Statements, like these, that negate an individual's racial realities have been referred to as microinvalidations (Sue et al., 2007). In this case, Linda's statement dismissed the centrality of Nicole's racial experiences in her life and the possibility that Nicole's experiences with racism impacted her wellbeing. Linda's statement also demonstrated her lack of awareness of the many studies that support that people of color do indeed experience discrimination regularly in their lives (see Sue & Sue, 2012; Carter et al., 2013) and that these experiences of racial microaggressions, like the ones that Nicole describes, are related to mental health issues (see Nadal, Griffin, et al., 2014).

When telling the story about her 20-year relationship with her husband, Nicole noticed that Linda's facial expression was one of surprise, which was followed by Linda asking Nicole about whether her daughter was born before or after she married David. While a seemingly innocent question, it is likely that Linda's reactions are based on her stereotypes about Black women. Perhaps Linda has biases that Black women do not have long-term romantic relationships or that all Black children are born to single mothers. Linda merely continued the therapy session without addressing the impasse that occurred. Nicole was annoyed by the whole interaction, but did not address it. If she did, it is possible that Linda would have denied that she committed a microaggression. Because Linda is committed to feminism and social justice issues, she may believe that she is incapable of discriminating against her clients; she may also be unaware of the biases she holds about other groups. As a result, the incident went unaddressed and Nicole continued to grow more disappointed in therapy. Given the previous studies that show a healthy client-therapy relationship and therapists' credibility are associated with their clients' perceptions that her or his therapist has the ability to work with issues of race and culture (Owen et al., 2011), it is likely that Linda's inability to discuss race may have led to Nicole's premature termination.

Another dynamic occurred in the therapeutic dyad that is worth noting. Nicole held assumptions about Linda that may have impacted her treatment. Nicole was surprised that her therapist was a White woman and had the preference of working with a person of color, particularly a woman of color. Here, we see potential underlying issues of mistrust, which could have been addressed right away. Given previous studies on some African Americans' perceptions of White therapists as "detached" and unlikely to be able to relate to their experience (Thompson et al., 2004), it would have been worthwhile for Linda to engage Nicole in a conversation in one of their first sessions. However, because Linda is in a place where she "does not see race," it did not occur and the cultural mistrust grew throughout their work together.

CONCLUSION

Racial microaggressions have been documented to be pervasive in the lives of marginalized groups (Nadal, 2011, 2013; Nadal, Mazzula, et al., 2014). Although relatively little has been documented on the manifestation of racial microaggressions in treatment (Owen et al., 2011), we discussed several types of racial microaggressions that could occur between White feminist therapists and clients of color. While APA's *Guidelines on Multicultural Education, Training, Research, Practice and Organizational Change for Psychologists* (2002) encourage psychologists to examine their own biases, assumptions, and worldview, we understand self-awareness is challenging, and more so in the context of racial microaggressions for White therapists due to the invisibility of Whiteness. Exploring personal biases, prejudices, and assumptions requires therapists to engage in thoughtful and deliberate self-reflection on their dominant social status and how their assumptions and worldviews influence interactions with clients.

The process of discovering our own biases and assumptions is a lifelong journey and commitment that transcends a prescribed set of skills (Mazzula & Rangel, 2011). For White trainees, who are just beginning to engage in feminist work, it is important for them to understand the lifelong nature of discovering and owning racist biases and assumptions; as well as the importance for a support system given the difficulties and challenges that may arise when engaging in this work (Smith & Redington, 2010). Increasing self-awareness and preventing racial microaggressions from occurring in the therapy room are critical when working with Clients of Color who have been documented to continue to encounter race-based experiences of discrimination on a daily basis (Carter, Forsyth, Mazzula, & Williams, 2005; Nadal, 2011). Providing a "safe space" for clients to discuss their own experiences with racial microaggressions can assist in building a healthy client-therapist alliance and break down cultural mistrust of system that has been historically oppressive to marginalized populations (Sue & Sue, 2012).

REFERENCES

American Psychological Association. (2002). *Guidelines on multicultural education, training, research, practice, and organizational change for psychologists*. Washington, DC: American Psychological Association.

American Psychiatric Association. (2014). *Diagnostic and statistical manual of mental disorders* (5th ed.). Washington, DC: Author.

Amodio, D. M., & Devine, P. G. (2006). Stereotyping and evaluation in implicit race bias: Evidence for independent constructs and unique effects on behavior. *Journal of Personality and Social Psychology, 91*(4), 652–661. doi:10.1037/0022-3514.91.4.652

Atdjian, S., & Vega, W. A. (2005). Disparities in mental health treatment in the U.S. racial and ethnic minority groups: Implications for psychiatrists. *Psychiatric Services, 56*(12), 1600–1602. doi:10.1176/appi.ps.56.12.1600

Bell, T. J., & Tracey, T. J. G. (2006). The relation of cultural mistrust and psychological health. *Journal of Multicultural Counseling and Development, 34*(1), 2–14. doi:10.1002/j.2161-1912.2006.tb00022.x

Bennett, M. J., & Stewart, E. C. (2005). *American cultural patterns: A cross-cultural perspective* (2nd ed.). Boston, MA: Intercultural Press.

Blume, A. W., Lovato, L. V., Thyken, B. N., & Denny, N. (2012). The relationship of microaggressions with alcohol use and anxiety among ethnic minority college students in a historically White institution. *Cultural Diversity and Ethnic Minority Psychology, 18*(1), 45–54. doi:10.1037/a0025457

Carter, R. T. (1995). *The influence of race and racial identity in psychotherapy*. New York, NY: Wiley & Sons, Inc.

Carter, R. T. (2007). Racism and psychological and emotional injury: Recognizing and assessing race-based traumatic stress. *The Counseling Psychologist, 35*(1), 13–105. doi:10.1177/0011000006292033

Carter, R. T., Forsyth, J., Mazzula, S. L., & Williams, B. (2005). Racial discrimination and race-based traumatic stress. In R. T. Carter (Vol. Ed.), *Handbook of racial-cultural psychology and counseling: Practice and training* (Vol. 2, pp. 447–476). New York: Wiley & Sons, Inc.

Carter, R. T., Mazzula, S., Victoria, R., Vazquez, R., Hall, S., Smith, S., ... Williams, B. (2013). Initial development of the race-based traumatic stress symptom scale: Assessing the emotional impact of racism. *Psychological Trauma: Theory, Research, Practice, and Policy, 5*(1), 1–9. doi:10.1037/a0025911

Chang, D. F., & Berk, A. (2009). Making cross-racial therapy work: A phenomenological study of clients' experiences of cross-racial therapy. *Journal of Counseling Psychology, 56*, 521–536. doi:10.1037/a0016905

Chow, J. C.-C., Jaffee, K., & Snowden, L. (2003). Racial/ethnic disparities in the use of mental health services in poverty areas. *American Journal of Public Health, 93*, 792–797. doi:10.2105/ajph.93.5.792

Dovidio, J. F., & Gaertner, S. L. (1986). Prejudice, discrimination, and racism: Historical trends and contemporary approaches. In J. F. Dovidio & S. L. Gaertner (Eds.), *Prejudice, discrimination and racism* (pp. 1–34). Orlando, FL: Academic Press.

Enns, C. (2004). *Feminist theories and feminist psychotherapies: Origins, themes, and diversity* (2nd ed.). New York: Haworth Press.

Gary, F. A. (2005). Stigma: Barrier to mental health care among ethnic minorities. *Issues in Mental Health Nursing, 26*, 979–999. doi:10.1080/01612840500280638

Greene, B. (1997). Ethnic minority lesbians and gay men: Mental health and treatment issues. In B. Greene (Ed.), *Ethnic and cultural diversity among lesbians and gay men* (pp. 216–239). Thousand Oaks, CA: Sage.

Hansen, N. D., Randazzo, K. V., Schwartz, A., Marshall, M., Kalis, D., Frazier, R., . . . Norvig, G. (2006). Do we practice what we preach? An exploratory survey of multicultural psychotherapy competencies. *Professional Psychology: Research and Practice, 37*(1), 66–74. doi:10.1037/0735-7028.37.1.66

Helms, J. E. (1990). *Black and White racial identity attitudes: Theory, research, and practice*. Westport, CT: Greenwood Press.

Hurtado, A., & Stewart, A. J. (2004). Through the looking glass: Implications for studying whiteness for feminist methods. In M. Fine, L. Weis, L. P. Pruitt, & A. Burns (Eds.), *Off White: Readings on power, privilege, and resistance* (pp. 315–330). New York: Routledge.

Jacobs, L. (2000). For Whites only. *British Gestalt Journal 9*(1), 3–14.

Mazzula, S. L., & Rangel, B. (2011). Cultural consideration for mental health treatment with women of color. In P. Lundberg-Love, K. Nadal, & M. Paludi (Eds), *Women and mental disorders: Treatments and research* (Vol. 4, pp. 75–91). Santa Barbara, CA: Praeger.

McIntosh, P. (2003). White privilege: Unpacking the invisible knapsack. In S. Plous (Ed.), *Understanding prejudice and discrimination* (pp. 191–196). New York: McGraw-Hill.

Nadal, K. L. (2011). The Racial and Ethnic Microaggressions Scale (REMS): Construction, reliability, and validity. *Journal of Counseling Psychology, 58*, 470–480. doi:10.1037/a0025193

Nadal, K. L. (2013). *That's so gay! microaggressions and the lesbian, gay, bisexual, and transgender community*. Washington, DC: American Psychological Association.

Nadal, K. L., Escobar, K. M. V., Prado, G. T., David, E. J. R., & Haynes, K. (2012). Racial microaggressions and the Filipino American Experience: Recommendations for counseling and development. *Journal of Multicultural Counseling and Development, 40*, 156–173. doi:10.1002/j.2161-1912.2012.00015.x

Nadal, K. L., Griffin, K. E., Wong, Y., Hamit, S., & Rasmus, M. (2014). The Impact of Racial microaggressions on mental health: Counseling Implications for clients of color. *Journal of Counseling & Development, 92*(1), 57–66. doi:10.1002/j.1556-6676.2014.00130.x

Nadal, K. L., Mazzula, S. L., Rivera, D. P., & Fujii-Doe, W. (2014). *Journal of Latina/o Psychology, 2*(2), 67–78. doi:10.1037/lat0000013

Nadeem, E., Lange, J. M., Edge, D., Fongwa, M., Belin, T., & Miranda, J. (2007). Does stigma keep poor young immigrant and US-born Black and Latina women from seeking mental health care? *Psychiatric Services, 58*, 1547–1554. doi:10.1176/appi.ps.58.12.1547

Neville, H. A., Lilly, R. L., Duran, G., Lee, R. M., & Browne, L. (2000). Construction and initial validation of the Color Blind Racial Attitudes Scale (CoBRAS). *Journal of Counseling Psychology, 47*, 59–70. doi:10.1037//0022-0167.47.1.59

Owen, J. J., Tao, K., Leach, M. M., & Rodolfa, E. (2011). Clients' perceptions of their psychotherapists' multicultural orientation. *Psychotherapy, 48*(3), 274–282. doi:10.1037/a0022065

Rivera, D. P., Forquer, E. E., & Rangel, R. (2010). Microaggressions and the life experience of Latina/o Americans. In D. W. Sue (Ed.), *Microaggressions and marginality: Manifestation, dynamics, and impact* (pp. 59–84). New York: Wiley & Sons.

Shelton, K., & Delgado-Romero, E. A. (2011). Sexual orientation microaggressions: The experience of lesbian, gay, bisexual, and queer clients in psychotherapy. *Journal of Counseling Psychology, 58*(2), 210–221. doi:10.1037/a0022251

Shim, R. S., Compton, M. T., Rust, G., Druss, B. G., & Kaslow, N. J. (2009). Race-ethnicity as a predictor of attitudes toward mental health treatment seeking. *Psychiatric Services, 60*(10), 1336–1341. doi:10.1176/appi.ps.60.10.1336

Smith, L., & Redington, R. M. (2010). Lessons from the experiences of White antiracist activists. *Professional Psychology: Research and Practice, 41*, 541–549. doi:10.1037/a0021793

Speight, S. L., Isom, D. A., & Thomas, A. J. (2013). From Hottentot to Superwoman: Issues of identity and mental health for African American women. In C. Z. Enns & E. N. Williams (Eds.), *The Oxford handbook of feminist multicultural counseling psychology* (pp. 115–130). New York: Oxford University Press.

Sue, D. W. (2004). Whiteness and ethnocentric monoculturalism: Making the "invisible" visible. *American Psychologist, 59*, 759–769. doi:10.1037/0003–066x.59.8.761

Sue, D. W., Bucceri, J., Lin, A. I., Nadal, K. L., & Torino, G. C. (2010). Racial microaggressions and the Asian American experience. *Asian American Journal of Psychology, S*(1), 88–101. doi:10.1037/1948-1985.S.1.88

Sue, D. W., Capodilupo, C. M., Torino, G. C., Bucceri, J. M., Holder, A. M. B., Nadal, K. L., & Esquilin, M. (2007). Racial microaggressions in everyday life: Implications for counseling. *The American Psychologist, 62*(4), 271–286. doi:10.1037/0003-066x.62.4.271

Sue, D. W., Nadal, K. L., Capodilupo, C. M., Lin, A. I., Torino, G. C., & Rivera, D. P. (2008). Racial Microaggressions against Black Americans: Implications for counseling. *Journal of Counseling & Development, 86*(3), 330–338. doi:10.1002/j.1556-6678.2008.tb00517.x

Sue, D. W., & Sue, D. (2012). *Counseling the culturally diverse* (6th ed.). New York: John Wiley & Sons, Inc.

Thompson, V. L. S., Bazile, A., & Akbar, M. (2004). African-Americans' perceptions of psychotherapy and psychotherapists. *Professional Psychology: Research and Practice, 35*(1), 19–26. doi:10.1037/0735-7028.35.1.19

Tuckwell, G. (2002). *Racial identity, White counsellors and therapists*. Buckingham, UK: Open University Press.

Wang, J., Leu, J., & Shoda, Y. (2011). When the seemingly innocuous "stings": Racial microaggressions and their emotional consequences. *Personality and Social Psychology Bulletin, 37*(12), 1666–1678. doi:10.1177/0146167211416130

Watkins, N. L., LaBarrie, T. L., & Appio, L. M. (2010). Black undergraduates experience with perceived racial microaggressions in predominantly White colleges and universities. In D. W. Sue (Ed.), *Microaggressions and marginality: Manifestation, dynamics, and impact* (pp. 25–58). New York: Wiley & Sons.

Worrell, J., & Remer, P. (2002). *Feminist perspectives in therapy: Empowering diverse women*. New York: Wiley.

The Unbearable Lightness of Being White

DIANE M. ADAMS

*California School of Professional Psychology, Alliant International University,
San Francisco, California*

In this article I explore the relationship between feelings of superiority, White privilege, White guilt, and a denied White racial identity and how these dynamics are enacted in therapy between White therapist and client. I discuss the concepts of White privilege, White guilt, color-blind racial ideology, and the invisibility of Whiteness and their importance in understanding problems in White identity development. Throughout this discussion I draw implications for clinical practice and training. I conclude by suggesting a process for identifying the dynamics of privilege and power in cross-cultural interactions through the use of self-reflection.

What I convey in this article is through the eyes of a Black woman and is influenced by my observations of the reactions of Whites to issues of race and diversity in racial awareness training, in clinical situations, and in my personal lived experience. As a Black person writing about Whiteness I approached this task with a sense of moral and social responsibility. Morally I felt the responsibility to speak with both candor and humaneness. In regard to the latter I paid special attention in writing this article to literature describing the subjective emotional experiences and opinions of White individuals about the issues I discuss. In regard to my sense of social responsibility, socially I always feel the responsibility to take any opportunity I am offered to speak about matters that will help illuminate, or at the least encourage dialogue about, the crisis that is race relations within the United States. Most often race dialogue is focused on the "other," or minority group members and their disadvantages. However, given that inequality in race relations is inherently comparative; this discussion can accurately be framed either in terms of dominant group privilege, or subordinate group disadvantage (Powell, Branscombe, & Schmitt, 2005). I focus on the concept of White privilege and the interrelationships between that concept and the phenomena of White guilt, color-blind racial ideology, and the invisibility of Whiteness.

The title of this article may be familiar to some who recognize it from the movie in the 1980s titled, *The Unbearable Lightness of Being*, based on the Pulitzer Prize winning novel by the same name. The film was produced by Ohlsson, Zaentz, and Zaentz, and was directed by Kaufman (1988). One critic in reviewing this movie said of the hero: "He feels life is light and that his actions have weightless consequences; he goes through life fleeing anything that might put on weight" (Elvira, 2000). It is the hero's experience of life as light, and as it turns out unbearably light, that metaphorically captures the experience of White privilege. Using similar imagery of lightness, McIntosh (1998) described White privilege as "an invisible weightless knapsack of advantages"(p. 148). Speaking both metaphorically and literally, White individuals who are unaware of their privilege, do not need to be burdened by a sense of social responsibility but can go through life "weightless," untroubled by issues of social equity, living life as if their actions have weightless consequence. There are consequences, however; and these consequences constitute the "burden" of White privilege. Paradoxically, I suggest that it is only when White individuals assume the burdens of social consciousness and responsibility that a state of freedom from the personal and societal consequences of racism and oppression can be achieved.

WHITE PRIVILEGE AND DENIAL

According to McIntosh (1998) White individuals are conditioned to not recognize their privilege, to remain oblivious to it while enjoying its benefits. She saw White privilege and male privilege as unconscious and as bolstered and sustained by denial. McIntosh (1998) listed 26 things that, as a White person, unlike people of color, she need not think about, and could remain confident would not affect her adversely. Her list of White privileges included such things as not being followed while shopping for fear that she would steal, or not being called a credit to her race for doing well, to being welcomed to buy property in any neighborhood she could afford. While McIntosh's (1998) list of privileges are familiar to most multicultural and feminist practitioners, I list them here because I find that contemporary doctoral trainees are unfamiliar with the concept of White Privilege and have never thought of social injustices as privileging them but only in terms of it disadvantaging others. Exposure to the concept of White privilege was eye-opening for many of these students who used it as a bridge for understanding the minority experience of discrimination. It became a way to connect with and see another worldview and provided another perspective on racism. McIntosh (1998) pointed out in describing White privilege that most White individuals are "taught to recognize racism only in individual acts of meanness ..., never in invisible systems conferring unsought racial dominance ... from birth" (p. 152). For some White students the exercise of thinking in terms of their advantages made racism more visible and its existence more legitimate in their minds.

In contemplating her list of privileges McIntosh (1998) ultimately arrived at the conclusion that White privilege like systemic racism confers dominance on White individuals and works to systematically disempower other groups. This premise provides a framework for exploring the dynamics of power and privilege in race relations that goes beyond individual acts of meanness. Race becomes an organizing structure for power relations within the culture, and racism comes to be defined and understood in terms of systematic and institutional oppression. Given this understanding of what it means to acknowledge privilege, one can see how denial would feature prominently in the dynamics of White race relations. Acknowledging White privilege requires acknowledging the existence of systemic racism, and this brings with it issues of culpability and responsibility, and challenges cherished notions, that in the United States choice and opportunity are equally available to everyone. The dynamic of denial in White privilege supports the American myth of meritocracy. This myth is the belief that success can be contributed to individual talent and effort, and that there is equal opportunity for all to pull themselves up from their bootstraps. This belief becomes an important one for understanding White racial identity development and race relation.

WHITE PRIVILEGE AND COLOR-BLIND RACIAL IDEOLOGY

Nowhere, is the dynamic of denial more manifest than in color-blind racial ideology. This set of ideologies supports the denial of White privilege and could even be considered to be a particular form, or manifestation of it that elaborates on social and institutional consequences. In spite of the fact that research has shown that the notion of color-blindness in people is inaccurate, and that perceptual differentiation of race occurs rapidly (in less than one seventh of a second) and emerges as early as 6 months of age (Apfelbaum, Norton, & Sommers, 2012, p. 205), color-blind racial attitudes are believed to have become the dominant post-civil rights racial ideology (Todd, Spanierman, & Poteat, 2011). This ideology reflects an unawareness of institutional racism and refers to racial attitudes that are based on the denial, distortion, and minimization of the importance of race and the existence of racism (Todd et al., 2011). Color-blind racial ideology is rooted in assertions that color-blindness can prevent prejudice and discrimination; however research has found that people exposed to arguments promoting color-blindness subsequently display a greater degree of both implicit and explicit racial bias (Apfelbaum et al., 2012; Chao, Wei, Good, & Flores, 2011). This ideology refutes the existence of a power hierarchy in race relations, and the notion of inequity, or an uneven playing field, and in the guise of equality and equal treatment of the races is the ideology used to overturn Affirmative Action policies and justify racial resentment. At best this kind of thinking takes the form of blithe denial, of social inequity, and supports the status quo, and at worst it takes the form of callous self-interest and blaming the victim.

Although one would think, in this day and age, that color-blind racial attitudes would not be prevalent among contemporary, liberal-minded, doctoral-level psychology students, White trainees in racial awareness classes often enter these classes with this mindset. In a recent racial awareness class I taught to psychology trainees, White trainees seemed astonished by statistics illustrating the extent of racial and social inequities in the health care system, saying they had not realized the magnitude of such disparities. They expressed the opinion that it was important to be "accepting of people of all races," emphasizing similarities rather than differences, and were in some instances appalled by the notion that race could be considered at all: "how dare someone judge me based on how I look instead of my behavior, said one White trainee commenting about a student of color who had grouped her (pejoratively) as like other White people. The student of color replied I am judged in that way all the time. Another White student in this same class gave examples of times that people of color had behaved toward her in "racist" ways, saying defensively that racism was a two-way street, and making no distinction between the experiences of racial minorities with racism and her experiences of race-related harassment. Sadly, her viewpoint reflects evidence suggesting that many White Americans today believe that Whites are as, or are more, victimized by racism than are Blacks (Apfelbaum et al., 2012, p. 207).

WHITE GUILT, WHITE PRIVILEGE, AND SOCIAL RESPONSIBILITY

In the movie *The Unbearable Lightness of Being,* it was convenient for the hero, a White male surgeon, not to examine the benefits of his White male privilege and his sexual philandering. It was only in coming to terms with his responsibility and impact on another that he was able to acknowledge that even for him life imposed some limitations, that he was not above a need for connection, and that he was accountable for his impact on others. In the end he was faced with the realization that it was a life absent the "burdens" of connection and responsibility that was unbearable. The experience of White guilt can contribute to this kind of awakening and be a pathway for White individuals in developing a sense of connection, accountability, and responsibility around issues of social justice and equity. From this perspective, White guilt, although an emotionally painful experience, is arguably a good thing, indicating acceptance of personal responsibility and connection. Before there can be a response of guilt there has to be an affective awareness of the other, a connection (Arminio, 2001). If you don't care or see anything wrong with the status quo or refuse to see any untoward consequences to others then you don't experience guilt.

The movement from denial to awareness of privilege for white psychology trainees is often a psychologically distressing experience, which is disorganizing and guilt provoking. White students undergoing this transition progress through stages of racial awareness, similar to Helms (1984) stages of White identity development in which they move from denial, struggle to embrace a non-racist White identity, and experience periods of confusion, disintegration, and superiority in the process. Arminio (2001) pointed out that once White individuals become aware of their privilege, they realize that their gains and advantages are not simply based on personal achievement and merit, but that they have a leg up, and may actually be benefitting from the disadvantages of others. With this awareness comes what she referred to as the "moral dilemma" of being White (Arminio, 2001, Literature review, para. 5): "They appreciate and enjoy its privileges, but realize those privileges are not extended to all people, and in particular (covert or overt) are denied to people of color" (Arminio, 2001, Literature review, para. 5). This realization results in the experience of guilt.

In her phenomenological study of race-related guilt, Arminio's (2001) study participants, six White graduate students, described the experience of White guilt as an emotionally painful one, using terminology such as, "a knife stabbing pain," as " feeling upset with myself," "feeling awful," "beating myself up," and the sense that "I have no backbone" (Naming Oppression section, para. 1). This latter theme, "I have no backbone," was echoed in another phenomenological study in which a group of White women against racism related their experiences of White guilt (Case, 2012). One of the most troublesome aspects of guilt they discussed was the guilt they felt about failures to speak out against racism when they were in all White social situations with other Whites who were making racist comments. Case (2012) suggested that for the women in her sample the urge to interrupt racism caused an internal conflict, and weighing of personal values of racial justice against the desire for social acceptance. It was an awareness of violating their personal values and the failure to act in a way consistent with those values that resulted in the experience of guilt and in a loss of self-esteem. These dynamics of White guilt suggest, at the least, that for White individuals who have anti-racist values it is important in order to preserve a personal sense of self-esteem and integrity that their behaviors be consistent with their values.

THE INVISIBILITY OF WHITENESS

The denial of White privilege and attempts to avoid the emotionally painful experience of White guilt are linked to the phenomenon of the invisibility of Whiteness and the disavowal of White racial identity. Whites can avoid the experience of guilt when they view themselves as individuals rather than as members of a race systematically linked with systems of oppression, domination, and unearned privilege (Case, 2012, p. 79). Denying systemic oppression or any personal benefits from it, circumvents not only the need to experience guilt but also to assume responsibility or accountability. I cannot say how often White trainees have said to me: I am not responsible for something my ancestors did 200 years ago. "In an intricate system of White privilege, Whites have the power to ignore and neutralize race when race benefits [them] Whites" (Case, 2012, p.79). As members of a dominant group, Whiteness can remain invisible to White individuals who never have to think about their race or the impact it has on their lives (Case, 2012; Dottolo & Stewart, 2013).

Research studies about White racial identification suggest that when explicitly asked about whiteness many White students are confused, defensive, or speechless (Dottolo & Stewart, 2013). In a study of 23 middle-aged White adults in a Midwestern city (Dottolo & Stewart, 2013), the authors found the participants seldom thought about their race. When asked about their racial identification they were taken aback, and their responses indicated that they had never given it much thought. In one instance the interviewer asked: "Do you think about your own racial identity much?" The White participant responded: "Pardon me?" The interviewer repeated the question: "Do you think about your own racial identity much?" Clearly, bewildered by the question the White participant responded: "My own racial identity" (Dottolo & Stewart, 2013, p. 108)? Another participant in this study when asked whether or not he thought about his racial identity or about being white responded, no, three different times when he was asked to reflect on the question, as if to emphasize he considered the question superfluous and that there was no need to think about it.

Recently, I was struck by the phenomenon of the invisibility of Whiteness and the ways in which it manifest. I was consulting the Publication Manual of the American Psychological Association (2009, p. 75) in reference to discussing preferential terminology for use with racial and ethnic groups. Ironically, I had consulted the publication manual in reference to a White student's question about what terminology to use when describing Whites. What wasn't discussed in the manual was as telling as what was.

While there was much discussion about what constituted appropriate language and terminology, for use with racial ethnic minorities, Whites were not included in this discussion. Alternative language and appropriate terminology was discussed for other racial ethnic groups, e.g., the use of Black, as opposed to African American, or Hispanic, as opposed to Latino, or Chicano, or the merits and appropriateness of using American Indian, Native American, or Native North American. The manual was virtually silent on language when discussing Whites as an ethnic racial group, only using the term White, without further elaboration or definition. I found this revealing because although the manual was silent on the issue, there are debates about, and alternative terminology used to refer to Whites, such as Caucasian, European American, Euro-Caucasian, or Anglo (McDermott & Sampson, 2005). Also research indicates that White individuals have geographical preferences about the use of such language, e.g., Whites in the Deep South strongly prefer use of the term "White," while the term Anglo is often preferred in the Southwest and Upper New England (McDermott & Sampson, 2005); also socio-economic status (SES) affects preference, the term Caucasian being preferred by more educated White respondents (McDermott & Sampson, 2005). I would suggest that the manual's silence on the issue reflects a pervasive and unconscious manifestation of the invisibility of Whiteness in this society. White is not thought of in terms of a racial, ethnic identity, but is taken for granted, and thus needs no defining. However, in not defining Whiteness, Whiteness becomes the unspoken parameter around which other groups are defined and compared, and contributes to a White identity that is unconsciously based on being in a superordinate position.

Unacknowledged feelings of superiority and the disavowal of a racial identity associated with the oppression of others contributes to problems in the development of a sense of racial and cultural identity for Whites as well as to the perpetuation of racism. White trainees most often do not consider themselves as members of a cultural group and culture is overlooked in the therapeutic relationship particularly the culture of Whiteness. In intercultural awareness trainings they seem to feel bereft of a culture, a sense of identification, affiliation, and belonging. In talking with a White colleague about this article and this phenomenon in particular, I was surprised and touched to see tears come into her eyes as she said that she longed for the sense of belonging that she saw among ethnic minority faculty in our institution. It seems that assimilation came at a cost for White individuals, as ancestors changed last names, lost accents, and strove to blend in, in order to achieve and become a part of the American Dream of economic success. Some authors propose that in order for White individuals to define themselves as cultural beings they need to acknowledge their own racial identity, and to define themselves in a process that mirrors that engaged in by minorities and draw upon unique aspects of their family heritage, and background in developing their identity (Apfelbaum et al., 2012, p. 208).

White trainees often become defensive about their own Whiteness, or guilty, and at the same time manifest an unconscious sense of superiority. As a result they can be unaware of their own biases and less sensitive to the complexity and importance of cultural differences in the treatment relationship. Research indicates that understanding one's own racial ethnic background and increasing awareness of one's own cultural assumptions and values can be a critical step in improving trainees' multicultural competence (Chao et al., 2011). This same research indicates that exposing

White graduate students to a course on Whiteness, covering such topics as; the history of race, systemic racial inequalities, White culture, power, privilege, and guilt, can bring about change in White racial identity, a new awareness of race, and a commitment to anti-racism (Chao et al., 2011). Exposure to multicultural coursework may be particularly important for the development of cultural awareness among White trainees, as research suggests that the development of this skill poses a steeper learning curve for White trainees than ethnic minority trainees, as at lower levels of multicultural training ethnic racial minority trainees report significantly higher scores than White trainees on multicultural awareness (Chao et al., 2011).

CLINICAL IMPLICATIONS

From a psychoanalytic point of view, it has been suggested that White racial superiority, White privilege, and a repudiated White racial identity are forms of pathological narcissism (Miller & Josephs, 2009). The argument is made that because of the competitive, individualistic nature of American society there must be Oedipal winners and Oedipal losers (Miller & Josephs, 2009), in other words, those who are ultimately successful and those who are not. Miller and Josephs (2009) used the term Oedipal, referencing the classic Freudian conflict of rivalry and competition, forbidden love, and retribution, and offered a racial interpretation. In classic Freudian theory, White men are the Oedipal winners who get to enjoy power, prestige, and wealth (Miller & Josephs, 2009) and White women are envious bystanders. Although Miller and Josephs (2009) do not discuss the controversial gendered aspects of Oedipal theory, which have been disputed and rejected by both feminist and contemporary psychoanalysts (Chodorow, 1992; Mitchell & Black, 1995), they do suggest the operation of a racialized form of Oedipal splitting in the United States that is based on the history of Black/White race and sexual relations.

In this racialized form of Oedipal splitting, Blacks become the quintessential epitome of all that is undesirable, devalued, forbidden, split off, and projected, and Whites come to represent all that is desired, idealized, valued, and sought after. In this view of things, Whites are the ultimate Oedipal winners and Blacks, and other people of color are the ultimate Oedipal losers, competence and success are unconsciously racialized to insure that there will always be someone who is a bigger Oedipal loser than they are (Miller & Josephs, 2009). In this paradigm, White winners can view Black losers as defensively using race to justify their lack of success, and any challenges to this viewpoint can pose the threat of narcissistic decompensation. Vulnerability to states of narcissistic decompensation are characterized by White shame and rage, and stem from instability in identity development from the splitting off and projection of repudiated aspects of the self. This disavowal of aspects of the self, results in a White identity that is fragmented and unintegrated and thus fragile and unstable (Miller & Josephs, 2009).

CLINICAL CASE EXAMPLE

The following case illustrates the dynamics of superiority, and the ways in which repudiated and projected aspects of White identity can remain invisible in a therapy while unconsciously being mirrored and enacted by White therapist and White client.

The case involves a 25-year-old White heterosexual female living in a residential drug treatment facility, working on sobriety. The client was referred for treatment by her case manager. Her stated goal was to be able to form stronger more intimate relationships with others. She described a history of lashing out at others, even those she cared about; she didn't understand why she did it, and wanted it to stop. She was having a great deal of difficulty adjusting to living in the residential treatment center. The therapist a young White woman described the client as guarded and as keeping people at a distance. At the treatment center she isolated herself from others and tried to avoid community meetings. The client came from an upper middle-class family and had traveled abroad in Europe. She continually devalued the other women in the facility calling them stupid, lazy and worthless. The other women were primarily Black and came from low socioeconomic backgrounds.

In spite of the fact that both she and her brother were drug addicts at an early age, she emphasized the fact that she came from a "regular, loving, and supportive, middle-class family." However, she had started using alcohol and smoking marijuana when she was 8 years old and was currently addicted to heroin. She described her brother as a "loser" and had no respect for how he obtained drugs, although she herself had been convicted of petty theft and shoplifting. The therapist described the transference and countertransference as positive. She identified with the client she said, because she resembled a close friend, they were similar in age, and the client had a higher level of intellectual functioning. This last statement, "a higher level of intellectual functioning," caught my attention and I inquired as to what she meant by it. Although the therapist stated she did not condone the client's isolative behavior in the treatment setting, nor the way she treated the other clients, she stated that she empathized with her because she had nothing in common with the other clients as they came from very different backgrounds. I pointed out that what they did have in common was that they were all drug addicts in recovery.

I then recalled that the therapist herself had, had difficulty adjusting to the treatment facility. She had been critical of the staff, the supervision she was receiving, and the way things were run. She had also reported at the beginning of the rotation having a hard time connecting with other clients at the residence, who she saw as "lacking insight," and "uncommitted" to treatment. (I was not the supervisor on the case but was teaching a small group case seminar where students presented cases from their clinical practica.) I began to explore more with the therapist what I had started to view as a shared sense of White superiority between her and the client that I was coming to see as interfering with fully exploring the client's interpersonal difficulties and social isolation. It seemed to me that the more the client distanced herself from the other clients and staff in the treatment facility the more likely she was to relapse. Since my role was to help the therapist with case formulation and consult on the case, not to supervise the psychotherapy, I encouraged the therapist to explore the cultural issues in the case. In this way she was able to address the racial issues in the case without being as threatened. She had balked when I had asked her what it was like to be a White therapist working in an agency where the majority of staff and clients were Black. She saw it less as an issue of race and more as an issue of class, training, and work ethic (the agency used peer counselors as well as licensed therapist to work with the clients).

The therapist was able to formulate that the client engaged in projection as a way to expel her negative feelings about herself and place them upon the other women in the facility. I took it a step further and suggested that Blackness in our culture has come to represent bad, forbidden, and unacceptable aspects of the self; we had done some readings in the class to this effect, and that based on these readings she entertain the idea that race was a factor in the client's reactions. We talked about the client's fear of falling out of the middle class and how important it was for her sense of self-esteem to hold on to the sense of privilege and status that being middle class and White conferred; and, that she feared becoming, like her brother, a "loser." I speculated how mortifying and threatening it must be to the client to be lumped in, in her mind, with a bunch of losers (low-income, Black addicts). However, we still had not addressed the issue of the therapist Whiteness and the client's Whiteness. This issue was invisible in that it was not spoken about but implicit in that it was being enacted. From my point of view the therapist was in collusion with the client in their unstated identification with each other's Whiteness and superiority and they were clinging together in a sea of Blackness in what Miller and Josephs (2009) referred to as a mutual admiration society.

I broached this idea with the therapist by suggesting that the client was not only using projection to bolster her self-esteem, but that she did in fact feel superior, and that this was an aspect of White racial identification, because in a racist society, such as the United States, Whiteness is considered superior. I went on to say that in our society race relationships are hierarchal and that in that hierarchy Whites see themselves as on top and Blacks and other minorities at the bottom. I suggested that there might be over-identification with the client, this was terminology familiar to the therapist, and that in some ways they were both feeling superior to clients and staff in the agency. I asked her to speculate in her case formulation about what this might mean for treatment. The therapist was able to entertain these ideas, and to concede that because of her identification with the client and her own uncomfortable feelings about the agency, she may not have fully explored her client's problematic interactions with other clients.

This case illustrates several concepts discussed in this article. The invisibility of Whiteness as a cultural factor can be seen in the therapist lack of understanding that this was a shared identification with the client. She could acknowledge similarities between her and the client in any number of ways, age, resemblance to friends, and intellect but could not acknowledge that they shared an identification of being White. This oversight is peculiar to White therapist working with White clients; ethnic racial minority therapists seldom fail to recognize or bring up the import of race in a treatment with like raced clients, usually exploring race as well as other intersecting aspects of their and their client's identity. Even more difficult for the therapist to acknowledge was that much of this identification stemmed from a shared sense of superiority. It is a difficult aspect of white racial identity development to acknowledge the racist foundations of White identity and many authors speculate that disavowed or repudiated White racial identification stems from the wish to separate the self from acknowledging White privilege, White dominance, and racism; creating as Bonilla-Silva (2003) said, the phenomenon of racism without racists. The therapist refusal to see that race was a factor in the treatment relationship even though she was able to acknowledge the impact of other intersecting identities, such as, age and SES, was an unconscious endorsement of the color-blind ideology that race doesn't matter.

CONCLUDING REMARKS: INTERSECTIONS AND CONNECTIONS

My final comments have to do with intersections and connections. In the movie *The Unbearable Lightness of Being* the hero is able to see one form of oppression but not another. At one point he and a group of his friends reflect on the complicity or innocence of those Czechoslovakians in the communist party in supporting a changing oppressive morality and regime in Czechoslovakia. Speculating that these individuals have to know what they are doing but are able to convince themselves of their innocence and can say our conscience is clear. In stark contrast the hero is unable to see and does no parallel reflection on the issues of gender oppression, his White male privilege, and his use of women purely as objects of sexual gratification. Being in touch with one form of oppression and privilege does not guarantee awareness of other forms (Case, 2012; McIntosh, 1998). This is not to say that there are not points of intersection between different forms of oppression, or between different groups and individuals experiences of oppression. However, the danger in assuming uniformity of oppression is in assuming that all people are equally knowledgeable of all kinds of oppression, thus "erasing any understanding of the need to listen to subordinated groups," about their particular experience of oppression (Case, 2012, p. 80).

McIntosh (1998) pointed out that because of the extensive use of denial in White privilege much of White oppressive behavior is unconscious and remains invisible to the perpetrator. She went on to reflect on women of color's accusations that White women are oppressive, and concluded that based on her reflections on the unconscious nature of White privilege they were justified. She speculated that the common denominator between White privilege and male privilege was denial. Case (2012) noted that women's gender oppression did not necessarily give them insight into racial oppression and pointed out the influence of multiple, intersecting identities. She noted that intersectionality among White women includes a privileged racial status and a subordinate gender status, as well as other intersecting identities, and that in different situations, at different times one aspect of identity can hold sway over, or be in conflict with another aspect.

Perhaps a point of common intersection for understanding White Privilege and other forms of oppression is a shared intolerance for injustice and oppression. One of the most often quoted sayings from *The Unbearable Lightness of Being* (Kundrea, 1984) conveys this notion: "when the heart speaks, the mind finds it indecent to object" (Goodreads, n.d.). The experience of White guilt can be thought of as the heart speaking, and as indicating an awareness of connection and concern for the experiences of another. As a Black woman I have often become impatient with White expressions of guilt particularly when it seems that Whites are staying mired in guilt, my feelings being "alright, already, get over it, and do what's righteous." Case studies of White guilt indicate that this attitude might be the right approach, if done in a way it can be heard, in that the experience of White guilt is brought about by either acting inconsistently or tolerating situations that are inconsistent with one's own personal values. In spite of my impatience, I believe it is necessary for White individuals to engage in these dialogues, particularly with each other. However, I believe they also have to move past dialoguing and experiencing, and make a conscious commitment to be agents of social justice.

I believe it is a difficult endeavor for White individuals to become aware of White privilege and move beyond it because its denial is so ingrained and unconscious in White identity. As I wrote this article I found that mentally I kept blocking in proposing solutions, and had to face that unconsciously, in spite of my multicultural commitment and training, I despair of solutions to race relations in the United States, but at the same time I feel that it is irresponsible to take a stance that is merely castigating, pointing out problems without offering any suggestions for change. In the interim, before I finished this article, I had an experience as a visiting scholar in Africa that gave me a new perspective on privilege and the power of self-reflection in increasing cultural awareness; and, although these experiences are tales for another time, and too lengthy to incorporate here, they provided me with new awareness and insight as I wrote. While in Africa I gained a personal appreciation of the ways in which culture and privilege organize power relations and the importance of self-reflection and cultural awareness in arriving at culturally sensitive approaches to resolving issues of power relations within cultural hierarchies. These experiences led me to think about strategies of intervention with White trainees into the phenomenon of White Privilege that I had overlooked.

Although I did not think about it at the time, the process that I underwent in resolving the conflicts I experienced resembled the use of a form of Liberation therapy that Arminio (2001) proposed as useful in the positive resolution of White guilt. She proposed a process for the transformation of guilt into action whereby the focus needs to be on: (1) helping individuals learn to see themselves in relation to cultural and contextual influences, in order (2) to move from acceptance of oppression to naming oppression (feelings of guilt), to (3) reflection and redefinition. While I was in Africa I went through this process spontaneously, as from the unfamiliar position of being the privileged, I navigated, issues of power, privilege, and gender in my interactions. My experiences highlighted for me the potential usefulness of Arminio's (2001) formula, particularly the equating of the experience of guilt with the naming of the oppression, and reminded me of the power of self-reflection and self-awareness in bringing about change.

Equating the experience of guilt with the naming of the oppression allows the individual to use their feelings of discomfort in cross-cultural interactions as a signal for the need to reflect on the cultural implications of the interaction. The appeal of this for me is that awareness and reflection are used as means to arrive at a cultural understanding; you do not need to already be culturally sensitive as a trigger for the reflection. However, you do need to reflect on and process the cultural and contextual influences on your feelings. The experience of guilt, or emotional discomfort, can serve like signal anxiety to alert to the potential of oppression, and help in identifying its source. Reflecting on the cultural context of those feelings facilitates the development of cultural awareness, and can compensate or circumvent the lack of it. Based on my own personal experience of confronting my privilege, I concluded that in order for White practitioners to competently address cultural and racial issues in their work they need to develop qualities of self-reflection, self-awareness, and a sense of social consciousness. I further concluded that their development of these qualities can be facilitated by exposure to multicultural training, by reflecting on the cultural context of cross cultural interactions, and by reclaiming a lost history and ethnic identity.

REFERENCES

American Psychological Association. (2009). *Publication manual of the American psychological Association* (6th ed.), Washington, DC: Author.

Apfelbaum, E. P., Norton, M. I., & Sommers, S. R. (2012). Racial color blindness: Emergence, practice, and implications. *Current Directions in Psychological Science, 21*(3), 205–209. doi:10.1177/0963721411434980

Arminio, J. (2001). Exploring the nature of race-related guilt. *Journal of Multicultural Counseling and Development, 29*(4), 239–252. doi:10.1002/j.2161-1912.2001.tb00467.x

Bonilla-Silva, E. (2003). *Racism without racists: Color-blind racism and the persistence of racial inequality in the United States.* Lanham, MD: Rowman & Littlefield.

Case, K. A. (2012). Discovering the privilege of whiteness: White women's reflections on anti-racist identity and ally behavior. *Journal of Social Issues, 68*(1), 78–96. doi:10.1111/j.1540-4560.2011.01737.x

Chao, R. C.-L., Wei, M., Good, G. E., & Flores, L. Y. (2011). Race/ethnicity, color-blind racial attitudes, and multicultural counseling competence: The moderating effects of multicultural counseling training. *Journal of Counseling Psychology, 58*(1), 72–82. doi:10.1037/a0022091

Chodorow, N. J. (1992). Heterosexuality as a compromise formation: Reflections on the psychoanalytic theory of sexual development. *Psychoanalysis and Contemporary Thought, 15*(3), 267–304.

Dottolo, A. L., & Stewart, A. J. (2013). I never think about my race: Psychological features of White racial identities. *Qualitative Research in Psychology, 10*(1), 102–117.

Elvira, B. (2000). Audience reviews for The Unbearable Lightness of Being [Review of the motion picture, The Unbearable Lightness of Being, 1988]. Retrieved from http://www.rottentomatoes/.../Unbearable_Lightness_of_Being

Goodreads. (n.d.). The unbearable lightness of being: Quotes by Milan Kundera. Retrieved from http://www.goodreads.com/.../quotes/4489585.nesnesiteln-lehkost.b

Helms, J. E. (1984). Toward a theoretical explanation of the effects of race on counseling: A Black and White model. *The Counseling Psychologist, 12*(4), 153–165. doi:10.1177/0011000084124013

Kundrea, M. (1984). *The unbearable lightness of being.* New York, NY: Harper & Row, Publishers.

McDermott, M., & Sampson, F. L. (2005). White racial and ethnic identity in the United States. *Annual review of Sociology, 31,* 245–261. doi:10.1146/annurev.soc.31.041304.122322

McIntosh, P. (1998). White privilege: Unpacking the invisible knapsack. In M. McGoldrick (Ed.), *Re-visioning family therapy: Race, culture, and gender in clinical practice* (pp. 147–153). New York: Guilford Press.

Miller, A. E., & Josephs, L. (2009). Whiteness as pathological narcissism. *Contemporary Psychoanalysis, 45*(1), 93–119. doi:10.1080/00107530.2009.10745989

Mitchell, S. A., & Black, M. J. (1995). *Freud and beyond: A history of modern psychoanalytic thought.* New York: Basic Books.

Ohlsson, B., Zaentz, P., Zaentz, S. (Producer), & Kaufman, P. (Director). (1988). *The unbearable lightness of being [Motion picture].* USA: The Saul Zaentz Company.

Powell, A. A., Branscombe, N. R., & Schmitt, M. T. (2005). Inequality as ingroup privilege or outgroup disadvantage: The impact of group focus on collective guilt and interracial attitudes. *Personality and Social Psychology Bulletin, 31,* 508–521. doi:10.1177/0146167204271713

Todd, N. R., Spanierman, L. B., & Poteat, V. P. (2011). Longitudinal examination of the psychosocial costs of racism to Whites across the college experience. *Journal of Counseling Psychology, 58*(4), 508–521. doi:10.1037/a0025066

"American" as a Proxy for "Whiteness": Racial Color-Blindness in Everyday Life

NELLIE TRAN

Department of Counseling & School Psychology, San Diego State University, San Diego, California

SUSAN E. PATERSON

Department of Educational & Psychological Studies, University of Miami, Miami, Florida

This article discusses racial color-blindness as it relates to a modern strategy used by both Whites and People of Color (POC) to mask their discussions of race and privilege. People who endorse racial color-blindness tend to believe that race should not matter and currently does not matter in understanding individuals' lived experiences. Therefore, racially color-blind individuals use strategies to justify their racial privilege and racist beliefs and attitudes. One such strategy is to use the term "American" as a proxy for "White" in describing instances of White privilege as norms and to hide discussions of race more generally. Study 1 findings show that there are many different socially constructed definitions for the term American. Study 2 findings reveal differences in definitions for American depending on an individual's race and generational status.

"I have a dream that my four little children will one day live in a nation where they will not be judged by the color of their skin, but by the content of their character." In the summer of 1963 atop the steps of the Lincoln Memorial, Dr. Martin Luther King, Jr. famously spoke these words of hope that the future would be a place where discrimination because of one's skin color no longer existed. Over 50 years later, though discrimination still exists, many scholars would argue that racism has nearly disappeared or at the very least, has become socially unacceptable (Zamudio & Rios, 2006). The phenomenon of *racial color-blindness* refers to a belief system that some individuals hold suggesting that race no longer matters and that the Unites States represents a meritocratic society where hard work is the sole determinant of success (Forman, 2004; Gallagher, 2003; Neville, Lilly, Duran, Lee, & Browne, 2000). In essence, those who endorse color-blind beliefs report not seeing "color" and that one's skin color does not matter in today's society. These individuals would also argue that Dr. Martin Luther King Jr.'s dream has been realized. During the 1960s Civil Rights Movement, color-blind beliefs began to emerge in the rhetoric of the "model minority" Asian American. This image suggested that the United States was color-blind because Asian Americans were not being held back but instead achieved success through their hard work (Kim, 2000). In this way, arguments that the United States systematically disadvantaged POC could be debunked based on the success of Asian Americans—a minority group that other groups ought to emulate.

The idea of the "American Dream" provides another example of how race has been removed from the discussion of achievement and replaced with proxy terms based on Americanism. In essence, the creation and maintenance of the American Dream was the first effort at producing racial color-blindness. The American Dream posits that success follows hard work, or that the harder you work, the more likely you are to be successful in achieving your goals. Success, in this sense, can be defined in a myriad of ways, including earning a high salary, having a prestigious job or even something as amorphous as freedom of action and speech (Hochschild, 1995). Philosophically, the American Dream is available to everyone (Hochschild, 1995); and everyone has equal access to it as long as they are willing to participate in trying to achieve success (i.e., work hard). In reality, the American Dream is unachievable for the majority of American citizens because of systemic racism.

This paper discusses racial color-blindness as it relates to a modern strategy used by both Whites and POC to mask their discussions of race and privilege. People who endorse high levels of racial color-blind ideology tend to believe that race should not matter, and more importantly, currently does not matter in understanding individual's lived experiences. Therefore, racially color-blind individuals use strategies to justify their racial privilege, and racist beliefs and attitudes. One such strategy is the use of the term "American" as a proxy for "White" to describe instances of White privileges as social norms and to hide discussions of race more generally. Empirical evidence will also be presented to support our claims.

RACIAL COLOR-BLINDNESS

Endorsement of a color-blind racial ideology goes beyond believing that race *should* not matter to also believing that race *does not* matter in today's society

(Neville et al., 2000). As a theory, Color-blind Racial Ideology stems from scholarly research in the legal field (Neville et al., 2000) in response to allegations of increased modern racism (McConahay, 1986), laissez-faire racism (Bobo, Kluegel, & Smith, 1997), symbolic racism (McConahay & Hough, 1976), and aversive racism (Gaertner & Dovidio, 1986). Color-blind Racial Ideology is conceptually different from racism, which is a construct that includes an ideological component and a structural or institutional component (Thompson & Neville, 1999). Color-blind Racial Ideology only includes an ideological component that suggests race should not and does not matter. Additionally, racism often involves beliefs in racial hierarchies and racial superiority of one group over others. While Color-blind Racial Ideology does not involve such hierarchies; instead it involves a denial of racial dynamics within today's society (Neville et al., 2000). Empirically, studies of racism are often interested in Whites' level of racism, and POC are not included. Color-blind Racial Ideology, on the other hand, is a cognitive schema developed for use with members of all groups to understand how people interpret racial stimuli (Neville et al., 2000). For example, when the U.S. military decides to ban certain types of hairstyles such as twists, locks, and large corn rows (cf. Cooper, 2014), a racially conscious individual might interpret the event as one that is racist because these are hairstyles that are popular and typically worn by Black women, especially those in the military. A racially color-blind individual, on the other hand, might rationalize the comment as one that is necessary for basic grooming standards in the military that mirror other regulations banning tattoos (cf. Cooper, 2014). In this way, the racially color-blind person is able to maintain their racist and sexist belief by masking it with the grooming argument.

It has been argued that Color-blind Racial Ideology allows Whites and U.S. institutions such as schools to maintain a racially progressive and tolerant stance while legitimizing racial injustice (Gallagher, 2003; Lewis, 2003a; Staiger, 2004; Williams, 1997). Schools accomplish this task by teaching color-blind racial beliefs implicitly and sometimes explicitly in their curriculum (Lewis, 2003a). Because schools are social contexts that are able to create their own rules and norms, it makes sense that schools would teach and value the high standard of a racially color-blind environment. Although arguably a worthy ideal to strive for, schools aiming to communicate this ideal may inadvertently neglect to prepare their students for the racial reality that exists beyond their school. In fact, research shows that Black parents who strive to provide mainly color-blind socialization messages to their Black children also tend to provide less preparation for bias in the real world (Barr & Neville, 2008).

Other studies also suggest that Color-blind Racial Ideology is highly correlated with ethnocentrism and less multiculturalism. Blacks, as compared to Whites, have been shown to be more likely to endorse a multicultural ideology such that individuals acknowledge the important influence of race (Ryan,

Hunt, Weible, Peterson, & Casas, 2007). Whites, on the other hand, are more likely to endorse a Color-blind Racial Ideology (Ryan et al., 2007). In this same study, participants who more strongly endorsed a multicultural racial ideology relative to color-blindness also reported less ethnocentrism (Ryan, et al., 2007). Additionally, researchers have linked endorsement of racial color-blindness with fewer educational diversity experiences (learning about other groups and histories of discrimination), less appreciation for diversity, more beliefs in meritocracy, more negative views of Affirmative Action policies, and less multicultural competency among counseling graduate students (Aberson, 2007; Neville, Spanierman, & Doan, 2006; Spanierman et al., 2008). Consequently, racial color-blindness is associated with more ethnocentrism and less cultural sensitivity.

For example, parents may strive to be progressive by teaching their child(ren) that race ought not to matter, but legitimize racial injustice by neglecting to teach them that race has been, and continues to be, an unfortunate factor that divides and subjugates POC. Consequently, Whites endorsing color-blind beliefs have been shown to report higher levels of disintegrated identities (Gushue & Constantine, 2007). A disintegrated identity is the status of White identity associated with little to no awareness of racial privilege (Helms, 1995). These individuals tend to be unaware of the privileges that racism affords them for being White, albeit unintentionally (Gushue & Constantine, 2007). Additionally, individuals high in color-blindness have been shown to endorse more modern racist attitudes (Awad, Cokley, & Ravitch, 2005). Modern racist attitudes include beliefs that racism is a thing of the past, POC are attempting to move too quickly into places they are not wanted, POC gain entry to these places unfairly through policies like Affirmative action, and that POC have gained progress through unfair means (McConahay, 1986).

Color-Blind Racial Ideology Among People of Color

Although Color-blind Racial Ideology is often used in reference to beliefs of Whites, it is an ideology that POC may also endorse. Some researchers have argued that POC adopt a Color-blind Racial Ideology promoted by their school as a means of survival to help students feel protected from, adapt to, and cope with setting norms (Lewis, 2003b). For example, a study of Korean American students at a predominantly White suburban school in New Jersey (Marinari, 2005) found that in order to be academically successful, Korean students had to be "symbolically White" and "culture free" (p. 376). The school promoted the notion that race should not and does not matter without acknowledging that it was really White, middle-class standards that they promoted as the norm. Korean students at this school reported that to be successful they had to adopt the color-blind ideology that the school promoted and assimilate to standards seen as representing White culture. On the other hand, White students at the school felt that "visible Koreans" not willing to blend in with the White norm and make "American" friends posed a problem to the school climate. This study highlights the potential benefits of adopting a Color-blind Racial Ideology because it does offer one path to success and survival. However, the study also shows that these students had to deny their heritage culture in order to achieve success and survive within the color-blind environment. The alternative is not to succeed by the setting's standards, but not have to deny their cultural identity. In another example, a study conducted at a predominantly White university found that more endorsements of color-blind racial beliefs was linked to reports of both better general campus climate and better racial-ethnic campus climate, irrespective of the participant's race (Worthington, Navarro, Loewy, & Hart, 2008). This finding suggests that color-blind racial beliefs may help to reduce perceptions of discrimination and increase positive perceptions of the climate. In other words, when Asian Americans are in the minority, they may adopt color-blind beliefs to protect themselves against what may be a racially hostile environment should they hold opposing views regarding the influence of race.

Additional evidence suggests that POC may use color-blind racial ideology as a protective mechanism. In response to stressful experiences, Asian Americans have been shown to use avoidant coping, where they avoid thinking about and dealing with the source of their stress and wishful thinking. Asian Americans have also been shown to refuse to believe in the negative aspects of their experience, more than Blacks (Sheu & Sedlacek, 2004). Though Blacks report being more likely to engage in positive help-seeking behavior when it comes to professional resources, they seek help for emotional concerns at lower levels (Sheu & Sedlacek, 2004). However, Asian Americans report using wishful thinking to cope with stressful experiences at similar rates as Whites (Sheu & Sedlacek, 2004). Specifically pertaining to racism as a stressor, Asian Americans also report using avoidant coping strategies (Noh, Beiser, Kaspar, Hou, & Rummens, 1999; Sanders Thompson, 2006). Although avoidant coping may be beneficial in preventing individuals from perceiving discrimination and the resulting stress individuals may associate with the discrimination, coping research suggests avoidant coping to be a psychological risk factor, resulting in harmful responses to stressful events (Holahan & Moos, 1987). Following the avoidant coping literature, endorsing a color-blind racial ideology may be an indicator that POC are avoiding racial explanations of stressful experiences or avoiding thoughts regarding their stressful experiences altogether.

In addition to potentially reducing perceptions of racism and racism-related stress, endorsement of color-blind racial beliefs has also been linked to higher levels of internalized racism (Osajima, 1993). Internalized racism refers to a type of oppression where POC accept the methods and stereotypes of those in the majority group (i.e., White Americans). For example, among Black college students, higher endorsement of color-blind racial beliefs is related to higher levels of psychological false consciousness as indicated by more victim blaming in situations of social injustices, high levels of anti-egalitarian beliefs to justify social inequalities, and internalizing of more racist messages about Blacks (Neville, Coleman, Falconer, & Holmes, 2005). Research has found that participants who reported high levels of psychological false consciousness, where they hold strong negative beliefs about their racial group, also tended to report preferences for having White friends over Black friends (Neville et al., 2005). Consequently, it is important to consider both positive and negative consequences of endorsing color-blind racial beliefs.

Despite the American Psychological Association's acknowledgement of the importance of studying an individual's color-blind racial attitudes and the association's call for more scholarship in this domain (American Psychological Association, 1997), attention still needs to be given to strategies that color-blind individuals use to hide their discussions of race.

Color-blind ideology has a number of impacts on both Whites and POC in how they approach, or avoid, issues of race. In addition to the mental health impacts, subsequent sections will also discuss how the use of color-blind strategies contributes to upholding color-blind ideology.

RACIAL-COLOR-BLINDNESS IN EVERYDAY LIFE

In theory, racial color-blindness appears harmless or even ideal because people believe that if race is truly invisible, or not noticed, then racist and prejudicial thoughts and behaviors cannot occur (Apfelbaum, Norton, & Sommers, 2012). However, in practice people use color-blind strategies as a mechanism to hide their racist and prejudicial thoughts, attitudes, and behaviors.

Color-blind strategies are used in many different ways and in varying contexts ranging from the interpersonal to the societal, with varying consequences. While striving to not seem racist, at the interpersonal level, Blacks report that Whites who use color-blind strategies seem more racist than Whites who openly talk about race (Apfelbaum et al, 2012). In addition, individuals who have been exposed to racial color-blind ideology show both more implicit and explicit racial biases (Apfelbaum et al., 2012). Therefore, when people do not believe that race matters, they tend to also hold beliefs that non-Whites are inferior to Whites. Color-blindness also has an inverse effect at the workplace. Relative to racially aware organizations, those that endorse a color-blind ideology tend to lead their employees of color to report more racism in the work environment (Apfelbaum et al., 2012). Such color-blind organizations are likely to have policies that require POC to leave their culture at home as described in the earlier example of the military banning certain hairstyles. In another example, Abercrombie and Fitch fired a Muslim woman for refusing to remove her Hijab headscarf while working in the stockroom (Ho, 2011). While deeming them unprofessional and inappropriate, activists have challenged that the problem is a lack of understanding of the Muslim religious practice and racist ideas about Muslims.

It is important to note that both examples we provide here also highlight the issues of intersectionality, such that women of color are often subjected to experiences that are simultaneously racist and sexist. This is no coincidence. Women of color experience more on-the-job discrimination than both women alone and POC more generally (Cortina, Kabat-Farr, Leskinen, Huerta, & Magley, 2013). This, in turn, leads to higher rates of women of color leaving their job. So while discussing racism-based discrimination in color-blind policies, it is important to note the often times multiplicative nature of intersectional experiences.

Legally, the U.S. government has adopted color-blind strategies as the primary approach to issues of racial bias. In effect, racially conscious policies are deemed inappropriate and race-based policies are consistently voted down (Apfelbaum et al., 2012). For example in Schuette v. Coalition to Defend Affirmative Action (No. 12-682), the Supreme Court upheld that it is unconstitutional for public universities to use race in college admissions decisions. Frequently, the justification against race-based policies is that Whites' legal rights may be violated. Therefore, policies that attempt to achieve racial parity, such as affirmative action, are used as evidence of reverse discrimination that would privilege minorities over majority group members (i.e., Whites).

Perhaps most importantly, racial color-blindness has changed the way U.S. society talks about issues of race. Racial color-blind ideology results in a shift from a belief in distributive to procedural justice. So, instead of a belief in equal outcomes, racial color-blind ideology encourages equal treatment, regardless of existing racial inequalities (Apfelbaum et al., 2012). Let's consider hiring policies as an example. Color-blind individuals, therefore, tend to advocate for Latinos and Whites to be evaluated in exactly the same way. Racially conscious individuals, on the other hand, tend to advocate for policies to recognize the oppressive educational and social system that makes it more difficult for Latinos to, on paper, look like a White applicant. Ironically, adopting a racial color-blind ideology has resulted in Whites feeling overwhelmingly discriminated against based on race. In fact, Whites report that they are more discriminated against than Blacks in terms of race (Apfelbaum et al., 2012). Without attention to outcomes, people ignore the historical oppression faced by POC in U.S. society that had led to policies on equal treatment in the first place.

The neglect of historical oppression also leads to the neglect of women of color's experiences of oppression within the women's movement and the racial minority movement. Consideration of the both gender and race simultaneously will ensure that women of color are visible within both the women's movement and the racial movement.

The forms in which color-blindness takes in everyday life are plentiful and may be easy to understand when they are highlighted as we have done here. However, color-blindness is often more difficult to spot on-the-go and is so widely integrated into everyday life that it seems impervious to criticism. The following sections provide one example of an everyday conventional term that is strategically and sometimes unintentionally used to disguise discussions of race, the racial hierarchy, and White privilege.

American = White

Use of the term "American" is problematic on several levels. First, the concept is ethnocentric and frequently used by people in the U.S. to refer to themselves to the exclusion of other North American countries, Central American countries, and the entire continent of South America. Second, and more relevant to the current paper, is that the term "American" is also used to represent Whiteness.

Research has repeatedly found that people across racial groups equate American to Whiteness. Across racial and ethnic groups, the term "American" is more frequently and automatically associated with White faces (Devos & Heng, 2009). White American children aged 6 through11 yeaars report three requirements to being American: loving America, following its rules, and being White (Brown, 2011). Second-generation immigrants from various ethnic backgrounds typically report "true Americans" to be White with blonde hair and blue eyes (Park-Taylor et al., 2008). White Americans, on an implicit level, equate "White" and "American" with their own group, while Asian and African Americans are less likely associated with the term "American" (Devos & Banaji, 2005). This association is reflective of numerous factors, including political power, length of immersion, and social status, that have conspired to ensure "whiteness" as the default experience not only of racial identity, but national identity as well (Devos & Banaji, 2005).

Perhaps more problematic then using the term "American" to mean White is that learning about American culture is also synonymous with learning about the racial hierarchy. U.S. history is fraught with ideas of White supremacy. For example, as early as the 1600s, White European settlers regarded their way of life as technologically and morally superior to natives who had lived on the same land for centuries (Zinn, 2003). Soon after, settlers began to support their economic system using slavery that resulted in the mass kidnapping and subjugation of African people. Even after slavery was abolished, racism continued to be a useful device for social control that would discourage rebellions and maintain the status quo (Zinn, 2003). Given this legacy and system of oppression, it is no wonder that newcomers such as immigrants continue to quickly learn about the racial hierarchy that puts Whites at the top (Olsen, 1997). As a result, newcomers and descendents of slavery learn and internalize that the only "real Americans" are Whites

(Lee, 1996; Olsen, 1997). So, although people may explicitly use the term "American" to mean one thing, American implicitly connotes a system that promotes White supremacy, and worse, the subjugation of POC.

The problem extends beyond *how* the term "American" is used, and reaches to how POC are treated and not accepted as Americans. Barlow, Taylor, and Lambert (2000) surveyed White American, African American, and Cuban immigrants about the extent to which they personally felt American and that other White Americans accepted them as Americans. Findings showed that White Americans both felt American and that others accepted them as American. African Americans, on the other hand, reported feeling American, but that White Americans did not accept them as Americans. Cuban immigrants reported neither feeling American, nor being accepted as Americans. Asian Americans also experience similar identity denial on a regular basis (Cheryan & Monin, 2005). Consequently, it is not enough to insist that POC and immigrants build more sense of their American identity. They do not feel as though others accept them to be American. Therefore, their use of American to mean White may reflect this racial reality.

EMPIRICAL STUDY

In this section, we briefly describe two studies, highlighting the relevance of understanding how American is used by different groups of people. The first study uses focus groups to understand the social construction and understanding of what is American. The second study uses the social constructions extracted from Study 1 to see if there are differences in how people define the term American while responding to a psychological measure of acculturation.

Both studies use the Language, Identity, and Behavioral American Acculturation Measure (LIB-A; Birman & Trickett, 2001). An individual "acculturates" when they come into sustained, long-term contact with a new culture (Berry, 1980). The measure includes three subscales including nine items for language use and comprehension, seven items on holding an American identity, and 11 items measuring participation in American behaviors. Extensive work has been done to understand this process with different immigrant groups (Beiser, 2006). However, results have been inconsistent across groups (Rogler, Cortes, & Malgady, 1991), making an acculturation measure the ideal tool for understanding how participants define American.

Study 1 – Social Construction of "American"

Participants discussed ways of defining American concepts in 1 of 15 focus groups. Each focus group included three to five participants. There were no restrictions on focus group compositions (e.g., race, gender, age, sexual orientation). An open listing for the study allowed Psychology Participant Research Pool students to sign up for studies without knowing the purpose of the study. Therefore, groups had a mix of participants representing different racial/ethnic groups and genders. The researcher facilitated discussion about what participants thought about when answering each question and how participants defined each use of the term "American."

Thematic analyses revealed many different definitions and socially constructed uses of the term American. They varied from being very fact-based, to include those born in the United States and those who are U.S. citizens to more socially constructed uses that included only Blacks and Whites or Whites only. Even more varied was the use of American to mean all those who are from a racial/ethnic group different from the participant. For example, a Filipino American may perceive all those who are not Filipino to be American.

Study 2 – Group Differences in "American" Definitions

Using the definitions that emerged during the focus groups of Study 1, this study quantitatively tested how participants defined the term "American" as they responded to the LIB-A measure. Participants included 278 (190 women, 87 men, 5 unknown) Psychology Subject Pool students from a large public university in Illinois. The sample included 20 Black students, 93 White students, 57 Latino students, and 98 Asian American students.

As expected, one-way ANOVAS followed by Tukey post-hoc analyses showed significant differences in levels of American acculturation by generational status; $F(3,264) = 3.86$, $p = .01$. Immigrants ($M = 3.00$, $SD = .44$) reported the least American acculturation, followed by second generations ($M = 3.40$, $SD = .37$), and third and fourth generation students ($M = 3.61$, $SD = .29$) reported the highest levels of American acculturation. The only racial group differences existed between Asian Americans ($M = 3.26$, $SD = .48$) on the low end and Whites on the high end ($M = 3.47$, $SD = .41$)

Next, chi-squared cross-tabulations analyses evaluated the extent to which groups differed in how they defined the term American for each question in the LIB-A measure. Definitions for American differed by race/ethnicity on items referring to American movies, songs, doctors, friends, and clubs/parties. Definitions for American also differed by generational status on items referring to American restaurants, movies, food, songs, doctors, friends, and clubs/parties. Some of the interesting findings include the following. First and second generation participants who tended to be Asian American or Latino were more likely to report that American parties were those that included people outside of their ethnic group or family. When it comes to who is considered an American friend, Asian Americans are likely to define them to be friends who are White/Caucasian (37%) or English-speaking (35%).

African American/Black, White/Caucasian, and Latino/Hispanic participants reported defining American friends as either friends born in the United States (44%, 46%, 34%) or U.S. citizens (44%, 43%, 44%). A closer look reveals that Asian Americans and Latino/Hispanics are about twice as likely to define American friends to be Whites. African American/Blacks and White/Caucasians are about twice as likely *not* to report defining them to be Whites.

CONCLUSIONS & IMPLICATIONS

"American" is a socially constructed word that has meant different things to different groups of people over different generations. Asian Americans and Latinos in the study presented here, and in most other studies, only represent the first and second generations, while Blacks and Whites tend to represent the third generation and beyond. Such generational differences, especially of non-White individuals, are likely a sign of the socialization that immigrants and POC receive about who gets to be American and what the term American actually means when the term is used.

Implications for Clinicians and Counselors

As we know, words carry meaning that extend beyond the dictionary and harbor social constructions that span history. Words like American, and concepts like being racially color-blind, mask racial realities of privilege and oppression. This is true for Whites and for POC. Within the counseling relationship, it is important to consider both the therapist's use of vague and value-laden terms such as American, while simultaneously exploring the client's use of such terms. Casual use of color-blind terms is very likely to lead to misunderstandings and mistrust between the therapist and client, especially those that are not race-matched. Clients of color, for example, may come into therapy with a White therapist ready to test the therapist's racial consciousness and recognition of White privilege. The therapist, who uses proxies for Whiteness such as "American," will be signaling that s/he is racially color-blind. This interaction will likely result in mistrust and hinder the therapeutic relationship. It is important that therapists consider how such subtle indicators of racial color-blindness may affect the client-therapist relationship. To ignore this dynamic will prevent healing for the client, or worse, it may exacerbate the situation.

Even when a therapist and client are race-matched, it is important that color-blind terms are not assumed to carry the same meaning for each individual. It is likely that the client has not deeply and critically dissected her/his understanding and usage of racially color-blind terms like "American." This is a particularly important reminder because our study findings suggest that other important demographic characteristics, such as generational status, may influence how an individual uses socially constructed terms that may mask more dangerous and politically difficult discussions around race and gender.

Therapist and researchers alike ought to also be wary of leaning too heavily on previously constructed, and even validated, measures. Unfortunately, reflexivity is not yet a common practice among psychological researchers outside of those who do qualitative work. Therefore, it is almost always unclear the racial consciousness of researchers who develop psychological measures published for therapists and researchers. When it comes to understanding racial experiences, we urge therapists to err on the side of being overly cautious and to be highly critical of measures that use terms that are vague and unclear. One way to practice extreme caution is to have clients work through measurement tools with the therapist and share their construction of terms and items in the measure.

Ultimately, uncovering and removing the racially color-blind strategies now embedded in our U.S. English language requires understanding one another's live experiences as racial beings. It requires therapists to acknowledge her/his experiences of privilege and oppression while having compassion and an open-mindedness about the lived experience of others. In this way, socially constructed terms that mask racial color-blindness become places for connection, discussion, and reflection, rather than places for correction and diagnosis.

REFERENCES

Aberson, C. L. (2007). Diversity, merit, fairness, and discrimination beliefs as predictors of support for affirmative-action policy actions. *Journal of Applied Social Psychology, 37*(10), 2451–2474.

American Psychological Association. (1997). *Can – Or should – America be color-blind? Psychological research reveals fallacies in a color-blind response to racism* [*Pamphlet*]. Washington, DC: Author.

Apfelbaum, E. P., Norton, M. I., & Sommers, S. R. (2012). Racial color blindness: Emergence, practice, and implications. *Current Directions in Psychological Science, 21*(3), 205–209. doi:10.1177/0963721411434980

Awad, G. H., Cokley, K., & Ravitch, J. (2005). Attitudes toward affirmative action: A comparison of color-blind versus modern racist attitudes. *Journal of Applied Social Psychology, 35*(7), 1384–1399.

Barlow, K. M., Taylor, D. M., & Lambert, W. E. (2000). Ethnicity in America and feeling "American". *The Journal of Psychology, 134*(6), 581–600. doi:10.1080/00223980009598238

Barr, S. C., & Neville, H. A. (2008). Examination of the link between parental racial socialization messages and racial ideology among Black college students. *Journal of Black Psychology, 34*(2), 131–155. doi:10.1177/0095798408314138

Beiser, M. (2006). Longitudinal research to promote effective refugee resettlement. *Transcultural Psychiatry, 43*, 56–71. doi:10.1177/1363461506061757

Berry, J. W. (1980). Acculturation as varieties of adaptation. In A. Padilla (Ed.), *Acculturation: Theory, models, and findings*, (pp. 9–25). Boulder, CO: Westview.

Birman, D., & Trickett, E. J. (2001). Cultural transitions in first-generation immigrants: Acculturation of Soviet Jewish refugee adolescents and parents. *Journal of Cross-Cultural Psychology, 32*, 456–477. doi:10.1177/0022022101032004006

Bobo, L., Kluegel, J. R., & Smith, R. A. (1997). Laissez-faire racism: The crystallization of a kinder, gentler, antiblack ideology. In J. Martin & S. A. Tuch (Eds.), *Racial attitudes in the 1990s: Continuity and change.* Westport, CT: Praeger Publishers.

Brown, C. S. (2011). American elementary school children's attitudes about immigrants, immigration, and being an American. *Journal of Applied Developmental Psychology, 32*, 109–117. doi:10.1016/j.appdev.2011.01.001

Cheryan, S., & Monin, B. (2005). "Where are you really from?": Asian Americans and identity denial. *Journal of Personality and Social Psychology, 89*, 717–730. doi:10.1037/0022-3514.89.5.717

Cooper, H. (2014, April 20). Army's ban on some popular hairstyles raises ire of Black female soldiers. The New York Times, A11. Retrieved from http://www.nytimes.com/2014/04/21/us/politics/armys-ban-on-some-popular-hairstyles-raises-ire-of-black-female-soldiers.html?_r=1

Cortina, L. M., Kabat-Farr, D., Leskinen, E. A., Huerta, M., & Magley, V. J. (2013). Selective incivility as modern discrimination in organizations: Evidence and impact. *Journal of Management, 39*, 1579–1605. doi:10.1177/0149206311418835

Devos, T., & Banaji, M. R. (2005). American = White? *Journal of personality and social psychology, 88*(3), 447.

Devos, T., & Heng, L. (2009). Whites are granted the American identity more swiftly than Asians: Disentangling the roles of automatic and controlled processes. *Social Psychology, 40*, 192–201. doi:10.1027/1864-9335.40.4.192

Forman, T. A. (2004). Color-blind racism and racial indifference: The role of racial apathy in facilitating enduring inequalities. In M. Krysan & A. E. Lewis (Eds.). *The changing terrain of race and ethnicity* (pp. 43–66). New York: Russell Sage Foundation.

Gaertner, S. L., & Dovidio, J. F. (1986). *The aversive form of racism.* San Diego, CA: Academic Press.

Gallagher, C. A. (2003). Color-blind privilege: The social and political functions of erasing the color line in post race America. *Race, Gender & Class, 10*(4), 1–17.

Gushue, G. V., & Constantine, M. G. (2007). Color-blind racial attitudes and White racial identity attitudes in psychology trainees. *Professional Psychology: Research and Practice, 38*, 321–328. doi:10.1037/0735-7028.38.3.321

Helms, J. E. (1995). An update of Helms' White and people of color racial identity models. In J. G. Ponterotto, J. M. Casas, L. A., Suzuki, & C. M. Alexander (Eds.), *Handbook of multicultural counseling* (pp. 181–198). Thousand Oaks, CA: Sage.

Ho, V. (2011, June 27). Abercrombie & Fitch sued over hijab firing. SFGate. Retreived from http://www.sfgate.com/bayarea/article/Abercrombie-Fitch-sued-over-hijab-firing-2366495.php

Hochschild, J. (1995). *Facing up to the American dream: Race, class, and the soul of the nation.* Princeton, NJ: Princeton University Press.

Holahan, C. J., & Moos, R. H. (1987). Personal and contextual determinants of coping strategies. *Journal of Personality and Social Psychology, 52*(5), 946–955.

Kim, C. J. (2000). *Bitter fruit: The politics of Black-Korean conflict in New York City.* New Haven, CT: Yale University Press.

Lee, S. J. (1996). *Unraveling the "model-minority" stereotype: Listening to Asian American youth.* New York: Teachers College Press.

Lewis, A. E. (2003a). Everyday race-making: Navigating racial boundaries in schools. *American Behavioral Scientist, 47,* 283–305. doi:10.1177/0002764203256188

Lewis, A. E. (2003b). *Race in the schoolyard: Negotiating the color line in classrooms and communities.* New Brunswick, NJ: Rutgers University Press.

Marinari, M. (2005). Racial formation and success among Korean high school students. *The Urban Review, 37,* 375–398. doi:10.1007/s11256-005-0019-x

McConahay, J. B. (1986). Modern racism, ambivalence, and the modern racism scale. In J. F. Dovidio & S. L. Gaertner (Eds.), *Prejudice, discrimination, and racism,* (pp. 91–125). New York: Academic Press.

McConahay, J. B., & Hough, J. C. (1976). Symbolic racism. *Journal of Social Issues, 33* (2), 23–45.

Neville, H. A., Coleman, M. N., Falconer, J. W., & Holmes, D. (2005). Color-blind racial ideology and psychological false consciousness among African Americans. *Journal of Black Psychology, 31,* 27–45. doi:10.1177/0095798404268287

Neville, H. A., Lilly, R. L., Duran, G., Lee, R. M., & Browne, L. (2000). Construction and initial validation of the Color-Blind Racial Attitudes Scale (CoBRAS). *Journal of Counseling Psychology, 47,* 59–70. doi:10.1037/0022-0167.47.1.59

Neville, H., Spanierman, L., & Doan, B. T. (2006). Exploring the association between color-blind racial ideology and multicultural counseling competencies. *Cultural Diversity and Ethnic Minority Psychology, 12*(2), 275–290.

Noh, S., Beiser, M., Kaspar, V., Hou, F., & Rummens, J. (1999). Perceived racial discrimination, depression, and coping: A study of Southeast Asian refugees in Canada. *Journal of Health and Social Behavior, 40,* 193–207. doi:10.2307/2676348

Olsen, L. (1997). *Made in America: Immigrant students in our public schools.* New York: New Press.

Osajima, K. (1993). The hidden injuries of race. In L. A. Revilla, G. M. Nomura, S. Wong, & S. Hune (Eds.), *Bearing dreams, shaping visions: Asian Pacific American perspectives* (pp. 81–91). Pullman, WA: Washington State University Press.

Park-Taylor, J., Ng, V., Ventura, A. B., Kang, A. E., Morris, C. R., Gilbert, T., ... Androsiglio, R. A. (2008). What it means to be and feel like a "true" American: Perceptions and experiences of second-generation Americans. *Cultural Diversity and Ethnic Minority Psychology, 14,* 128–137. doi:10.1037/1099-9809.14.2.128

Rogler, L. H., Cortes, D. E., & Malgady, R. G. (1991). Acculturation and mental health status among Hispanics: Convergence and new directions for research. *American Psychologist, 46*(6), 585–597. doi:10.1037/0003-066x.46.6.585

Ryan, C. S., Hunt, J. S., Weible, J. A., Peterson, C. R., & Casas, J. F. (2007). Multicultural and colorblind ideology, stereotypes, and ethnocentrism among Black and White Americans. *Group Processes Intergroup Relations, 10,* 617–637.

Sanders Thompson, V. L. (2006). Coping responses and the experience of discrimination. *Journal of Applied Social Psychology, 36*(5), 1198–1214.

Sheu, H., & Sedlacek, W. E. (2004). An exploratory study of help-seeking attitudes and coping strategies among college students by race and gender. *Measurement and Evaluation in Counseling and Development, 37*(3), 130–143.

Spanierman, L. B., Poteat, V. P., Wang, Y. F., & Oh, E. (2008). Psychosocial costs of racism to white counselors: Predicting various dimensions of multicultural counseling competence. *Journal of Counseling Psychology, 55*(1), 75–88.

Staiger, A. (2004). Whiteness as giftedness: Racial formation at an urban high school. *Social Problems, 51*(2), 161–181. doi:10.1525/sp.2004.51.2.161

Thompson, C. E., & Neville, H. A. (1999). Racism, mental health, and mental health practice. *Counseling Psychologist, 27,* 155–223. doi:10.1177/0011000099272001

Williams, P. J. (1997). *Seeing a color-blind future: The paradox of race.* New York: Noonday Press.

Worthington, R. L., Navarro, R. L., Loewy, M., & Hart, J. (2008). Color-blind racial attitudes, social dominance orientation, racial-ethnic group membership and college students' perceptions of campus climate. *Journal of Diversity in Higher Education, 1,* 8–19. doi:10.1037/1938-8926.1.1.8

Zamudio, M. M., & Rios, F. (2006). From traditional to liberal racism: Living racism in the everyday. *Sociological Perspectives, 49,* 483–501. doi:10.1525/sop.2006.49.4.483

Zinn, H. (2003). *A people's history of the United States: 1492-present.* New York, NY: Pearson Education.

Slicing White Bre(a)d: Racial Identities, Recipes, and Italian-American Women

ANDREA L. DOTTOLO

Psychology Department, Rhode Island College, Providence, Rhode Island; and Women's Studies Research Center, Brandeis University, Waltham, Massachusetts

This article focuses on Italian-American women and on how they construct, understand, and maintain their ethnic identity in relation to Whiteness and White privilege. Since language cannot serve as symbol for these women because speaking Italian was often forbidden in their homes, or spoken only between adults in covert communications, they often must cling to other symbols of Italianness in order to preserve their sense of gendered ethnic identities. I argue that one such symbol is food, wherein participants manipulate recipes and use food to navigate and negotiate being both Italian and American, Whiteness, femininity, and social class. Implications for therapy about how we understand our multiple identities in relation to others as part of larger systems of power and privilege are explored.

Andrea: Is there anyone you would not give the recipe to?
Sophia: No, no, no no. I mean, nobody ever [asked], you know... oh, I got this great pasta and beans recipe, I mean, it's simple. Even a medigan could do it. [Laughter]

Sophia sits at her kitchen table in this interview—feisty, unassuming, full of laughter, and speaking with ease. This quote is an excerpt from an interview which is part of a study on Italian American women, identity and food that is the focus of this article. I begin this article with the words of Sophia, one of the women, in order to set the stage, to introduce and contextualize this study.

(All names of interviewees are pseudonyms.) This article explores previously unexplored aspects of Italian-American women's racial identity and its connections to food from a psychological perspective, including the following research questions: How do Italian-American women see themselves as both similar and different from "White" women? How do Italian-American women both cling to White privilege, while simultaneously distancing from White Anglo Saxon Protestants (WASPs)? How do Italian-American women use food as a medium through which to understand themselves as "real" Italians, and as different from women who are not of Italian ancestry? Why is it important for therapists to consider variations of Whiteness in their practice?

A term that is important here, related to the quote above, and central to this study, is *medigan*. It is Italian-American slang for "American." Imagine someone with a thick Italian accent pronouncing the word, and it sounds like "Ah-med-i-gan," which then became truncated to *medigan*. It is never a compliment in any context, but a derogatory term used to mark those who are not Italian. This is obvious in the quote above, where Sophia explains that the recipe is so simple that "even a *medigan* could do it." It is used most often as a noun, to technically (and disdainfully) describe anyone who is not Italian, but the most usual application is WASPs (White Anglo-Saxon Protestants) or other "Whiter" groups. It is almost never used to describe a person of color, or even anyone whose ethnicity is readily identifiable (other than White). This composes a complicated message about race, class, history, ethnicity, and culture, as it is used to distinguish Italian Americans from Whites as "Other" (implying some sort of cultural superiority). It might also be used as patronizing, as in, "the poor *medigans,* they just don't know any better" (implying that "real" Italians do). And in the expression from Sophia, above, it is also about gender and performances of femininity, as she is also implicitly referring to non-Italian women in the discussion of recipes and cooking.

While there have been significant contributions about Italian-American women in the fields of history, sociology, and literature, (e.g., Bona, 1999; di Leonardo, 1987; Gabaccia & Iacovetta, 2002; Giunta, 2002; Guglielmo, 2010) very little research has been conducted from a psychological perspective. Given the paucity of scholarship in psychology as a whole about Italian-American women, there is an even greater absence of literature in psychology interpreted through a feminist lens focusing on this population.

This article focuses on Italian-American women and on how they construct, understand, and maintain their ethnic identity in relation to Whiteness and White privilege. Since language cannot serve as symbol for these women because speaking Italian was often forbidden in their homes, or spoken only between adults in covert communications, they often must cling to other symbols of Italianness in order to preserve their sense of gendered ethnic identities. I argue that one such symbol is food, wherein participants manipulate recipes and use food to navigate and negotiate being both Italian and

American, Whiteness, femininity, and social class. Exploring the mechanisms through which women understand who they are in relation to others, and how their multiple identities are situated within systems of power and privilege has important clinical implications for therapy.

SOCIAL IDENTITIES

This study is situated in social identity theory, where scholars often credit much of the groundwork in the field to American psychologist Henri Tajfel (1981), who described social identity as "that part of an individual's self-concept which derives from his *[sic]* knowledge of his *[sic]* membership of a social group (or groups) together with the value and emotional significance attached to that membership" (p. 255). It is group membership that informs, constructs and maintains social identity. Jenkins (1996) offers a similar characterization, "Social identity is our understanding of who we are and of who other people are, and, reciprocally, other people's understanding of themselves and of others (which includes us)" (p. 5). Group membership and group relations serve as interpretive signifiers, directing social navigation. This is especially relevant when considering how Italian-American women understand their own Italianness and Whiteness in relation to others who are both similar and different from them.

However, social identities cannot be examined in a vacuum. Feminist theories of intersectionality inform us that our multiple social identities intersect and are mutually constitutive, so that I cannot examine Whiteness without also considering gender and class, for example (Crenshaw, 1995; Combahee River Collective, 1977/2005; Dottolo & Stewart, 2008).

Marecek (1995) provides an illustrative example of intersectionality, highlighting its significance to scholars of social identity:

> To say that I am a White, middle-class, North American woman is not to say that I am part woman, part White, and part late 20th century North American. If I were fitted out with skin of a different color, or transported into a different moment of history, I would no longer be the woman I am now. (p. 163)

Marecek (1995) demonstrates not only the importance of including multiple identities and institutional structures in our analyses, but also highlights how our insights might be lacking, that our appreciation for narratives of identity will inherently exclude or ignore potentially significant dimensions in capturing a fuller, more accurate account. While she does not indicate her ethnic origin, Marecek describes herself as "White," using that term, which is also different from the Italian-American women in this study. This is not to say that they claim that they are *not* White, but that they situate themselves in relation to a particular American, WASP ideal of Whiteness.

Similarly, in Kaschak's (2011) discussion of a "mattering map," a model of contextual feminist therapy, she explains, "there are multiple energetic forces impinging upon an individual and any social interaction" (p. 11). This study aims to employ these feminist theories in order to examine the implications of White ethnic identities in a therapeutic context.

WHITENESS

One of the most notable qualities of Whiteness is precisely its "unremarkableness." Because Whiteness is seen as "natural" or a default identity in many national and international contexts, it often goes unnoticed, hidden, taken for granted as "normal." McIntosh (2001) characterized White privilege as "an invisible package of unearned assets" (p. 30). Whiteness, as well as all other racial categories, is not static but shifting, fluid, always a product of socio-historical context. In other words, many groups in the United States who are now considered White, especially the Irish, Jews, and Italians, did not always have access to all of the privileges granted to them, and their racial status was the target of much debate.

Jacobson (1998) traces the political history of Whiteness in the United States from the early years of the Republic through the Civil Rights era. A series of particularly significant historical moments in the making of Whiteness resulted from the flood of European immigrants that arrived in the mid-late 19th and early 20th centuries. By 1924, the United States had had "enough" of the new immigrants for a few decades, and the time had come to revise its immigration policy. The Johnson-Reed act of 1924 enforced a quota system restricting entrance of Eastern and Southern Europeans, who were questionably, or not-quite-all-the-way White, as well as those officially considered non-White. These new categories were a result of "racial science" and the law joining forces, dividing people into three racial possibilities: "Caucasian, Mongoloid and Negroid" (Jacobson, 1998, p. 94). Partially because Italians were never legally deemed non-White, and for the most part happened to have arrived before 1924, Italians became firmly situated as White or "Caucasian." Guglielmo (2003) articulates the particular histories of the Roman Empire and the Renaissance in Italy as crucial in attributing Whiteness to Italian-ness. He states, "anti-immigrant racialists had to exercise caution in their color-questioning of Italians, for if Italians were not White, a good deal of Western civilization might not have been either" (p. 41).

Jacobson explains, "to become 'Caucasian' in the 1920s and after ... was not simply to be 'White' ... it was to be *conclusively, certifiably, scientifically* White. 'Caucasian' identity represents a Whiteness discovered and apprehended by that regime of knowledge whose cultural authority is greatest" (p. 95). (For a discussion of the making of Whiteness for these specific groups, see Ignativev, 1995 on the Irish; Brodkin, 2004 on Jews; and Guglielmo, 2003 on Italians). This racial status continued to grant those groups lucky enough to be included in the new definition all the advantages that Whiteness had to offer.

Many disciplines, including psychology, perpetuate a regime of "scientific" Whiteness in their research, often in allowing Whiteness to go unmarked. Brekhus (1998) employs the terms "marked" and "unmarked" to describe the social and academic categories to which we pay more or less attention, depending on our classifications. Brekhus (1998) offers

> The marked represents extremes that stand out as either remarkably "above" or remarkably 'below' the norm. The unmarked represents the vast expanse of social reality that is passively defined as unremarkable, *socially generic,* and profane. (emphasis in original, p. 35)

In privileging the unmarked, the marked becomes articulated and foregrounded, receiving disproportionate attention and exaggerating its distinctiveness, making them also less "normal." Marked groups are often homogenized, and "characteristics of a marked member are generalized to all members of the marked category but never beyond the category, while attributes of an unmarked member are either perceived as idiosyncratic to the individual or universal to the human condition" (Brekhus, 1998, p. 36). Brekhus (1998) argues that our disproportionate attention to marked categories reproduces the "epistemological blindspotting" of unmarked categories (p. 39). Morawski (2004) refers to this in relaying psychology's obsession with showing differences. Therefore, Brekhus calls for an intentional "reverse marking" as an "explicit strategy for foregrounding the unmarked as though it were unusual and ignoring the marked as though it were mundane" (p. 43). Focusing on the unmarked is not intended to reinscribe privilege, but precisely to destabilize it, bringing attention to mechanisms and technologies of power and control. My intention for this research is to integrate this as an overt political strategy. I am continually aware, as Apple (1998) warns

> We must be on our guard to ensure that a focus on Whiteness doesn't become one more excuse to recenter dominant voices and to ignore the voices and testimony of those groups of people whose dreams, hopes, lives, and very bodies are shattered by current relations of exploitation and domination. (p. xi)

Many Whites do not recognize or acknowledge race as a self-descriptor (Dottolo & Stewart, 2013). When Whites *do* access social identities related to race, they are often in the form of ethnic or cultural identities. Although there are many interesting historical accounts of the ways in which many European ethnic groups *became* White according to official U.S. policies as described above, (Brodkin, 2004; Guglielmo, 2003; Ignatiev, 1995), many of these ethnic communities remain and ethnicity serves as a central social identity for its members. For example, when Sue (2004) asked Whites on the street about race, he found that, "a significant number of respondents denied being White by saying "I'm not White; I'm [Irish], [Italian], [Jewish], [German] ... " It was obviously easier for them to acknowledge their ethnicity than their skin color ... " (p. 764). Although many White ethnics may not *deny* their Whiteness, ethnic and cultural identifiers might be more readily available to them. This is to say that, for instance, being Irish, Italian and Jewish are still meaningful identities for many Americans. The distinctions between these (White) groups serve as important markers of "us" and "them" in many places, (most notably in east-coast urban neighborhoods.) Even though declaring "I am Irish" or "I am Italian" is, in essence, stating "I am White," the cultural meaning, I argue, intended by the speaker and interpreted by the listener does not convey that message. Indeed, the women in this study who talk about being Italian are often able to point to specific foods, rituals, values, and cultural practices that mark their "Italian-ness" as unique. In addition, there are phenotypes associated with each group, where an individual might "look" Irish or Italian, also placing them in relative proximity to a physically White ideal. Either way, for "ethnic" and "non-ethnic" Whites, it is precisely their Whiteness that it hidden from view.

Italian insistence on retaining a cultural identity led many to continue to emphasize the ways in which they were distinct from Whites. However, because of the obvious advantages of White privilege, many Italian-Americans went to great lengths to "assimilate" into American Whiteness, often by adopting more American food tastes and products. This is not unique to Italians, and many ethnic immigrant groups have historically done the same. In the HBO series *The Sopranos,* the lead character, Tony Soprano, played by the late James Gandolfini, reveals his resentment of the attempt by other Italians, specifically Dr. Cusamano, his neighbor and physician, to Whitewash himself when he calls him a "Wonderbread WOP." It is precisely this disdain that Tony has toward Italians who want to assimilate that contributes to the racial ambiguity in Italian-American culture.

"WOP" is a slur historically used against Italians, popularly thought to date from the inscription for "without papers" stamped by Ellis Island officials on to immigration documents. Contrary to popular belief, that is likely *not* the derivation of the term, but from the Neopolitan word "guappo," or one who is arrogant, overbearing, and brash, often to the point of inducing a fight. It can also refer to members of the "Guapperia," a Neopolitan crime organization. Either way, "WOP" acts as a class indicator, representing those who are institutionally marginalized. Tony Soprano's use of the phrase "Wonderbread," is also significant, stemming from the idea that "real" Italians would always and only eat Italian bread, and never processed American "white" bread. In this way, white bread equals White bred. Food represents ethnic identity, and in reference to the title of this article, variations of Whiteness, different "slices" of racial formations. Tony further accuses Cusamano of "eat[ing] his Sunday gravy [meaning tomato sauce] out of a jar," which even more seriously attacks his Italian authenticity. Ruth Frankenberg makes a related argument about the use of food and commodities as a metaphor for race. She notes that Whiteness is often signified in narratives by commodities and brands. "Wonderbread, Kleenex, Heinz 57. In this identification, witnesses came to be seen as spoiled by capitalism, and as being linked to capitalism in a way that other cultures supposedly are not" (Frankenberg, 1993, p.199).

METHOD

It was important that the method for this study on Italian-American women and food was rooted in the words of the women themselves, since their narratives of identity were the central feature. Qualitative methods, especially interviews, were most coherent with the research questions.

Participants

Interviewees were 13 "baby boomer" women who self-identified as Italian American living in Syracuse, New York. All are working class and heterosexual. The "baby boom" generally refers to individuals born between 1945 and 1965, which would place the women in their 50 s and 60 s at the time of interview. Through interview prompts, participants reflected upon messages received from their parents' generation, implementation of recipes, understanding of identity in their own generation, and discussion of their wishes and intentions of ideas and feelings to convey to future generations, including their children and possibly grandchildren. Their life stage and generation enables examination of their understanding of their situated Whiteness. Focusing on this sample allows for exploration of Italian-American femininity in a particular socio-historical context and geographical location. Women of this era came of age in the 1950s and 60 s, marking a particular moment in American nationalism, while negotiating being the grandchildren of Italian immigrants, some of whom likely faced more overt discrimination of Italian "conditional" Whiteness (Jacobson, 1998).

All participants self-identified as Italian American, naming one or more grandparents as emigrating from Italy. That is, all interviewees and their parents were born in the U.S., and for some, several grandparents as well, making the women in this study several generations removed from migration. None of the participants could speak Italian, and were the product of parents and grandparents ensuring the Americanization of their daughters by purposefully not teaching them their language. In most cases, Italian language was reserved for covert communication between grandparents, and sometimes parents, but, as children, excluded the women interviewed.

Why Syracuse?

Syracuse is an industrial city in central New York, and derives its name from Siracusa, a city on the eastern coast of Sicily. Italians in Syracuse settled on the North Side of the city, mostly around the turn of the 20th century, as they did in many other American cities. The significant population of Italian Americans allowed for an ethnographic approach to this study, exploring the ways in which ethnic and immigrant identities are connected to place and space. Syracuse also represents one of the many cities on the east coast of the United States that contains White ethnic enclaves, which is not as omnipresent in other regions such as the west coast of the United States. The women in this study grew up within a large community of other Italian Americans, suggesting that their ethnic identity development and constructions of Whiteness may have been different than those who were the only Italians in their neighborhood or community (Laurino, 2000). Furthermore, my own family of origin has long established roots in Syracuse, and it is where we were born and raised. These connections and relationships to the community facilitated trust in the participants as well as the use of snowball sampling (Dottolo & Dottolo, 2015).

The Interview

Participants were recruited through family and community relationships, and each woman was asked to bring a recipe to the interview. Participants were informed that they would be asked questions about the recipe of an Italian dish that they brought to the interview, questions about their ideas and feelings about food in general, and being Italian American. Interviews averaged about 30 minutes in length, were audio recorded and transcribed verbatim.

Other ethnic identity researchers have also employed methodologies that focus participants on an object or cultural product, such as a photograph (Nenga, 2003). For example, Banks (2000) explores how Black women's narratives and conversations about hair and hairstyling practices are especially representative of the politics of race, gender, class, identity, self-esteem, social control, and power. While Banks might have asked her interviewees questions about these topics directly, discussions about hair seemed to allow women to freely discuss a familiar topic while revealing significant and symbolic meanings. This study is inspired by Banks' work, in that the research design was intended to engage Italian American women in discussion about a familiar and tangible topic that is rich with multiple meanings and connections to ethnicity, immigration, gender, generation, and class.

Verbatim transcripts were coded for Italian American identity in terms of expressions reflecting: 1. The use of the term *medigan*, or "American," and 2. Responses to the question, "Do you think food plays a more significant role in your life as an Italian compared to women who are not Italian?" Specifically, if participants mentioned a referent group in their answer, comparing the role of food to another specific ethnic group "who is not Italian," then this was also coded. The categories were not mutually exclusive, so a participant might both use the term *medigan* as well as name a particular non-Italian referent group, and each were coded accordingly. Several subcategories emerged as instantiations of these two major themes, which will be described in the results section.

If It's Not One Thing ... It's Your Mother

A unique element of this project is that I am working with my mother, Carol, who co-created the interview protocol with me. Carol also still lives in Syracuse, where she, her mother, and her grandmother lived all their lives. Carol was a key recruiter of participants, as she is a "baby boomer" herself, and she also conducted a majority of the interviews. It was important that the participants felt they were speaking to a peer, who could relate and remember alongside them. She also contributed to the analysis along the way (Dottolo & Dottolo, 2015).

RESULTS: CONSTRUCTING ITALIAN AMERICAN WHITENESS

Medigan

As noted in the introduction and epigraph of this article, *medigan* is Italian-American slang for "American," although its use is derogatory, comparative, and complex. It is used by Italian Americans to refer to three somewhat different but potentially overlapping groups: 1) White Anglo Saxon Protestants, or WASPs; 2) any "Whiter" person with a non-identifiable ethnic identity (such as those who say they are "just White," "mongrels," or "a little bit German, a little bit Irish, English, French and Dutch ... "—importantly, each of these components are White ethnic groups); or 3) those clearly identifiable "Whiter ethnics" that are not Italian, such as those groups mentioned above. It is important to note that the women in this study grew up in Syracuse in a time when there were strong German and Irish neighborhoods. In fact, there is still a prominent Irish contingency on the West side of the city, known as "Tipperary Hill."

Five of the interviews contain the use of the term *medigan*, but none mentioned the word "White." On the one hand, this is a feature of their White privilege, in that they certainly understand themselves as White, especially in this large Italian-American community, and do not need to assert their Whiteness, an indicator of its invisibility. On the other hand, they use this slang term for "American" to refer to those "Whiter" than themselves, albeit in a disdainful way. This might reflect Jacobson's (1998) idea of Italian American status as conditional, though certifiably White. To use another example from the television series *The Sopranos,* in a therapy session in the first season, Tony complains to Dr. Melfi, his therapist, that his wife, Carmela, wants him to make new friends by attending a neighborhood barbecue near their suburban home. Tony dreads such occasions because, "the medigans are boring." Dr. Melfi, who is also Italian American, understands yet misinterprets his statement and asks, "So do you not consider yourself White?" She may also be challenging his

White privilege in this therapeutic moment. Tony replies, "I don't mean White, like Caucasian, I mean *medigan*." Tony's derision is also class-based, as his *medigan* suburban neighbors talk about stock options and golf at these gatherings, topics Tony finds both uninteresting and alienating.

The following excerpt is from an interview with Annie for a recipe for "stuffed calamari":

> Andrea: Do you know if there is a more authentic or more Italian version of the recipe?
> Annie: There might be. In Italy, you make things different than we do here. So they might do it without the sauce. I do know that they put the tentacles in. And there are some of us who don't....[points to her husband, who is sitting at the table. He shakes his head, as if to say, "no way!"]
> Andrea: So you don't eat the tentacles at all?
> Annie: He's half *medigan*, remember? [Laughter].
> … …. But I mean, I'm not opposed to eating the tentacles, especially, you know, you can fry them, and whatever. But, no, I don't put them in there because we have some people in our family… my son-in-law is Slovakian-Czechoslovakian. And the kids, I don't know how the kids would react to that. The grandkids.

Here Annie reveals that she doesn't know if there is a more authentic version of the recipe ("there might be"). She knows that "in Italy they do things differently there," but she doesn't exactly know what that means, revealing her American socialization and status. She points out that her husband refuses to eat the tentacles, marking him as not a "real" Italian, more specifically, (and maybe worse) he is half *medigan*. In this case, his mother was German, which is an especially representative type of non-Italian other, especially since there was also a significant German population in Syracuse. However, Annie *is* a "real" Italian because she would eat the tentacles. Other than her husband, there are other non-Italians that she has to contend with, contributing to her omission of the tentacles in the dish. Her son-in-law is not Italian at all, *medigan* ("Slovakian- Czechoslovakian"), and clearly marked as non-Italian "other," though clearly White. Also, her grandkids will also likely reject such a version of the dish, both because her children have married non-Italians, and also because the subsequent generations are just more Americanized, becoming more "Whitewashed" with time and acculturation (Dottolo & Dottolo, 2015).

Similarly, Rita admits that when she was married to her husband and raising children that her cooking "was more *medigan*." When I asked if her husband was Italian, she said:

> He was Irish and Polish. … It's funny because he thought his mom made the best sauce in the world, but it was really like salsa. [Laughs] Because they put everything in it. And then he had mine and he loved it.

She laughs at the ridiculousness of an Italian tomato sauce likened to salsa, and that her husband didn't know any better but to like it. But once he was "educated" about her "authentic" food, he couldn't help but "love it."

Connie uses the term *medigan* twice in her interview with Carol, where she explains that she is really the only person in her immediate family, other than her mother, who likes to cook:

> Connie: My sister is not an Italian cook. She cooks very *medigan*.

She continues to lament that her daughter is not interested in learning the traditional Italian recipes, preserving the culture, but that her son's girlfriend, who is not Italian, often asks Connie questions and demonstrates interest:

> Connie: She could definitely be the one who would carry on recipes, and do things the Italian way... so my *medigan* future daughter-in-law would be the one to carry things on! Who knew?

Again, this is especially gendered, as it is the non-Italian women learning to cook for their Italian husbands that is part of this heteronormative script.

While *medigan* is used to refer to non-Italian White others with disgust and/or pity, the word "American" was used differently, and in the case of one woman, Paula, an American woman seemed to signify progressive, liberated, and fashionable. She recounts that when she left home to go to school she lived with roommates of Irish and English descent, where they taught her to cook different kinds of foods. When she returned to Syracuse to care for her mother, she introduced these foods to her mother, foods like "broiled meat and fish, vegetables, rice... less pasta, some casserole..." She explains that these were foods never eaten in a traditional Italian meal repertoire, especially "never a casserole," and describes this food as "more Americanized." Upon further reflection, she notices that there are many ways that her mother was "less Italian," and when I pressed her, she said:

> Paula: Well, she didn't wear the black dress and black stockings I can tell you that... you know, my mother was always dressed. I mean, she worked downtown in a women's department store. And she [had] the hats, and, you know, the gloves... even when she was young. She just, she wasn't the stereotype Italian that you think of.
> Andrea: Can you think of other ways that she became more American, other than her food?
> Paula: ...Going back to work. I mean, that was unheard of back then... that was unheard of at that time. You know, the woman stayed home. You know, she took care of the house. But, she went back to work. ... 'Cause my father worked in construction, and he didn't work in the winter. And that's when, you know, you needed, you

know, that's when health insurance started to come out. And you needed that stuff. So she went back to work when I was ten.

Paula refers to the traditional practice of Italian widows dressing entirely in black, confined to the role of widow, mourning their husbands for the rest of their lives. Even after Paula's father died, her mother continued to work outside the home, and did not conform to these feminized scripts that seem outdated according to Paula.

Even though Paula's mother worked outside the home out of economic necessity, she equates her mother's "Americanness" with dressing well and entering the workforce. She speaks with admiration about these qualities, which differ in tone and content from those of a *medigan*. In this case, an "American," *White,* woman is admirable, successful, and liberated- perhaps even something to aspire to, maybe representing an idealized and desired condition of middle class Whiteness.

WOMEN WHO ARE NOT ITALIAN

Toward the end of the interview, participants were asked, "Do you think food plays a more significant role in your life as an Italian compared to women who are not Italian?" Responses to this question provide information about who comes to mind for these women when asked to discuss non-Italian others, especially related to the ways in which they might situate their Whiteness. Social identity theorists are concerned with understanding both in-group and out-group boundaries, and in this case, who gets referenced as "not us," or "them" (Tajfel, 1981; Jenkins, 2000). Seven participants mentioned, either implicitly or explicitly, other White groups in response to this question, mostly those considered *medigan*. None mentioned racial minorities. One set of responses demonstrates an interesting case about perceptions of Jews.

Explicit Naming of a White Other

One of the more colorful responses to this question was about the Irish, mentioned by two different women. As mentioned previously, there is a significant Irish immigrant settlement in Syracuse, and these women grew up with the Irish, probably as their most contentious White ethnic rival. I grew up hearing the saying, "The Italians and the Irish—they either are killing each other or getting married." Rita's response demonstrates that both might be true:

> Andrea: Do you think that food plays a more significant role in your life as an Italian, compared to women who are not Italian?

Rita: Yes... Um well food is used like, you know, when somebody's sick you bring them food. When somebody dies, you bring them food. If they've had a baby and they can't cook, you bring them—it's a comfort. It just how we were raised, it's just what we do. You know, other nationalities might drink, but you know, food's just always been that way. You know, people come to your house after a death and the first thing they do is come in with, you know, god knows, a wheel of cheese or lasagna or whatever. So uh yes, I think Italians definitely.

Andrea: And you mentioned that other nationalities might drink. Are there other comparisons that you can think of how... Italian women use food differently than other nationalities might?

Rita: Well, like in our family, if somebody dies and you go back to somebody's house, there's not a bar set up. Whereas I've been to other funerals and everybody just gets drunk. And that upset me tremendously, so I said, 'I'm not doing this anymore.' You know, there were a couple of instances and I just said, "No more, I won't go," because it's too upsetting to me.

Andrea: So you associate that with a particular ethnicity?

Rita: Mm hmm.

Andrea: Irish, I'm guessing?

Rita: [Nods].

Andrea: Yeah, yeah. Yes, I understand.

Rita: And not all... because I have a lot of friends. But this was my ex-husband and his friends and how they—how they handled it. That's what they—and I'd never been exposed to anything like that. I'd only been exposed to Italians.

Andrea: Do you think that drinking is seen differently in Italian culture?

Rita: Yes, definitely. I mean with us, it's just—you know, you just have a glass of wine with dinner and that's enough, whereas other people, they just have to drink to block the pain or whatever. It's just their way of coping. I mean when I read *Angela's Ashes*, I was like, "This is worse than I ever thought." And I worked with this Irish guy who married an Italian girl, and I'd go in every day and say, "I cannot believe the poverty I cannot believe the poverty and how you drink away your"... and just how these men would earn a living, living in complete poverty, but they would go drink away their earnings. And it just—because in an Italian family, your family comes first. That's just how it is. So uh you know, and it was a big issue between my husband and I, you know, the drinking and so on. And even when I was around his family—but his father's side, which is Polish, that was a lot different. You know, it was just the Irish and Italian.

Rita contrasts the role of food and drink between Italian and Irish culture, and is especially disturbed by the centrality of alcohol for the Irish, namely in the social circle of her ex-husband.

It is notable that Rita does not mention the name of the group specifically until she is pushed. She attributes these differences to core values in both groups, and uses this to mark those who are different from her. Perhaps she knows that alcoholism is part of a stereotype for the Irish, and worries that it might be in bad taste to be so specific. But once the interviewer mentions the group name, she continues to describe her emotional responses of shock, discomfort, and perhaps even disgust, resulting in her refusal to attend similar events.

Food for Rita represents family, as was the case for many other participants, and her observations of the ways in which the Irish use food and alcohol symbolically translate into their lack in valuing family. She also mentions the Polish as another White other, who are "different" from the Irish, perhaps implicitly "not as bad," but different nonetheless. Rita's deep connection to food and family values is revealed in her explanation of the central role of food in intimate life events, including birth and death. For Rita, the Irish serve as a powerful example of a different kind of Whiteness, one that is especially emotionally loaded for her.

Implicit Naming of White Other

Sometimes participants did name a specific ethnic group, but implicitly referred to non-Italian, *medigan* others in their response. Similar to Rita, Karen discusses the central role of food for Italian women, especially its emotional significance and ties to family:

> Andrea: Do you think food plays a more significant role in your life as an Italian, compared to women who are not Italian?
> Karen: Absolutely.
> Andrea: And how do you see that?
> Karen: Um...I think Italian women think more of—think of food in a more emotional way than non-Italian women. I think Italian women think of it more as a way to gather your family and to please your family. And I think non-Italian women don't look at it that way. I think it's more of a means to an end.

When the interviewer tries to get Karen (who currently lives in the southeast United States) to name a particular group, instead of indicating their ethnic origin, she names their home state:

> Andrea: Have you seen examples of—that you might be able to speak to —of women who are not Italian, and if they weren't Italian, what ethnicity they may have been—that you can see a comparison?
> Karen: (sighs) Well um...let me think about this a minute. I mean my friends here—and you know the south is very much a melting pot—I have one very good friend who's from Oklahoma, I have another very good friend who's from Pennsylvania. They're both non-Italian. I'm not even sure of their ethnicity...

Particularly for Italian Americans who settled in the northeastern United States, any region that rings of the Midwest, (or is not New York, New Jersey, or New England) comes to stand in as bland, White other, the prototype of *medigan*. In this case, Karen names Pennsylvania (likely not Philadelphia or Pittsburgh) and Oklahoma to most closely mark the ethnic identities of her friends. This is also an example of White privilege, in that what is not said, what is invisible, is that these friends are White. It is precisely that they are unmarked (Brekhus, 1998) that reveals their Whiteness. Even while mentioning that the south is a "melting pot," a (problematic) term used to indicate racial diversity and immigrant "assimilation," those who come to mind for Karen that are not Italian are unidentifiable White others:

"You're from Ohio, so what?"

Karen's response also speaks to the importance of region of the United States in the development of Italian ethnic identity. For east coast Italians, there tends to be a belief that the further away you are from Ellis Island, the most common entry point for Italians upon immigration, the less authentically Italian you can be. This idea is informed by the notion that an authentic Italianness is diluted through distance and consistent intermingling with the *medigans*.

Jews

Two women named Jews as a group that are not Italian, but did so in contrasting ways:

> Andrea: Do you think food plays a more significant role in your life as an Italian compared to women who are not Italian?
> Annie: Yes. [Answers immediately]
> Andrea: ...and how? You think of examples?
> Annie: Just because of the way we were raised. You know? I mean, Italian mothers... are more concerned with their kids eating than studying, I think.

Similar to Rita, Annie does not mention the name of a specific group at first:

> Andrea: Can you think of examples where you saw a contrast between Italians and others?
> Annie: Uh, yes. I had a Jewish friend when I was young—[she] didn't think about lunch. I was, I remember being in awe of that! [Laughter] That—[she] was more concerned with having every book in their arms—in her arms, and having homework done.

I mean really...studious, compared to—I mean, food was like, back on the burner. It was something to keep you alive.

Annie notices that her Jewish friend is different from her because of her focus on scholastic achievement ("studious") and apparent lack of interest in food ("didn't think about lunch" and food "back on the burner"). Again, we cannot know if Annie hesitates to be more specific at first because of her invoking of an ethnic stereotype, but she does seem to notice this as a difference in values from her own experience. Annie notices a cultural difference of the value of education that enabled many Jewish immigrants to succeed soon after arrival to the United States as compared to Italians, generally speaking (see Brodkin, 2004). In contrast, Louise sees the Jews as similar to Italians, and does not hesitate to name ethnic names:

> Carol: Do you think food plays an important role in your life as an Italian compared to women who are not Italian?
> Louise: Yes.
> Carol: How?
> Louise: I believe that Italian women and Jewish women together—food was a prize, a goal, a reward. Um, it was offered like on holidays and it was offered as celebrations—in celebrations—as rewards for doing something good. Getting a good report card? What kind of a pie would you like? Or what kind of a dessert would you like? Or what do you want for dinner? Where do you want to go for dinner? Yeah, I do think so. Yeah.

Importantly, Louise sees Italian and Jewish women "together" because of their shared emphasis on food. While Rita mentioned previously the role of food in birth and death for Italians, Louise continues to explain its significance in holidays, celebrations, and rewards. While Annie notices a difference between her and her Jewish friend, Louise groups Italians and Jews in the same "boat." While Jews obviously have a different religion, cultural tradition, and are often from different nations than the Italians, they do share a similar kind of conditional Whiteness, as traced by several historians, (for example, Jacobson, 1998 and Brodkin, 2004).

The referent groups that the women mention as "not Italian" reveal a complicated set of ways in which they situate and understand their ethnic identity and White privilege. On one hand, their own White privilege and internalization of institutionalized racism is embedded in the fact that they do not even consider non-Whites as a comparison group. They are so "certifiably" White that they do not even have to assert it. It might also indicate that they might think that minority racial groups do indeed use food similar to Italians, as they do have some exposure to Black, Latino and Asian Americans as well as immigrant groups who clearly value food. On the other hand, their naming of other "Whiter" groups might also demonstrate that they compare themselves to those who have relatively more power and prestige, albeit their disgust of the *medigan*, or even perhaps precisely because of it. For example, historically speaking, mass migration by the Irish to the United States took place some fifty years before the wave of Italian immigrants. By the time the Italians arrived, the Irish were already firmly established as White, often having advanced to positions of institutional power and privilege. For example, while Carol remembers growing up around nearly all Italians, the teachers, principals, and bosses in her community were usually not Italian, but *medigan*. They had already become "American."

In the case of the Jews, Annie notes their difference when discussing a cultural feature that contributed to their upward mobility, while Louise sees their similarities around food. Perhaps the fact that these Italian American women named other White ethnics as markers of difference indicates an upward social comparison, and in doing so, also results in a necessary pity and disgust of their "lack" of culture, identity, family, and values, represented in the linguistic function of *medigan*.

This sentiment could only happen in a large Italian community, the disgust or disdain of the other who are more privileged.

DISCUSSION

These narratives about Italian-American ethnic identity have important implications for women and therapy. They illustrate within group variation around gender and Whiteness, and the complexity of racial formations shaped by immigration, region, and community. Therapists might consider how White ethnics might use their ethnicity to claim otherness, while also benefitting from White privilege and/or certainly not denouncing their Whiteness. This is related to ways in which individual experiences of marginalization and alienation can be simultaneously situated alongside invisible privilege and "conferred dominance," (McIntosh, 2001) all around ethnic identity.

Therapists, especially those that are psychodynamically trained, are taught to pay attention to that which is not said, cannot be spoken, the unspeakable. This therapeutic lens offers particular strengths and insights, needs to be applied to individual experiences of social identities and their relationships to institutional power and privilege. We need to pay more attention to those identities that are deemed "normal," the standard by which others are measured, in a therapeutic context. Whiteness, masculinities, heterosexualities, middle- to upper-class status, and citizenship, for example, all affect how we understand ourselves- our traumas, histories, and resilience—just as much as those without such privilege.

This research also points to the need for therapists to reflect upon their own race, gender, class identities in relation to the client. Therapists might consider their assumptions, for example, about the identities they share with their clients, and the ways in which they may or may not facilitate insider or outsider status, similarity and difference. For example, I once had a therapist who was also an Italian American woman, and at first I was relieved to share these common identities. I quickly learned, however, that our notions of Italianness and gender were dramatically different, shaped by social class, region of the United States, and the regions of Italy from which our ancestors had descended. Shared identities should be approached as both a potential strength as well as a caution.

Practitioners in immigrant communities should also pay attention to Whiteness. It is important to note that the distance from immigration greatly affects relationships to Whiteness. For example, for some immigrant groups deemed White in a North American context, their descendants are automatically granted White privilege, and the ability to become "Whitewashed" over the generations. Language, accent and citizenship status might be markers of "otherness" for White ethnics, but they have the privilege of changing that over time. While many immigrant groups try to get rid of their accents, we know that therapists often react to clients who speak a language different from their own, and that accents are valued differently, laden with meanings about race and class (Espin, 2013). Although the women in this study do not have an Italian accent, they certainly speak with an upstate New York working class accent, and an Italian American way of speaking, including slang like "medigan." In contrast, immigrant groups that are not considered White will never be granted such unearned advantage. For example, the descendants of slaves who have been in the United States for many generations do not have the luxury of shedding their accent in order to become White.

The community and region of the United States in which ethnic identity is developed is also an important consideration. The Italian American women in this study came to understand their ethnicity in a large community of similar others, which is necessarily different from those who were the only Italians (or family of any ethnicity) in their community. This understanding of self and relevant others also has implications for where the client currently resides. For example, I was raised among these many Italians in Syracuse, but then lived on the west coast and the Midwest for some time, in areas without similar others nearby. This greatly affected many of my experiences in those contexts, without necessarily being a salient cue all the time.

This study also implications for therapist and client explorations of boundaries of social identities, who is considered "us" and "them." For the Italian American women, "they" were clearly *medigans,* those non-Italian White others. These themes have implications for therapy around issues of conflict, violence, separation, identity, community, and home. However, it is important to consider that this is who they named in the context of discussing food, recipes, and being Italian American. For them, food symbolically represented family, morality, culture and home. "Taste" was lacking among the *medigans,* especially related to food in these ways. If, however, this study had focused on a different set of topics, such as crime, or the police, for example, it is likely not *medigans* who would be most salient, but other racialized minority groups, especially men (Dottolo & Stewart, 2008).

Clinicians might also implement the strategy of having clients speak about a cultural object in order to invoke narratives about other important themes such as race, class, gender, sexuality, bodies, home, family and morality. The narratives of these women are rich with insight, contradiction, history, and emotion—both explicit and implicit, both spoken and unspoken. Innovative tools that might illicit narratives in a therapeutic context should continue to be explored, not only for the sake of telling one's story, which can have healing and transformative effects, but stories *are* our identities, situated within "plots" of culture and institutional structures. (Espin, 1999, Polkinghorne, 1988). As clinicians, practitioners and researchers, we must continue to interrogate the many layers of meaning around privilege embedded in our stories and in our realities, work that psychology has just begun to do. Hopefully training programs will no longer reference "diversity" as a mere stand-in for the racially marginalized, but also require an unpacking of masculinities, heterosexualities, the cis-gendered, the able-bodied, and the middle and upper classes, all alongside Whiteness.

REFERENCES

Apple, M. W. (1998). Foreword. In J. L. Kincheloe, S. R. Steinberg, N. M. Rodriguez, & R. E. Chennault (Eds.), *White reign: Deploying whiteness in America*. New York, NY: St. Martin's Press.

Banks, I. (2000). *Hair matters: Beauty, power, and black women's consciousness*. New York: New York University Press.

Bona, M. (1999). *Claiming a tradition: Italian American women writers*. Carbondale, IL: Southern Illinois University Press.

Brekhus, W. (1998). A sociology of the unmarked: Redirecting our focus. *Sociological Theory*, 16(1), 34–51. doi:10.1111/0735-2751.00041

Brodkin, K. (2004). How did Jews become White folks? In M. Fine, L. Weis, L. P. Pruitt, & A. Burns (Eds.), *Off White: Readings on power, privilege, and resistance* (pp. 17–34). New York, NY: Routledge.

Combahee River Collective. (1977/2005). A Black feminist statement. In W. K. Kolmar & F. Bartkowski (Eds.), *Feminist theory: A reader* (2nd ed., pp. 311–316). Boston, MA: McGraw Hill.

Crenshaw, K. W. (1995). Mapping the margins: Intersectionality, identity politics, andviolence against women of color. In K. W. Crenshaw, N. Gotanda, G. Peller, & K. Thomas (Eds.), *Critical race theory: The key writings that formed the movement* (pp. 359–383). New York, NY: The New Press.

di Leonardo, M. (1987). The female world of cards and holidays: Women, families, and the work of kinship. *Signs: Journal of Women in Culture and Society*, 12(3), 440–453.

Dottolo, A. L. & Dottolo, C. (2015). Legacies of migration: Italian American women, food and identity. In O.M. Espin & A. L. Dottolo (Eds.), *Gendered journeys: Women, migration, and feminist psychology* (pp. 281–301). New York, NY: Palgrave MacMillan.

Dottolo, A. L., & Stewart, A. J. (2008). "Don't ever forget now, you're a Black man in America": Intersections of race, class and gender in encounters with the police. *Sex Roles, 59*, 350–364. doi:10.1007/s11199-007-9387-x

Dottolo, A. L., & Stewart, A. J. (2013). "I never think about my race": Psychological features of White racial identities. *Qualitative Research in Psychology, 10*, 102–117. doi:10.1080/14780887.2011.586449

Espin, O. M. (1999). *Women crossing boundaries: A psychology of immigration and transformations of sexuality*. New York, NY: Routledge.

Espin, O. M. (2013). Making love in English: Language in psychotherapy with immigrant women. *Women & Therapy, 36*(3–4), 198–218. doi:10.1080/02703149.2013.797847

Frankenberg, R. (1993). *White women, race matters: The social construction of Whiteness*. Minneapolis, MN: The University of Minnesota Press.

Gabaccia, D., & Iacovetta, F. (2002). *Women, gender, and transnational lives: Italian workers of the world*. Toronto, Canada: University of Toronto Press.

Giunta, E. (2002). *Writing with an accent: Contemporary Italian American women authors*. New York, NY: Palgrave.

Guglielmo, J. (2010). *Living the revolution: Italian Women's resistance and radicalism in New York city, 1880–1945*. Chapel Hill, NC: The University of North Carolina Press.

Guglielmo, T. A. (2003). *White on arrival: Italians, race, color and power in Chicago, 1890–1945*. New York, NY: Oxford University Press.

Ignatiev, N. (1995). *How the Irish became White*. New York, NY: Routledge.

Jacobson, M. F. (1998). *Whiteness of a different color: European immigrants and the alchemy of race*. Cambridge, MA: Harvard University Press.

Jenkins, R. (1996). *Social identity*. New York, NY: Routledge.

Jenkins, R. (2000). Categorization: Identity, social process and epistemology. *Current Sociology, 48*(3), 7–25.

Kaschak, E. (2011). The mattering map: Multiplicity, metaphor and morphing in contextual theory and practice. *Women & Therapy, 34*, 6–18. doi:10.1080/02703149.2010.532688

Laurino, M. (2000). *Were you always an Italian?: Ancestors and other icons of Italian America*. New York, NY: W.W. Norton.

Marecek, J. (1995). Gender, politics, and psychology's ways of knowing. *American Psychologist, 50*(3), 162–163. doi:10.1037//0003-066x.50.3.162

McIntosh, P. (2001). White privilege and male privilege: A personal account of coming to see correspondences through work in women's studies. In L. Richardson, V. Taylor, & N. Whittier (Eds.), *Feminist frontiers V* (pp. 29–36). Boston, MA: McGraw Hill.

Morawski, J. G. (2004). White experimenters, white blood, and other white conditions: Locating the psychologist's race. In M. Fine, L. Weis, L. P. Pruitt & A. Burns (Eds.), *Off white: Readings on power, privilege, and resistance* (pp. 215–231). New York, NY: Routledge.

Nenga, S. K. (2003). Social class and structures of feeling in women's childhood memories of clothing, food, and leisure. *Journal of Contemporary Ethnography, 32*(2), 167–199. doi:10.1177/0891241602250884

Polkinghorne, D. E. (1988). *Narrative knowing and the human sciences*. Albany, NY: State University of New York Press.

Sue, D. W. (2004, November). Whiteness and ethnocentric monoculturalism: Making the "invisible" visible. *American Psychologist*, 761–769.

Tajfel, H. (1981). *Human groups and social categories: Studies in social psychology*. Cambridge, United Kingdom: Cambridge University Press.

Index

Note: Page numbers in *italic* type refer to tables
Page numbers followed by 'n' refer to notes

Abercrombie and Fitch 168
ableism 46–8
abuse 47–8
accent 195
Adams, D.M. 5, 149–62
addressing model 105–6
Africa 160–1
African-Americans 12, 25, 45, 103, 110–11, 130–44, 154, 170
Akbar, M.: Thompson, V.L.S. and Bazile, A. 133
Albrecht, G.L.: and Devlieger, P.J. 49
alcoholism 191
ambivalence theory 80
American Civil War (1861–5) 9
American culture 34
American Dream 155
American Psychological Association (APA) 96, 106, 131, 144, 154, 168; *Guidelines on Multicultural Education Training Research Practice and Organizational Change for Psychologists* 131–3, 144
American Psychologist 17, 132
Americanism 164
Americanization 184, 187–8
Americanness 189
Americans 4–5, 139, 179, 185, 188, 193–4; European 42, 43–6; *medigan* 179, 185–9, 192, 195–6; Native 9; socialization 187
Ancis, J.R.: and Syzmanski, D.M. 95
Anglo-Whites 139
ANOVAS (Analysis of Variance) 172
anti-racism 80, 133, 156
Apple, M.W. 182
Arminio, J. 153, 161
Asia 33, 110
Asian women 29–41
Asian-Americans 135, 139, 164, 167, 170–3

autonomy 142
Awad, G.H.: *et al.* 103

baby boomers 184–6
Balan, S.: Haritatos, J. and Mahalingam, R. 33
Banks, I. 185
Banks, M.E. 3–4, 42, 49
Barlow, K.M.: Taylor, D.M. and Lambert, W.E. 171
BARNGA 108–9
Bartoli, E.: *et al.* 4, 68–84
Bazile, A.: Akbar, M. and Thompson, V.L.S. 133
Belin, T.: *et al.* 134
Bentley-Edwards, K.L.: *et al.* 4, 68–84
Berrill, K.: and Cummings-Wilson, D. 79
bias 117–29; gender 138; racial 118, 135, 138, 152
biological taxonomy 21
Bluemet, J.: *et al.* 103
Bonilla-Silva, E. 159
Brekhus, W. 182
Brooks, J.E.: *et al.* 103
Bucceri, J.M.: *et al.* 136–9
Buddhism 30
Burns, A.: *et al.* 2, 5

Cadena, M. de la 16, 20–1
Caenguez, K.: *et al.* 20
California (USA) 102; Los Angeles 121
Cameron, R.P.: *et al.* 45–7
Campbell, F.K. 45–8
Canada 15n
Canary Islands 25
capitalism 184
Capodilupo, C.M.: *et al.* 17, 136–9
Carter, R.T. 17, 20–1, 24, 120–3
Case, K.A. 4, 85–100, 153, 160
Caucasians 181, 187

INDEX

Chang, C.Y.: and Hays, D.G. 102
Christianity 10, 30
citizenship 91, 194–5
civilization 30
class 1, 29, 38, 185; identity 194; middle 20, 49, 92, 141, 157–8, 189, 196; social 3–5, 19–21, 124, 178–80; upper 20, 196; working 184, 195
Class Divided, A (1985) 121
classism 14
classroom teaching strategies 117–29
clinical psychology 88, 97, 125
clinical training programs 4, 85
Cohen, B.B.: Díaz-Lázaro, C.M. and Verdinelli, S. 18
Collins, P.H. 89
colonization 8, 12, 18, 37, 42
Color of Fear, The (1994) 121
color-blind ideology 159, 168; racial 5, 149–52
color-blindness 12, 72, 75, 79, 101–16, 132, 136; racial 5, 43
communities: indigenous 18; marginalized 93, 134
Compton, M.T.: *et al.* 133
Constantine, M.G.: *et al.* 97
Costa Rica 11–12
counseling 68–84
Crash (2004) 121
Crawford, D.: *et al.* 45–7; and Ostrove, J.M. 44
Crenshaw, K. 89
critical race theory 16
critical whiteness theory 29
cross-cultural psychology 105–8
cultural diversity 101
cultural identity 34, 113, 124, 155, 167, 183
cultural responsive training 101, 113–15
cultural sensitivity training 4, 101
culturally responsive therapy 5, 130
culture 188; American 34; Irish 190; Italian 190; popular 22
Cummings-Wilson, D.: and Berrill, K. 79
Curry, M.A.: *et al.* 47
Czechoslovakia 159

Davis, J. 9
Delgado-Romero, E.A.: and Shelton, K. 140
democracy 142; racial 22–3
Denny, R. 106
Devlieger, P.J.: and Albrecht, G.L. 49
Diagnostic and Statistical Manual of Mental Disorders (DSM-V) 131
Díaz-Lázaro, C.M.: Verdinelli, S. and Cohen, B.B. 18
didactic teaching strategies 120
difference: ethnic 113
Disabilities Act (USA, 1994) 43

disability 1–3, 44, 92; people with (PWD) 45–9; women with (WWD) 43–4, 47–9
discrimination 46–9, 94–5, 112, 150–1, 167–9; racial 19, 87, 94
diversity 77, 88–90, 101, 107
Dottolo, A.L. 5, 178–98; and Kaschak, E. 1–6
double marginalization 42–53
Druss, B.G.: *et al.* 133
Duan, C.: and Nilsson, J. 103

East 31
Edge, D.: *et al.* 134
Eisenhower, A.: *et al.* 20
Ellis Island (USA) 183, 192
emigration 18
empowerment 55, 131, 135
Empowerment Feminist Therapy 18
England, S. 20
English language 37, 174
Enns, C.Z. 49
enslavement 9
equality 9, 18
Ervin, A.: *et al.* 4, 68–84
Esquilin, M.: *et al.* 136–9
ethnic differences 113
ethnic groups 1, 11, 24, 44, 71, 154, 170–2, 191
ethnic identity 5, 49, 155, 161, 178–81, 185–6, 192–4
ethnic minorities 14, 44, 71–3, 133, 155–6
ethnic stereotyping 193
ethnicity 5, 14, 38, 42, 43, 111–12, 183–5, 190–1
ethnocentrism 165–6
eugenics 22, 45
Europe 17–19, 157
European Americans 42, 43–6
exoticism 31
exoticization 39
experiential teaching strategies 121–5

Facebook 96
femininity 3–5, 7–9, 42–5, 49, 178–80, 184
feminism 78, 135, 143
feminist psychotherapy 13
feminist theory 4, 68, 140
feminist therapy 4, 7, 12–13, 81, 104, 130–48, 181
fifteenth century 10
Filipino Republic 32–4
Fine, M.: *et al.* 2, 5
fixed racial categories 3
Flores, M.P.: *et al.* 103
Fongwa, M.: *et al.* 134
Frankenberg, R. 18
Frazier, R.: *et al.* 136
Freudian theory 156

INDEX

Fu, M. 4, 101–16
Fukui, M. 39

Gandolfini, J. 183
García, A.M.: et al. 4, 68–84
gender 8, 29, 38, 185; bias 138; identity 91, 103; norms 70; socialization 72
Gernat, C.A.: et al. 89
Gibson, J. 48
Gringas 11
groups: ethnic 1, 11, 24, 44, 71, 154, 170–2, 191; marginalized 2, 144; minority 111–12, 149, 164, 196; racial 68, 71, 75, 87, 118, 125, 154, 170–2
Guapperia 183
Guglielmo, J. 181
Gulbas, L.E. 19
Guthrie, R.V. 2

Hammar, L.: et al. 89
Hansen, N.D.: et al. 136
Haritatos, J.: Mahalingam, R. and Balan, S. 33
Harris, R.S. 17, 25
Hays, D.G.: and Chang, C.Y. 102
Hays, P.A. 105
healthy disability identity 4, 42, 43, 48–9
Hebrews 10
hegemony 33
Heller, W.: Mukherjee, D. and Reis, J.P. 44
Helms, J.E. 132, 153
heritage: mixed 38
heterosexual privilege 91, 97
heterosexual relationships 3, 29–41
heterosexuality 1
hierarchy 158; racial 3, 14, 73, 165, 170; social 2, 45
Hijab 168–9
Hispanics 20, 133, 154, 173
Hoetnik, H. 22
Holder, A.M.B.: et al. 136–9
homogenization 29, 33
homophobia 97
Hooker, J. 19
Hughes, R.B.: et al. 47
human beings 8, 111–12
humanity 42
Hurd, T.L.: and McIntyre, A. 103–4

idealization 33, 72
identity: American 171; class 194; cultural 34, 113, 124, 155, 167; ethnic 5, 49, 155, 161; gender 91, 103; healthy disability 4, 42, 43, 48–9; idealized 33; marginalized 78, 89, 137; multicultural 125; non-racist 132; non-racist White racial 4, 117; personal 70; privileged 2, 90, 92–3; racial 5, 22, 49, 69–70, 87–8, 103, 124–5, 132, 154–8; racial-ethnic 2; social 3, 89–95; white 76; white racial 85–6, 117, 149
ideology 151–2, 166; color-blind 159, 168; color-blind racial 5, 149–52, 164–9; multicultural 165; racial 151
Illinois (USA) 172
immigrants 18–20, 33–4, 93, 170–3, 181, 194; Latina 16–28
immigration 19–21, 38, 42, 185, 195
imperialism: Western 39
inclusive privilege studies 91–2
incomplete white consciousness 86–7
India 32, 35–6
indigenous communities 18
indigenous people 9
individual racism 137–8
inequality 2, 19, 30–1, 70, 103–4, 149, 168, 169
injustice: social 140, 150
internalized racism 34
intersectional learning 92–3
intersectional privilege: awareness training model 85–100; studies 90–7
intersectional theory 89–90
Irish culture 190
Italianness 178–80
Italy 181, 184, 187; culture 190; Sicily 184
Ivey, A.E.: Liu, W.M. and Pickett Jr, T. 89

Jacobson, M.F. 181, 186
Japan 30–1; Nagasaki 30–2
Jenkins, R. 180
Jews 189, 192–4
Johnson-Reed Act (USA, 1924) 181
Josephs, L.: and Miller, A.E. 156–8
Juby, H.L.: et al. 97
justice: racial 68, 73, 86; social 69–78, 81, 88, 132, 135, 143, 152, 160

Kalis, D.: et al. 136
Kaschak, E. 3, 7–15, 181; and Dottolo, A.L. 1–6
Kaslow, N.J.: et al. 133
Kaufman, P. 150
Kincheloe, J.L. 9, 30, 35
King Jr, M.J. 163–4
King, R. 106
Kwan, P. 32

Lamberghini-West, A.: et al. 88
Lambert, W.E.: Barlow, K.M. and Taylor, D.M. 171
Landrine, H. 104
Lange, J.M.: et al. 134
language 195
Language Identity and Behavioral American Acculturation Measure (LIB-A) 171–3
Latin America 15n

INDEX

Latina immigrants 16–28
Latinos 12, 169, 173, 193
learning: intersectional 92–3
lesbian gay bisexual and transgender (LGBT) 133, 140
Leu, J.: and Mahalingam, R. 35–7
Lewis, V.L. 59
Liang, J.J.-C.: *et al.* 97
Liberation therapy 161
Liu, W.M.: Pickett Jr, T. and Ivey, A.E. 89
Long Island (USA) 10
Lorde, A. 78
Los Angeles (USA) 121
Lucchese, F.: *et al.* 20
Lykes, M.B.: and McIntyre, A. 102

McClain, S.: *et al.* 72
McIntosh, P. 4, 54–67, 86–8, 107, 119, 150–1, 160, 181
McIntyre, A.: and Hurd, T.L. 103–4; and Lykes, M.B. 102
Madame Butterfly 3, 29–32, 39
Mahalingam, R.: Balan, S. and Haritatos, J. 33; and Leu, J. 35–7
Marecek, J. 180
marginalization 34, 73, 194–6; double 42–53; racial 74
marginalized communities 93, 134
marginalized groups 2, 144
marginalized identities 78, 89, 137
marginalized population 130, 145
marginalized social identity 93
Marhsall, M.: *et al.* 136
masculinity 1, 7–9, 13, 97, 196
Mazzula, S.L.: and Nadal, K.L. 5, 130–48
medigan 179, 185–9, 192, 195–6
men with disabilities (MWD) 44
mental health care 117
meritocracy 119, 166
Michael, A.: *et al.* 4, 68–84
microaggressions 4–5, 17, 73
microcosm 112
middle class 20, 49, 92, 141, 157–8, 189, 196
Midwest (USA) 192, 195
migration 194
Miller, A.E.: and Josephs, L. 156–8
Mindrup, R.: *et al.* 88
minorities 2, 69; ethnic 14, 44, 71–3, 133, 155–6; racial 133, 152; racial-ethnic 134
minority groups 111–12, 149, 164, 196
Miranda, J.: *et al.* 134
Mirrors of Privilege: Making Whiteness Visible (2008) 121
misogyny 13–14
mixed heritage 38
mixed race 3, 16, 19

Mona, L.R.: *et al.* 45–7
Montañez, L.: *et al.* 22–3
Morawski, J.G. 2, 182
Mukherjee, D.: Reis, J.P. and Heller, W. 44
multicultural competencies 4, 85–9
Multicultural Education Training Research Practice and Organizational Change for Psychologists, Guidelines (APA) 131–3, 144
multicultural identity 125
multicultural ideology 165
multicultural psychology 11
multicultural training 4, 68–70, 87
multiculturalism 48, 69–72, 90, 132, 165
multiple identities 178–80
multiple subjectivities 80
Muslims 169

Nadal, K.L.: *et al.* 17, 136–9; and Mazzula, S.L. 5, 130–48
Nadeem, E.: *et al.* 134
Nagasaki (Japan) 30–2
National Multicultural Conference Summit (NMCS, USA) 106
National SEED Project on Inclusive Curriculum (USA) 56, 59
nationalism 23, 184
nationality 11–12, 38, 54, 190
Native Americans 9
Neville, H.A.: *et al.* 103
New Jersey (USA) 139, 166
New World 9–10
New York (USA) 184, 195; Syracuse 184–9, 195
Nichols, E.G. 19–22
Nilsson, J.: and Duan, C. 103
nineteenth century 19, 22, 31, 181
non-racist identity 132
non-racist White racial identity 4, 117
norms: gender 70
North America 7
Norvig, G.: *et al.* 136

Oahu (Hawai'i) 101
Oedipal theory 156
Ohlsson, B.: Zaentz, P. and Zaentz, S. 150
Oklahoma (USA) 191–2
Orient 31
Orientalism 32
Oschwald, M.: *et al.* 47
Ostrove, J.M.: and Crawford, D. 44
Other 2, 81, 149, 179, 187
Otherness 1–2

Padrón, E. 3, 16–28
Paisley, K.: and Rose, J. 102
participation: social 45–6
Paterson, S.E.: and Tran, N. 5, 163–77

INDEX

patriarchal society 8
patriarchy 33
pedagogy 9, 59
Pennsylvania (USA) 191–2
people of color (POC) 17, 25, 74–7, 80, 163–6, 171–3
people with disabilities (PWD) 45–9
personal identity 70
Pewewardy, N. 86
phenotypes 183
physical ability 54
Pickett Jr, T.: Ivey, A.E. and Liu, W.M. 89
Pollock, G.H. 18
popular culture 22
population: marginalized 130, 145
Porter, N. 3, 29–41
poverty 30–2, 47, 92, 190
power: dynamics 102–4, 151; relations 55, 151, 160–1
Powers, L.E.: *et al.* 47
prejudice 118, 121–2, 133, 136–7, 144, 151
privilege analysis: white 54–67
privileged identity 2, 90, 92–3
Pruitt, L.P.: *et al.* 2, 5
psychology 2–3, 69–71, 93, 104, 136, 141, 152, 179, 182, 196; clinical 88, 97, 125; cross-cultural 105–8; multicultural 11; white 153
psychotherapy 48, 68–71, 80, 130, 133, 140, 158; feminist 13; training programs 68–84
public sphere 26
Puchner, L.: and Roseboro, D.L. 102

Quintero, P. 22

race 2–5, 21–2, 68–84, 103, 117–20, 142–4, 149–51; mixed 3, 16, 19; relations 56, 149–52
racial being 76–7, 119
racial bias 118, 135, 138, 152
racial categories 3, 7–8
racial color-blindness 5, 43, 163–77
racial continuum 19–20
racial democracy 22–3
racial designations 2, 8
racial discrimination 19, 87, 94
racial groups 68, 71, 75, 87, 118, 125, 154, 170–2
racial hierarchy 3, 14, 73, 165, 170
racial identity 5, 22, 49, 69–70, 87–8, 103, 124–5, 154–8, 178–98; non- 132
Racial Identity White Counsellors and Therapists (Tuckwell) 132
racial ideology 151
racial inequality 169
racial justice 68, 73, 86
racial marginalization 74
racial microaggressions 130–48

racial minorities 133, 152
racial mixing 18–19, 22
racial socialization 4, 14, 73, 136
racial stereotypes 48
racial whitening 22
Racial-Cultural Counseling Laboratory 122
racial-ethnic identities 2
racial-ethnic minorities 134
racism 2–3, 21–4, 77–80, 85–90, 102–4, 111–12, 117–25, 151–3, 164–7; anti- 80, 156; internalized 34; societal 48
Randazzo, K.V.: *et al.* 136
RCT (Relational Cultural Theory) 24–6
Reis, J.P.: Heller, W. and Mukherjee, D. 44
Renaissance 181
Renker, P.: *et al.* 47
reproductive rights 44
responsibility: social 149–53
Robinson-Whelen, S.: *et al.* 47
Roman Empire 181
Rose, J.: and Paisley, K. 102
Roseboro, D.L.: and Puchner, L. 102
Ruiz, E. 24–6
Rust, G.: *et al.* 133

Said, E. 32
Salinas, J.F.: *et al.* 22–3
Sánchez, L.M.: *et al.* 22–3
savagery 30
Schwartz, A.: *et al.* 136
segregation 72
self-identity 21–3, 26, 49
self-reflection 54, 149
seventeenth century 9
sexism 11–12, 32, 46, 138
sexual orientation 1, 8, 42, 135, 138
sexuality 54, 70, 90–1, 108, 196
Shar, R.: *et al.* 72
Shelton, K.: and Delgado-Romero, E.A. 140
Shim, R.S.: *et al.* 133
Sicily (Italy) 184
Sight Unseen (Kaschak) 8
sixteenth century 18
skin color 163
slavery 9, 20–2
social action 95–7
social class 3–5, 19–21, 124, 178–80
social hierarchy 2, 45
social identity 3, 89–95, 180–2, 189, 195; marginalized 93
social identity theory 180
social inequality 168
social injustice 140, 150
social justice 69–78, 81, 88, 132, 135, 143, 152, 160
social participation 45–6

INDEX

social status 45–6
social work 88, 97, 125
socialization 11–13, 102, 173; American 187; color-blind 165; gender 72; racial 4, 14, 73, 136; white racial (WRS) 68–84
societal racism 48
socio-economic status (SES) 155
Sopranos, The (HBO series) 183, 186
Spain 10
Spray, B.: *et al.* 88
status: social 45–6; socio-economic (SES) 155
stereotyping 3, 45, 77, 85–8, 121–2, 136–40, 167, 188; ethnic 193; racial 48
sterilization 45
Stevenson, H.C.: *et al.* 72
subjectivity 80
Sue, D.W. 17, 118, 132, 182; *et al.* 17, 136–9
superiority 9, 36, 149, 155–9; white 158
supremacy: white 9, 31, 120, 170
Suyemoto, K.: *et al.* 20
Swank, P.R.: *et al.* 47
Syracuse (New York) 184–9, 195
Syzmanski, D.M.: and Ancis, J.R. 95

Tajfel, H. 180
Tatum, B.D. 76
Taylor, D.M.: Lambert, W.E. and Barlow, K.M. 171
teaching strategies: classroom 117–29
Thailand 32
therapeutic ally-ance 85–100
therapy: culturally responsive 5, 130; feminist 4, 7, 12–13, 81, 104, 181; Liberation 161
Thompson, V.L.S.: Bazile, A. and Akbar, M. 133
Torino, G.C. 4, 117–29; *et al.* 17, 136–9
training: clinical programs 4, 85; cultural responsive 101, 113–15; cultural sensitivity 4, 101; intersectional privilege awareness model 85–100; multicultural 4, 68–70, 87; psychotherapy programs 68–84
Tran, N.: and Paterson, S.E. 5, 163–77
Tuckwell, G. 132
twentieth century 19, 180–1, 185

Unbearable Lightness of Being, The (1988) 5, 150–3, 159–60
United Kingdom (UK) 17
United States of America (USA) 3–5, 8–11, 15n, 16–25, 29–32, 35–8, 58–60, 149–51, 156–60, 192–5; African-Americans 12, 25, 45, 103, 110–11, 130–44, 154, 170; American Dream 155; American Psychological Association (APA) 96, 106, 131, 154, 168; Americanism 164; Americanization 184, 187–8; Americanness 189; Americans 4–5, 139, 170–3, 179, 185, 188, 193–4; Asian-Americans 135, 139, 164, 167, 170–3; California 102; Civil War (1861–5) 9; culture 34; Disabilities Act (1994) 43; Ellis Island 183, 192; English language 174; European Americans 42, 43–6; identity 171; Illinois 172; Johnson-Reed Act (1924) 181; Language Identity and Behavioral American Acculturation Measure (LIB-A) 171–3; Long Island 10; Midwest 192, 195; National Multicultural Conference Summit (NMCS) 106; National SEED Project on Inclusive Curriculum 56, 59; Native Americans 9; New Jersey 139, 166; New York 184, 195; Oklahoma 191–2; Pennsylvania 191–2; Supreme Court 169
upper class 20, 196
Utesy, S.O.: *et al.* 89

Venezuela 3
Verdinelli, S.: Cohen, B.B. and Díaz-Lázaro, C.M. 18
virtue 61, 107

Weis, L.: *et al.* 2, 5
well-being 36, 56, 60–1, 130, 143
West, T.C. 44
Western imperialism 39
White Anglo Saxon Protestants (WASPs) 179–80, 186
white cultural values 135–6
white identity 76
White Privilege: Unpacking the Invisible Knapsack (McIntost) 56, 60
white racial socialization (WRS) 68–84
white/black divide 7–15
Williams, M. 49
Wise, T. 92
Woan, S. 39
womanhood 44–5
women with disabilities (WWD) 43–4, 47–9
WOP 183
working class 184, 195
World War II (1939–45) 10
worldview genogram 109–10
Wright, W.R. 20

Youtube 96–7

Zaentz, P.: Zaentz, S. and Ohlsson, B. 150